In Strength and Shadow

Mervyn Davies was born in 1946 and played for London Welsh, Swansea, the British Lions teams of 1971 and 1974, and the Welsh national side. He is currently chairman of the Welsh Rugby Former International Players Association.

David Roach runs a copywriting agency called Red 10 Creative. He was born in Wales but now lives in Oxford. In 2002, he collaborated with former Llanelli and Wales scrum-half Rupert Moon on the acclaimed *Full Moon: Rugby in the Red.*

MAINSTREAM *SPORT*

IN STRENGTH AND SHADOW

THE MERVYN DAVIES STORY

MERVYN DAVIES AND **DAVID ROACH**

MAINSTREAM
PUBLISHING
EDINBURGH AND LONDON

This edition, 2005

First published in Great Britain in 2004 by
MAINSTREAM PUBLISHING COMPANY (EDINBURGH) LTD
7 Albany Street
Edinburgh EH1 3UG

ISBN 1 84596 031 9

A catalogue record for this book is available from the British Library

Typeset in Baskerville Book
Printed and bound in Great Britain by
Cox & Wyman Ltd

Contents

Acknowledgements

The authors wish to thank the following for their time, help and encouragement:

Mervyn: Jeni Davies, Christopher Davies, Laura Davies, Betty Davies; Peter Thomas and J.J. Williams of the Welsh Rugby Former International Players Association; John Dawes, David Parry-Jones, Willie John McBride, Bobby Windsor, John Taylor, John Hughes; Rob Cole at the Westgate Sports Agency, the *Western Mail*, Robert Davies; Bill Campbell, Graeme Blaikie, Lizzie Cameron and Ailsa Bathgate at Mainstream Publishing; Green Umbrella Video, Christopher Davies Publishers, Nick Davis.

David: Katy Gordon, William and Isabella; Linda, Jean and Beryl Brown; Cerys and Roger Clarke; Kevin, Mandy, Jamie and Rhianna; John Roach; Sandy Taylor and Duncan Lawson; Richard Tomlin, Muffin Gordon, Callum and Rosa; Ali and Neil MacGregor; David Couch for his Maori nous; David Gedge; Tanya Lidstone; and Jack Gordon and Diana Hawkins for going beyond the call of duty.

Foreword

In every great team there are three or four key players that a captain can rely on to deliver the goods. These players are often unfussy types, preferring to get their heads down and do the job they are selected for. They must be unflinching in their commitment to the wider cause, for without their unbending efforts, the whole shape and structure of the team could fall apart. I was fortunate enough to play with men of such outstanding calibre throughout my long career: men reliable enough that I barely had to give them a second thought once the starting whistle blew. And no one did more for his team, or for me, than that prince of number 8s, Mervyn Davies.

Mervyn was unquestionably the greatest number 8 of my era. His particular playing talents are well documented: almost invincible at the back of the lineout, with a passion for tackling and the soft, basketball hands of an instinctive ball player. But the hidden parts of Mervyn's game equally impressed me: the stuff that went on away from prying eyes. His anticipation was unique and the skill he had to off-load the ball in ridiculously tight situations was unmatched. And his mental strength, too . . . his will to fight and to win lifted him up to the heights of the very great.

I played alongside him in New Zealand in 1971 when his performances on that momentous tour catapulted him onto the world stage. My, how the New Zealand press admired him: the harshest critics in world rugby were won over by the man who stood as straight and as strong as a steel girder. Three years later, in South Africa, he was even better. As his captain I could rely wholeheartedly on his support and consistency. My number 8 would do his job, and do it brilliantly.

Away from the pitch Merv is an affable, easy-going fellow. He is quiet without being reserved, and he enjoyed – and deserved – the respect and the friendship of his fellow players. As a captain for Wales he led like a Lion and I am sure he would have been the difference between success and failure on that tour of New Zealand in 1977.

The events of an earlier spring robbed rugby of one of its greatest ever players, and the men who shared time with Mervyn – both on and off the field – were sad for the sport, but remain grateful that we still have him around. His status as a sporting legend is guaranteed . . . but playing is just one small part of the Mervyn Davies story. I am proud to be associated with this exceptional man and to have played a small role in his extraordinary tale.

Willie John McBride

I

A Matter of Balance

Port Elizabeth, South Africa
July 1974
I suck in the air. The smell of sweat and liniment engulfs me as I make my way to the back of the lineout. The call comes; the ball isn't going my way. I glance to my right and see the boys lining up, ready. Benny shouts into midfield, but I cannot make out his words. They are not directed at me . . . they do not concern me. Winning the ball, protecting the men who stand before me: that is my immediate concern. We have to watch each other's backs out here, especially in the lineout. A man weighing 15 or 16 st. is at his most vulnerable when he is airborne. With his arms raised up high above his head he cannot protect himself from the low and nasty punch that comes stealing in under his ribcage. He needs his mates. This is a brutal business. My ribs and midriff are proof: they carry the bruises from a series of well-placed whacks.

I tense my body, waiting for another blow to come, but it doesn't. I glance at the Boks beside me and they look exhausted. They are breathing hard. For 40 minutes, they have hit us with all their fury, but we have held firm. Now they look lost. Maybe we've knocked the fight out of them. Then again, desperate men can be dangerous foes so there must be no let-up until we leave the field. I can hear some frantic Afrikaans; all is not well in their ranks. Bobby prepares

13

to throw, and I can see fruit arcing out of the crowd towards him. A foot comes stamping down on mine so I lean in with my shoulder and shake my assailant off. These boys are bruisers, not rugby players; Christ knows where they've come from . . . they've been pushed onto the pitch to do us over, but they will not. We have been punched and kicked across the field, but we haven't yielded a single yard. Little do they realise that we are feeding off their hatred, growing stronger with every blow.

Bobby throws the ball in, but I lose sight of it as Gordon powers up and taps it back to Gareth. Now it is gone. Now my work begins. The lineout breaks up and I turn and push past Kritzinger. He reaches out to pull me back, but I repel him with my arm and break free. The ball is zipping left; I visualise it flying through the hands of our back line: Edwards, Bennett, McGeechan, Milliken and then to J.J. Williams. It is a play we practise – getting the ball out quickly to our fastest runner. I move in support, joining a measured stampede of red jerseys. I feel strong and alert, aware of every obstacle as I pick my way through the backtracking Boks. I feel alive; each heartbeat pounds out the powerful, rhythmic drumming of an unstoppable march. My mind works on split-levels: I can see the exact patch of grass where I need to be, without losing sight of J.J.'s run. I can also sense where my flankers are, but I can't explain how I can comprehend all three elements at once. If I could explain it, then I might lose the magic.

J.J. feeds J.P.R., who heads wide. J.P.R. squeezes past the number 10 and for a fraction of a second I think he is going to ground. I check my run; a green arm tries to wrap itself around my neck but fails. I go on, ready to support my full-back, but the ball is back with J.J. I am not needed. He is through. I slow down and smile. The red machine, full of cut and thrust, has sliced apart the South Africans yet again. My gaze goes up and over J.J. as he touches down, then on towards the thousands of black and coloured fans penned in behind the posts. They raise their arms and salute him, cheering wildly as the green dream cracks and falls. Then it hits me: the match and the series are both won. Whatever the Boks try now, their efforts will be fruitless. Each Lion, each man in red, grows with every step. We stand tall. We stand supreme. We will go on.

Traffic noise. Too much traffic noise. Cheerful hellos. Christopher wriggling in my arms. The sun feels hot on my face and it hurts my eyes. I wish I had found my sunglasses. I wish I were invisible. The noise and the crowds confuse me. Go away. My mouth is dry and I have no sense of smell. I miss the aroma of bakeries, the smell of fresh bread. I miss the smell of my boy. I put him down on the pavement and rest my left arm. It feels weak. I can't hold anything properly. There is too much noise.

I want to walk across the road. Such a simple task: first one foot, then the other. But I am nervous. The cars seem different, faster and bigger, yet somehow also smaller. They confuse me. I have to squint against the sun, but I cannot judge how fast they move. I am too scared to guess. But it is just a road. A road I've crossed 1,000 times. The colours dazzle me. People stare. Someone stops and talks. I cannot hear her words clearly so I mumble my stock response and try to flee. I look bad, crooked and frail. I try to stand tall, dragging up a mental picture of the man in the white headband . . . trying to change from the inside what I project on the outside. But the image gets scrambled and lost. Leave me alone. I want to cross that bloody road.

I pick Chris up and walk to the kerb. I look left and right and left again, like a child, and then I put my right foot forward; but I misjudge the distance from kerb to road. The sensation starts . . . not again, not now! My knees crumple and I fall. I twist and protect my boy as I land painfully on my shoulder. More faces, more pity. Christopher is gathered up by a passer-by. He's crying. A crowd forms around me. Cars stop. The town stops. Saturday stops. A hand is thrust towards me but I push it away. I don't need any help. I will get up. I will get up. I need to cross the road. I will go on.

II

The Swansea Boy

To hear it said, at least the way I have heard it said, it would be easy
to believe that the word 'Mervyn' carried more significance than just
a name. I've heard it used to encourage, to chastise – and even to
praise. I dare say it has also been employed as an insult (flanked by
a few expletives), particularly in the bear pit of Murrayfield or down
Dunedin way. 'Mervyn' is a good word for shouting, you see . . .
letters well grouped so that one can open the lungs and really go for
it. It is the way the syllables sit; it allows the vocalisation to begin
with a murmur and develop into a roar. And despite what the smart-
alecs on the terraces might have believed (you know the type – boys
with a quip for every lost lineout ball) no one could shout out my
name like my mother. The end to many a day was signalled by her
call as it rose up the hill from Trewyddfa Road and into Parc
Llewellyn, the place where I would loiter and cling to the last of the
evening sun.

I was born in Gorseinon Hospital, Swansea on 9 December 1946:
Thomas Mervyn Davies, a post-war baby boomer like fellow Wales
internationals Terry Cobner, Bobby Windsor and Ray 'Chico'
Hopkins. The town of my birthplace, the town where I still live, is
the place I've called home throughout the larger part of my life. It is
my patch, an area of Wales where sea, sky and soil meet head on.
From the easy sweep of Swansea Bay arcing out towards the

Mumbles to the high hills that rise up seemingly from the sand, this 'ugly, lovely town' as (I believe) Dylan Thomas once called it, has a uniqueness, a salty freshness that sits well with me. It is here where I can sit down with a pint and be 'Merv', the local boy who once captained his country. In my heart and in my thoughts Swansea remains a game old town where people are drawn to work, to holiday, to escape . . . and I have done all three in her generous environs.

My early Swansea memories are flashback images rather than crystal-clear certainties. Because my memory has been partly stolen from me, there's a particular pleasure when it provides snapshots of what I did when I was young: trundling around on a three-wheel trike, rolling stones along the gutter, scraping sticks against the brickwork of our street. I think I can even recall a moment in my mother's shawl but that might be received wisdom from family reminiscences. I do remember watching the Queen's coronation at a neighbour's house, staring goggle-eyed at the television set in the days when the set itself was a great novelty – a tiny, blurred screen in a big, brown cabinet. Some memories remain strong because they form the building blocks that helped construct the man I am and they are the ones I hold especially dear – of my father, my mother, my brother, the relatives, friends and the action that was found in and around Trewyddfa Road.

The Davies family wasn't well off; we were a solid working-class Welsh breed, chapel-goers all, who stuck together through thick and thin. Our house was small and warm and always gave a good welcome to anyone who happened by. David John (Dai), my father, worked as a welder in a local power station. Back then in the '50s and '60s Swansea was a place of heavy industry and export, so there was always a job for a man willing to bend his back into some hard graft. One only had to peer down the valley at the industrial sprawl to see how easy it was to earn a few quid.

In the years before the war, my father had been a reluctant coal miner. I say reluctant because he loathed life underground. To him, the call to arms was a godsend, a chance to flee from the pit and enlist in the armed services. He once said the mines would have killed him if he'd stayed there a moment longer. Although mining was a reserved occupation, I think he preferred taking his chances against the Germans rather than having to haul his 6 ft-plus frame to the coalface. My father seldom spoke of his wartime experiences – and now that he is gone I regret not asking him – but I do know he was shipped out to north Africa to fight with Montgomery's Eighth. After a few encounters with the enemy, he was taken prisoner and joined a large number of his fellow Desert Rats who were plucked off the scorched sands and bundled back to Germany for the duration. Whilst others were fighting their way across France, Italy and Burma, my father spent his war trapped behind barbed wire. Although in many ways his war could have been much, much worse, it was an ironic fate to befall a man who had joined up because he felt imprisoned in the pit.

When news of his capture eventually reached his wife Mary Elizabeth (Betty) – my mam – she must have felt a strange sense of anxiety and relief. All she could do from then on was gather together the occasional – and meagre – Red Cross parcel and hope its arrival would help him through his stretch. Like countless others across the world, they had to wait for an end to the whole business before they could be reunited.

In common with other industrial towns and cities on the home front, Swansea was always potentially a wartime bombing target. Its foundries and refineries, and its strategic access to the open sea where a lifeline of food and materials could be landed, had flagged its presence on many a Luftwaffe map. Local historians, who work hard to chronicle the town's numerous lives, reckon Swansea suffered over 40 serious air raids between the outbreak of hostilities and the end of 1943. The worst incident was a sustained attack known as 'the Three Nights Blitz', which rained bombs for three consecutive nights in February 1941. Some 30,000 incendiary bombs destroyed centuries of history in a few hours. My mother – like so many other men and women fighting the domestic battle – did what she could and joined the local fire service.

As with others of my generation, I am thankful that I was born in quieter times. The war had ended by the time I arrived, but they were still years of hardship, rationing, rubble and rebuilding. Both Mam and Dad, and my nan who lived with us, worked hard to stretch whatever resources we had. We weren't the only ones living in this way; the whole country was rubbing its eyes and slowly coming to terms with the future.

For the first few years of my life we were a Welsh-speaking household, and then, when I was four years old, an important decision was made about my education. The obvious option would have seen me heading to the Welsh school in Llansamlet some three miles away but that would have involved two separate bus journeys there, and two more back. My parents looked down the hill instead and settled on Plasmarl Juniors, the 'English place'. There may have been financial reasons behind my parents' choice – the opportunity to save a few bob a week on transport must have been attractive – but, knowing the way my parents thought, I suspect that their decision was in all likelihood mainly influenced by my future prospects. They were quite traditional in that respect: both wanted their eldest child to go on and achieve the kind of education that they had never had. Throughout childhood, adolescence and even adulthood they sacrificed much for both me and for my younger brother, Dyfrig.

It was a shocking upheaval for a four year old to find himself suddenly in an alien environment, unable to communicate with his peers. My teachers and classmates thought I was backward during those initial months because I knew no English at all. But it is easier for the very young to pick up new words and slowly, painfully slowly, my English came.

Irrespective of any natural ability to learn, there were two factors that helped me settle in at Plasmarl: first, my Aunt Sal taught reception class and kept a watchful eye on her bewildered nephew; and second, my parents ceased speaking Welsh at home. I gained one language but lost another. For every new anglicised term that lodged in my brain a Welsh word was ousted. I did retain some Welsh, but I am hardly fluent. Most of the Welsh I spoke in adulthood was rooted in rugby, because Gareth Edwards and I would use Welsh calls in set-piece plays to confuse the opposition. Losing one's birth-language was not too much of a hindrance in multi-cultural Swansea, where people like my grandparents had migrated from Devon, and others came from Ireland or the

Midlands in search of work. But if I had been born a few miles further west into Carmarthenshire, across the Loughor say, then Welsh would undoubtedly have remained my native tongue.

Schoolwork wasn't a high priority for me, there was too much of the outdoor boy fighting to be free. Parc Llewellyn was a great, wooded hilltop where streams ran into ponds that were alive with newts and frogs. The trees were made for climbing and gangs of boys would use the thick undergrowth to hide and ambush any approaching foe. It was a place where a boy with a penknife and a ball of string could while away the hours from sunrise to sunset. And the park was somewhere dens could be built that would keep the rain out and the conspiracies in; a great advantage when the big westerly fronts rolled in off the Atlantic (as they often did: Swansea is one of the wettest places in Britain).

Even at such a tender age I showed a zealot's love for the physical side of life. My size put me a good head, and some shoulder, above my friends. My mother was a tall woman – 5 ft 9 in. – so it seemed I was destined to inherit my parents' stature. Later, my height made me an awkward adolescent and my gangly frame threatened my fragile teenage psyche, but as a boy, I was surprisingly well coordinated – especially when one considers the distance between my brain and my feet.

Like almost every other small boy I played lots of sport, but times were different then – far different from today. Back then there was no hero worship or cult of celebrity to follow. We didn't have the access to – or the interest in – what the sporting stars of the day got up to. We saw sport as something to do, a game to pile into, and the need to watch live sport barely entered my consciousness; I saw maybe a couple of Swansea matches down at St Helens, but being in a crowd did not stir my interest the way that playing did. I had to do something, anything, to burn off the restlessness. And if I did have a particular sport of choice when I was a boy then it would have to be soccer: to this day I have a terrific fondness for the round ball game. Most Welsh people do, yet we are caricatured as a nation interested only in their rugby. Witness the biennial ordeal we endure when attempting to qualify for the final stages of the World Cup or the European Championships; that collective angst is a good indicator of what the Welsh feel about the 'other' game. I enjoyed my cricket too, but only if I could bat or bowl: I was the kind of boy who would try to slope off somewhere if required to field. Unless I was trying to obliterate a batsman's stumps or launch my willow at a poorly delivered longhop, cricket had too much space, and too slow a pace, to engage my attention fully. Even then I preferred the claustrophobic thrill of being right in the heart of the action.

At Plasmarl the only part I played in a team game was for the soccer XI. Our school had no grass whatsoever, so we had to play football out in the concrete playground. We would play a few fixtures away against other local schools and I remember on one occasion turning out as centre-forward (the first example of my height dictating my playing position) up at Paradise Park. Never has there been a more ill-suited name for such a rough piece of wasteland: it revealed Swansea's civic planners' gifts for irony. It was at Paradise Park where I scored my one and only goal for Plasmarl Juniors, and it was also where I ripped the skin off my leg after attempting a sliding tackle on that terrible, razor-edged asphalt. The one benefit (not appreciated at the time, of course) was that in my later rugby career the rock-hard pitches of the South African high veldt held little fear for a man who had once left bits of his flayed skin all over Paradise Park.

The specific memory from my boyhood that did draw me to rugby is still clear in my mind, the significance of which has grown with the passing years. I must have been aged ten or thereabouts and up to no good in my parents' bedroom. I recall pulling open a large, heavy drawer at the foot of my father's wardrobe. I don't know what I could have been looking for – perhaps some relic from his army days? But there, neatly folded at the bottom of the drawer, beneath his good shirts, was a blood red jersey with a golden three-feather crest. When I opened it out on the bed and turned it over, I saw a large, beautifully stitched '8' in a creamy, off-white colour. Perplexed by the significance of this find, I trailed it downstairs to my parents for answers. My dad's immediate response was to raise his big paw and show me – in quite explicit terms – what happens to nosey little boys who go snooping about. But he quickly calmed down and said, in his matter-of-fact way, that it was his Welsh shirt, the one that he had worn on Cardiff Arms Park.

Although my father seldom revealed his inner thoughts or past experiences to his children, I don't want to paint him as a distant or aloof man, because he wasn't. People have to remember that the dynamics of the parent–child relationship were quite different then. I think that the first time my father watched me play rugby was when I turned out in my first senior game for London Welsh. Nowadays, parents are expected to follow everything their children do, to be there yelling encouragement from the sidelines – but my father was working when I played. He also never, ever pushed me into anything. I respect him for his restraint as much as I do for his achievements. Many a promising child has been lost to sport because of a father's pressure, and the lesson I learnt from Dai was one I was anxious to follow with my own children. I digress, but by all accounts my father was a more than useful player – better than me, according to many who saw us both play (a view that he shared too, incidentally!). He played for Swansea before the war and was regarded as a tough, uncompromising lock or number 8. His height allowed him to move between the two positions when circumstances required (the curse of the tall, mobile player). Adolf Hitler rudely interrupted his club career with Swansea, and for four dull years there was little opportunity to play rugby in the prison camp. After his repatriation and return to Swansea, he took to the field again – this time as captain of the All Whites. Not long after, when some semblance of normality had returned to people's lives, he was invited to represent Wales in a series of 'Victory Internationals'. These matches were played in 1946 in place of the Home Internationals. Although the Wales players wore Welsh shirts and played at Cardiff Arms Park or Murrayfield in front of capacity crowds, the games were not awarded full international status. That meant that the players did not get their caps. The matches were seen as a chance for the players, the public and the game itself to get back to some kind of normality after the rigours of war. 'Wales' even played the New Zealand Expeditionary Forces before they set off on their long journey back to the southern hemisphere: an encounter that was undoubtedly as hard fought as any between those great rugby foes.

I gather he played the game properly: with hardness, skill,

enthusiasm, commitment and fairness. I suspect he was just happy to shake off the years of confinement and run free again. If he was anything like his son, then he would have viewed each match as a release, a place to put the stress and strain of life and work and family away for a couple of hours each Saturday afternoon. He played the game at the highest level, he achieved his sporting goals, and then, when it was time to finish, he walked away and got on with his life. My father didn't brag or boast about what he had done. Nor did he hide within the aura of it. A rugby match was just a rugby match . . . a small – but highly enjoyable – part of his weekly life.

If I were the romantic type, then I would have used the 'jersey in the drawer' discovery as *the* defining moment of my childhood. It wasn't, and I may be guilty of over-playing its significance now. Yet knowing that my father – the man I would see walking in exhausted from work or shaving at the sink, that same man I saw lost in his newspaper or larking about with my mother – had played for his country, made me believe I could do it too. We were of the same stock: if he could achieve something so big, then so could I. Doing what he had done – what I could easily regard as the impossible – was, in fact, feasible. I did not set myself a timetable to follow – I was far too lazy to put that amount of effort in – but I knew that it could be done. Holding his Wales shirt didn't fill me with a desire to don one myself, it just brought home that someone from someplace like Trewyddfa Road could actually go on to play for his country.

Betty and Dai were good people; they demanded that Dyfrig and I worked hard and were respectful to others. My father wasn't afraid to use the big paw, and the memory of it finding its spot beneath a mountain of blankets when Dyfrig and I gave him cause to act makes me laugh even now. My brother and I shared a bed as children, and because he is nearly five years younger than me I had the responsibility of an elder brother to dictate what went on in our bedroom – so I was usually to blame for my father's irritation. Dyfrig and I fought and played together in the riotous and loud way that brothers do, both inside the house and out, and I reckon we were quite a handful. Yet both of us always knew that our parents loved us and would do whatever they could to give us the best start in life. Being a parent is in some ways the hardest job in the world: the hours are unforgiving, the rewards are not always obvious and there's no formal training for it. You can only do your best for your children, but I realised quite early on in life that my parents' best was more than good enough.

III

Picking Up the Ball

There are numerous reasons why Wales fell away as a rugby power after the Golden Era of the 1970s. Ask any Welsh person, or any rugby lover for that matter, and they will put forward their own theories. Many people are quick to point out the gradual decline of heavy industry in the valleys and along the coastal areas from Fishguard to Newport. True, one must concede recession did have a grave impact upon the stuttering national game, denying a generation of amateur players the uncompromising training ground that men like Dai Morris and Bobby Windsor grew up on in pit and steelworks respectively. But I feel – in purely rugby terms – Wales was hit as much by the loss of school rugby (especially grammar school rugby) as she was by the loss of her steelworks, her docks and her collieries.

Grammar schools across Wales were the great rugby academies, places where the game could be studied and picked apart with an almost puritanical eye. Games masters would bully and blather away, shaping the minds and bodies of their eager young charges, creating players who would pit their skills against equally adroit boys from other schools. Competition was fierce . . . and the common need to excel raised the standard of the game with each flowering generation. Of course, I never studied at a grammar school so it is feasible that my view is somewhat over-simplified or just slightly skew-whiff. But I have a hunch it isn't, because whatever district trial I was invited to attend (and there were a fair few in the Swansea of my youth), I never once got a look in. It didn't matter what I – or the players from my school – did on the field; the shirts we tried out for were already earmarked for the grammar school boys. Five minutes into a trial match and it was all over: the district selectors (mainly with grammar school connections) had already booked their boys their places. Just as it was in England, Ireland and Scotland, many of the youngsters who would one day go on and represent Wales at rugby union came from a grammar school background.

My parents never hid from me their wish that I should go to the grammar school. They longed for me to be the one who broke the mould in terms of the Davies family education. I would have gone, but fate had something else lined up. The greatest demand Dai and Betty placed upon my young shoulders was that I pass my eleven-plus. They gave me no choice. If I was going to get anywhere in life, if I wanted to avoid a dirty, dangerous future, if I wanted to get well away from the acrid smoke of the smelters' yard or the blackness of the mine, then I would have to 'think' my way out. My father didn't want either one of his boys toiling away like him.

Despite my reluctance to study and the latent nature of any academic leanings I might have possessed, I did what I was told and put the graft in. Whether it was the fear of failure (and disappointing my parents) that spurred me on, or just having a lucky knack of being able to learn parrot-fashion, I passed. Incredibly, I managed to focus my wandering attention long enough to get the grades that would take me into a new kind of Elysian world. Well, that's what I thought would be coming my way. That is what my folks thought too – young Merv polished up and pushed off to a grammar school like Dynefor or Bishop Gore. The local education authority however, had a different idea. A seismic change in attitudes towards post-war schooling had taken place. Looking back now, the late '50s/early '60s resemble an almost egalitarian age where society seemed gripped by the need for change. In my own small way I was part of a grand social experiment, an experiment that would take the cream off the top of the junior schools and spread it about a bit. I was chosen for an entirely new kind of educational experience. Like modern-day pied pipers leading the way, boys of all abilities and from all types of different backgrounds were rounded up by the local education authority and led up the hill to a brand new concrete monstrosity called Penlan Multilateral.

By the time I arrived there in 1958, Penlan had been in existence for little more than a year. The principle behind its foundation – as with other secondary moderns and then comprehensives – was to provide a rounded education to a cross-section of society. We were assessed at junior school and then streamed accordingly. There were two ways to go when new students reached Penlan: either with the school 'swots' or off with the also-rans to do 'tech'. As with other eleven-plus passers, I was popped straight into the top set. Was this the brave new world our fathers had fought for? To see the hopeful looks on our eager young faces as we were bussed in from all over Swansea, one might have thought yes. But – as is often the case with education – idealism and reality found themselves poles apart. The great gleaming citadel to inclusiveness and togetherness that was Penlan was, in fact, a rough-and-tumble zoo where the strongest – or the sneakiest – survived. I am not only talking about physical strength because the pack nature of the stalking student body would often reduce the biggest game to easy meat. No, at Penlan a boy needed alertness, mental sharpness, a quick understanding of the rules and some luck to get through each day. If he was too brainy, too dull, too short, too tall, too fat, too thin, too quiet, too loud, too hard, too soft . . . if he was anything that allowed the other pupils to hang a label upon him, then he was a target. The best way to get by was to blend in because if you possessed anything that set you apart from the mob then, by God, you were going to get it. My physical size certainly got me the treatment in my first few weeks until I swallowed hard and decided to give back as good as I got.

The school building itself was five storeys high and well over 200 yards long. It was a massive structure, bigger than any other place I had ever entered. It was also quite impossible to navigate and one lived in fear of disappearing down some godforsaken corridor never to be seen again. The brutality of the bricks and mortar mirrored perfectly the atmosphere inside, for if there was ever a school of hard knocks then it was Penlan. A feral law ruled which fast-tracked many of the boys straight to badness. A few of my fellow pupils were so rough, so hyped-up on front, they even gave some of the more hapless masters a pasting. It was Wild West Glamorgan; full of bandits on the inside – and there were even horses on the outside. I would often stare out of the window, blocking out the chaos around me, looking at these manky old nags wandering around the school. I half expected to see Alan Ladd or James Stewart come ambling into view to round up some of the ruffians. But it was sometimes funny too; especially when the shout went up for a breakout and we'd cheer on one larrikin or another as he made his daring escape, leaping aboard a scraggy mount and disappearing off into the sunset.

For all my criticism of Penlan it did provide me with a good education – and not just in the formal sense. It taught me one of life's most valuable lessons: it made me streetwise. I learnt more about the scheming tendencies of my fellow man in those few formative years than I did before or since. Take, for instance, the annual cross-country race. Because of the newness of the school, there was no grass anywhere on the premises, just vast tracks of glutinous mud. And on that soggy wasteland the teachers could inflict a little bit of retribution on the little sods that caused them such misery each day. The cross-country 'track' itself wasn't even a track; it was a quagmire that bordered the entire school grounds and we were instructed to run it . . . all three strength-sapping miles of it. The underfoot conditions were guaranteed to be abysmal and the weather to be inhuman: the run always seemed to coincide with the foulest day of the year. Yet no matter how much I loathed running – in particular that aimless, looped running which seemed to go on forever – I could not keep my competitive streak in check for long. In my first year I finished third out of 200. In the second and third years I finished third or fourth but when, 12 months later, the teachers told us to drag ourselves around the course twice, I thought 'bollocks to that' and strolled in a hugely satisfying 104th. Never had outright failure felt so good. Whether with Wales, the Lions or running up and down the seafront with Swansea RUFC, my loathing for training runs was born in the Penlan mud.

It is true to say that the sporting facilities at Penlan were somewhat spartan. The theory was that once the school had settled, the grass had finally grown and the pupils could make it safely to the gym without sliding all the way down the hill to Swansea town, our facilities would be the envy of every other school in the area. But my year, the year above and the year that followed, had to make do till nature worked. Yet, as the saying goes, 'what doesn't kill you makes you stronger', and the hardships we faced doing what other pupils in other schools did with comparative ease instilled in us a sense of true grit. Gym class was universally popular, and although I was keen to participate, my height didn't suit work on the apparatus. There may not have been a rugby or football pitch at that time, but one man was determined to do something positive about it and he can lay claim to unearthing my playing talent. Well, I know he dined out on that story a few times over the years and I never begrudged him because he did have a profound influence on the direction my life would eventually take.

Gwyn Watts was quite a teacher – and quite a character, too. He was the role model teacher I might have aspired to become if I had possessed one iota of his natural teaching talent. Teaching is a tough job – one could argue perhaps the toughest – but good teachers have a gift that makes it seem effortless. And that was how Gwyn taught: with little fuss and apparently a lot of ease.

Like his colleagues around him, Gwyn must have viewed the student body of Penlan with extreme frustration. We were a fidgeting mass of dissent and aggression. What we needed – and what the school needed – was an outlet, somewhere or some way all that testosterone could get channelled and burnt off. But the school had no form, no history, no infrastructure in place . . . it had no well-worn pathway that would have given the boys ideals – or achievements – to aspire to. The school had no network of fathers – or even elder brothers – that would have laid down its own traditions; the school, and everything inside it, was still too new. Men like Gwyn knew that Penlan needed to have something we could all be proud of, and he felt sport was the best way to build it. His attitude was: 'if we don't have our own traditions, then let's make some'. He had a lifelong love of rugby and decided that was what we needed . . . so he put a team together.

In those days, it didn't matter how short, tall, fat or thin you were; there was always a position for you on the rugby field. Nowadays, players are quite uniform in their physical appearance: wingers are as big as locks; props are the size of flankers. But back then a hooker was as different from a centre as a pit bull terrier is from a racehorse. Rugby used to be a great physical leveller: it provided common ground where players of different shapes and sizes could all fulfil roles of equal importance. On one matter, however, I must take issue with Mr Watts' claims to being a true rugby scholar. He may well have been a respected referee in his day and he became a trusted friend, but when Gwyn Watts first picked me for Penlan Seniors the daft bugger put me on the wing. I say 'picked' but I mean 'bullied'. He cast his eye over the various classes at his disposal and said, 'you, you, you, you' before bussing us down to the rock-strewn fields of Waunarlwydd. I was 12 years old and about to begin my first proper game of rugby.

Initially, I had mixed feelings about the sport. Part of me felt I was born to play it, especially after discovering my father's Wales shirt in his wardrobe. But another part of me felt strangely detached; rugby seemed an alien activity that didn't have much place for individuality. My few previous rugby experiences had involved chucking a ball around the street, but that never truly appealed to my sporting instincts. Football and cricket did, because one could see what an individual contributed to the wider team, from hitting boundaries to scoring last-minute winners, but rugby – the rugby I knew, the rugby I was about to play – seemed to disintegrate into a shapeless mêlée. And from my exiled position out on the wing it looked even worse than that – just a frenzy of arms and legs. What did I feel in that first match? A rush of adrenalin as the ball came my way? A strange mix of fear and excitement as I threw myself at the onrushing boots? The cocky bliss, perhaps, of beating a man on the outside? No. I'll tell you what I felt: boredom. I had never been so bored in all my life. At least in the football matches I had played for Plasmarl there was always a faint chance the ball would come my way if I loitered in or near the opposition box. But rugby, schoolboy rugby . . . I might as well have been fielding at third man up at Parc Llewellyn. Despite Gwyn's noble intentions to have the game played properly, those first two matches for Penlan descended into free-for-alls. If rugby was going to engage me then I had to be where the ball was. Gwyn said that it was *his* inspired decision to bring me in off the wing and put me at number 8. But I seem to recollect demanding to make the move. Between us, though, we found the position I would occupy for the rest of my rugby life.

What was it about the nuts and bolts of playing number 8 that enthused me in those early years? I loved the robustness of the role, the need to exert a strong physical presence. Being alert too, always on one's mettle; that also appealed. I relished the turmoil that would often engulf the back row, whether going toe-to-toe in the lineout or waiting to pick up and dump an opposing flanker. Number 8 tested my strength, my courage, my instincts and my sense of self. Away from the pitch I was never a fighter. I would walk away from bother with barely a look over my shoulder. Away from the pitch I was too tall, too skinny, too covered in spots to have any real self-confidence – I was shy and awkward and offered little more than a lumbering presence in mixed company. But that was away from the pitch: on it, I was an entirely different being. I swaggered; I welcomed the hardness, the bruises, and the lumps being knocked out of me. I enjoyed the struggle and the team ethos, the need to contribute something big to each match. Away from the pitch I was moseying through my adolescence with little care or concern, but on the pitch some deep, deep pleasure was awakened by the crash, bang, wallop of rugby.

Number 8 also suited my size. I could have slotted into the second row and dominated the lineout but number 8 fitted my rangy physicality far better. Besides, if I was to be an effective lock then I would have needed more beef and none was forming on my beanpole frame. I lacked the zip to play flanker, but I did have good stores of natural stamina, which is a vital part of a back-rower's armoury. The key to effective back-row play, however, is to remain right on top of the action, and my best quality as a player – right across the arc of my career – was an instinctive ability to read the game. From the number 8 position I was in the optimum place to gauge what was going on. Let the flankers sprint and peel off the scrum, let them annoy, niggle and nail the fly-half; but let the number 8 get on with his job . . . setting the tempo, chasing the ball, snuffing out problems, bridging the gap between forwards and backs.

Being tall; now there's a thing I couldn't train for. But without my height I doubt I would have made any kind of impact upon the game. Tall people in rugby are often lampooned as great big lurches whose sole purpose is to win lineout ball. At Penlan I used my height well around the rugby field and in other areas too. At this time I started playing basketball, a sport I have always had a terrific love for. Technically, basketball is a non-contact game but it is a sport where one can impose one's physical presence. There are other aspects of basketball that I fed into my development as a rugby player. An understanding of spatial awareness for one: in basketball you have to continually seek out the gap . . . and essentially, that's the basis on which good rugby is built. Basketball also demands dexterity; an ability to handle the ball quickly and deftly just as you would in the 15-man game. Basketball is a contest where decisions have to be made instantly: dither and the play is gone. I very much enjoyed making decisions on the rugby field; after all, why should thinking be the sole domain of the backs? After I started playing basketball at Penlan I pursued it even further in college. If I had not got into London Welsh as a rugby player, then maybe I might have tried my hand at basketball with Crystal Palace. Why not? I certainly had the size, the understanding and the love of the game.

The older I got, the easier the going seemed to become. It was often commented that I was so laid back I was practically horizontal. But what, in all honesty, did I have to trouble me? Home life was good, and my only regret was that my understanding of the Welsh language had diminished: the only time I was exposed to Welsh was every Sunday at chapel, or when my grandmother would revert back to her native tongue. Chapel-going was tough, but we did form a good social group and the group would often go out dancing or to the cinema on a Saturday night. But when I wasn't in school or larking about with my mates, I used to enjoy my own company and go off for miles on my bike exploring the Carmarthenshire countryside. I was a perfectly normal youth with very little – except my size – to set me apart. About the most dramatic thing that happened to me was getting stabbed – and even that was an accident. It happened walking back one afternoon from Penlan with some friends. Behind us there were some lads from a younger year messing about with a penknife. The next thing I knew I felt a sharp pain in my calf. I turned around, looked down, and saw a knife sticking out of the back of my leg. It was not a deliberate act or a malicious assault, it was just boys being boys and pushing a silly game too far. But it did have quite serious repercussions; a large chunk of muscle was sliced open and it consigned me to a couple of months at home.

It was while I was languishing indoors that I developed an interest in a hobby that not many other international sportsmen could claim to have: tapestry. I would sit, leg up, watching my mother hand-stitch these wonderful creations, often of a religious scene. There is a famous tapestry often seen in Welsh chapels of an old woman with a shawl, and in her shawl can be seen the face of the devil. I was bored, and naively thought that tapestry looked easy. I watched my mother completely lost in concentration and that willingness to lose herself in something so intricate and colourful mesmerised me. I asked her if I could have a go and, after a few lessons – and the obligatory bloody fingers – I discovered a world of perfect stillness and utter peace, emanating from an activity that involved great imagination and considerable care. I went on to complete a few tapestries over the years . . . although not in the presence of my playing colleagues.

When it was time for me to finally leave Penlan, my parents still set the agenda. In essence, I willingly abdicated responsibility for that part of my life to them: 'Great,' I thought, 'let someone else worry about it.' They were both keen for me to go on to university but my A level grades in Geography and Applied Maths weren't too encouraging. I did consider getting a job or taking a year out to re-sit because I had no real ambition or direction regarding my future. But then, at the very last moment, I applied to Swansea College of Education. I'd never had any previous desire to be a teacher, but I had spent most of my life around them and thought, 'that looks all right, why not?' I hadn't excelled at school, but it was a comfortable environment to be in (once the ropes had been learnt) so I concluded that it couldn't be that bad to work in either. Besides, six years at Penlan had exposed me to the worst kinds of tomfoolery a pupil could perform, so I had lots of relevant teaching experience already – or so I thought. Part of me wanted to get away from Swansea and live a little, but my laziness prevented me from being more proactive so I took the easy option and stayed at home for the next three years of my life.

My college days were excellent. I had money in my pocket thanks to a full grant from the education authority and free board at my parents. Their generosity continued to amaze me. My father arranged for me to get holiday work with him up at the Swansea and Vale International Nickel Works manufacturing zinc, and I had a fantastic time. There was something exciting about doing physical – and very dangerous – work. My father had always advised me against a life in manual labour but at that time I found it exciting, and knowing it was only a short-term measure heightened the appeal. The money was the real reason I eagerly left the house each morning. At one stage I was even bringing home more pay than my father and yet they still refused to take a penny from me. I managed to buy myself a car – although learning to drive with my father wasn't the most enjoyable way to spend an afternoon. He was a stubborn bugger on occasions, just like me, and many lessons ended in stony silence or with one of us getting out of the car and walking away in a huff. But I passed, and I saved up and bought myself a cheap little Mini. They weren't built for drivers sized 6 ft 5 in., but it was the best set of wheels I ever had. They were fun days, and whenever we had the chance a gang of us would go off down the Gower to Broughton or Llangefni to swim, dive, surf and have beach parties. The surf culture has been thriving in Swansea for longer than people might think. I might be knocking on a bit now but I've still got my Bilbo fibreglass board hanging in my mother's garage. Riding the waves . . . now in my mind's eye *that* is where I really earned the nickname 'Merv the Swerve'.

The friends I made in college – Chris Morgan, Colin Williamson, Norman Sanders, John Turley, Keith Richards and Colin Jakeman – have remained my lifelong friends. I knew as soon as I met them that they would. College was a place where a person could subtly reinvent himself should he choose to; there was no need to carry the baggage of adolescence anymore. And in truth, I was glad to jettison some parts of my past. I did, however, continue to carry some of the self-consciousness I felt about my size, a feeling which slowly dissipated only some years later when I was a regular for Wales. But there was a legitimate reason to feel a little coy about my personal appearance, because Swansea College of Education had a female to male ratio of 5:1. All those lovely girls; they frightened and fascinated me.

My areas of study were Geography, Physical Education and Divinity . . . and it soon became apparent in which subject I would specialise. Even after I qualified, I don't think I ever taught Geography. I found college work very demanding and all-encompassing – especially in and around teaching practice time. I have been up against some of the toughest, roughest rugby players who have ever graced the game but they were pussycats compared with the kids we taught on teaching practice. These kids could smell a student teacher from a mile away and they revelled in the dark arts of fear and dread. Luckily, I had the gym as my salvation, a place where I too was well practised in the art of sweet revenge.

The work was gruelling, but my friends and I always made time to enjoy ourselves. It was the mid-'60s and although Swansea might not have been swinging like London or Liverpool, or even Cardiff, it could certainly rock a fair bit. We did our duty and threw ourselves into living the student life. Friendships were formed that would never be broken. You would do anything for each other. I remember being with Chris – who was a native of Aberfan – on that terrible day in October 1966 when 144 people, 116 of them children, were killed when a tip of coal waste slid onto the village. We jumped in the car and headed north-east, desperate to help. All we could do was offer our willing hands, but, like the countless others who tried, we were turned back because there was nothing that could be done. The whole country lived through a nightmare, but it was harder for locals like Chris, who knew some of those lost as people and not just as names.

Like Penlan, Swansea College had little or no rugby heritage to speak of. It didn't have the reputation of Trinity College

Carmarthen, UWIC, Caerleon or Barry. But the college was asked to send a few players off to trial matches and yet again I was one of those who was dispatched – though more out of habit than hope, I think.

We didn't have a bad side, but inconsistent would be the best description for us. We played all the other colleges, and beat many of them. But we also met teams like the South Wales Police or Lampeter, and we endured games where 18-year-old boys suddenly came face-to-face with grown men. I remember one occasion when we were leading a match 20–0 at half-time and were full of ourselves. Come the second half we were methodically beaten up for the next 40 minutes and ended with a completely demoralising defeat. But I still enjoyed it – the get-togethers, the games and the post-match drinks with my teammates. In my view, a rugby match didn't end at the final whistle . . . it ended when the boys dispersed from the bar later that night. The game itself was often the catalyst for the get-together. Sure, I played hard but college rugby (unlike the other rugby I played in my career) wasn't only about winning. I thrived on doing my bit for the team; but in all honesty, to do that I had to achieve *my* aims, play the game *my* way. I worried about my performance first and then the team. Some players are screamers, they need to be stoked up on tension before they activate; but me, I could detach myself, bring a veil down and be cool, calm and collected. I would always be thinking about what was happening around me. One can learn so much from the opposition if viewed at close hand, and I would study mine intently. My game was a game of strategy – of feints and thrusts . . . it unfolded like a chess match.

In many ways I found basketball more exciting than rugby, mainly because the number 8 role I played in college was so negative. These were the days of the 'corner-flagging' player . . . of playing the game in a box within a box. The number 8 was seen as the great architect of defence. Once the opposition won the ball and spun it out along their three-quarter line the number 8 would ignore everything around him and hare off towards his own corner flag because that is where the ball was heading. The great exponent of this defensive art was Alun Pask, a man once described by rugby encyclopedia and friend, David Parry-Jones as 'a snorting shire horse'. Pask was a marvellous defensive number 8 – there have been few better in my opinion – but his game wasn't mine. My game would be more attack focused, more about gaining and moving the ball. But I am getting ahead of myself; the role of the number 8 – and the way I did it – wouldn't evolve until I met John Dawes at Old Deer Park.

In college colours I learnt first hand what a savage game rugby could be. I was seldom injured and rarely got involved in any nonsense. I was of the opinion that if an opponent punched, kicked, gouged, stamped or bit then he did so out of fear. His violent action resulted from his feeling of inferiority. And I also learnt there was little point in retaliating. I played during the days when linesmen were mute onlookers and what television cameras there were, were trained exclusively on the ball. Referees missed much of what went on in a ruck or maul, but you could bet your beer money that they would always see the bloke who hit back. They were good lessons to learn: in all the rugby I played I was only ever sent off once, for fighting when Penlan School were playing against Gowerton Grammar and Mr Pugh sent their lock and me off for ten minutes to cool our tempers. I learnt that there was little point in pursuing personal vendettas, but if you were particularly incensed by an underhand action, a chance to dig in a bony shoulder or elbow would soon arise.

There are some injuries you cannot do a thing to avoid . . . and in my case a broken jaw was one. We were facing Trinity College at Ashley Road playing fields, Swansea and I was trapped at the bottom of a ruck. I saw the ball shoot across the field and tried to disengage my body so I could head off to the corner flag. It was at that precise moment, just when my attention was momentarily elsewhere, that some sneaky little so-and-so sent a well-aimed boot straight into my face. I knew instantly what he'd done because I felt – and heard – the bone break. Bad luck. Bad timing too, because this was the morning of the Wales v England match. I hobbled into the nearby Singleton Hospital only to be told to travel to the other side of Swansea to Morriston. As soon as I entered the deserted casualty department I knew there was little chance of immediate treatment. My suspicions were confirmed when a kindly nurse told me 'all the doctors have gone up to Cardiff for the match'. Wonderful. They bandaged me up like Desperate Dan with toothache and packed me off home. Not only did I have to give up my match ticket but I also had to endure a nightmare 24 hours before a doctor could see straight enough to fix me. My jaw was wired up and I was out of rugby for three months. I never did discover who put the boot in. Believe me, I would love to know.

I implied earlier that I felt virtually ignored by the great and the good of the Swansea rugby establishment, but that is not strictly true: whilst I was incapacitated with my busted jaw I was asked to turn out for the All Whites. I had done so a few weeks earlier, at New Year in fact, against the Scottish touring side Watsonians. No one wanted to play rugby over the New Year period and Swansea struggled to raise a team. Someone, somewhere, mentioned this lanky young number 8 plying his trade for the college up on the hill. It was a strange experience turning out for my father's old club. I wanted to play for my hometown even though I was aware I was their last resort. The match was played in good spirits on a freezing cold mid-winter night, but I enjoyed it. I didn't find it remotely challenging and put it down to experience. What that game did give me, however, was a letter of introduction from Swansea Rugby Football Club stating that I had represented them. It was a letter that would prove useful because, as my college days were drawing to a close, I was determined to leave the comfortable life I had enjoyed in South Wales. New challenges were coming my way and I was in a hurry to meet them.

IV

London Calling

A rugby player's life at the top of his game is often a short one. Mine was. I started late and finished early. But I can be satisfied knowing that the game took me all over the globe; it made me an army of friends, brought with it plenty of success and provided much happiness. And whilst my rugby life was unfolding I always felt in control of events. Well, almost always. There was a brief period of time between September and December 1968, a few short months in fact, when I didn't know what the hell was going on. It was all that I could do to hang on and see where destiny (or pure luck) would eventually lead. It was a time when my rugby life suddenly went into hyperdrive.

Rewind to the late summer of that year and the moment when I finally left the town where I had grown up and studied. I was ready to stretch my legs and walk away from the easy, familiar environment that had cocooned me through my first 20-something years, and I did what so many other young teachers from Wales do; I upped sticks and headed off across the border. It might not read like a momentous change but, internally, I felt as if I had reached a watershed. I could have easily remained in Swansea, languishing in the status quo, but for once I felt a real urge to do something different. My new professional status would open a few doors, although I had little hope of finding a teaching position in Wales, because there were few available. Instead, I joined a mini-exodus to England to get a job.

Wales has always enjoyed a reputation for producing good teachers, and the education authorities around the Midlands, Manchester, Bristol, London and the Home Counties made it known to the numerous Welsh teaching establishments, through their recruitment circulars, that there were jobs waiting for those prepared to relocate. With the blessing of my folks and the reassuring presence of my mates beside me, I couldn't wait to give it a go.

Four of us – Chris, Norman, Colin Williamson and I – had a grand plan to stick together; we'd formed a close bond in college and felt no challenge was insurmountable if we faced it together. After a careful reconnoitre of what was available, we applied en masse to the education authority of Surrey. It worked a treat; we all got jobs in the county. About eight other mates from college got jobs in the neighbouring county, so the next part of our grand plan was to scour the map and find a suitable base within easy reach of all our schools. In Guildford, we found it.

As I mentioned in the previous chapter, I was no natural in front of the chalkboard, but I fell on my feet somewhat at Mytchett County Primary School, Frimley Green. The tall, dark-haired new-boy with the strange accent was brought in to teach 10 and 11 year olds, and I faced my first professional placing with some trepidation. College and teaching practise could only impart so much; doing it for real, now that is where a teacher learns his or her craft. The breadth of teaching disciplines required in junior school unnerved me. In fact, when I moved on to a secondary school post in the Emanuel School a couple of years later, I found the luxury of focusing on one or two subjects far more rewarding than concentrating on the whole curriculum. But that first class in that first crucial year was a trial by fire. I was fortunate my group were a nice bunch of middle-class kids from a nice middle-class area, because my first tour at the chalk-face could have been much worse. A junior schoolteacher has to be all things to all pupils, and it is an unenviable task trying to hold the attention of the class hour after hour, day after day. True, you do quickly get to know them . . . but they also get to know you. Luckily for me, Chris Morgan also taught at Mytchett, so we hunkered down, analysed the mistakes we made and tried to learn from each one – and from each other.

Mytchett was a pleasant place to work – a cosy and gentle place even – where the presence of our predominantly female colleagues helped curb the wilder instincts of two Welsh boys. What my colleagues thought of this strange twosome from the depths of South Wales I will never know. If we annoyed or irritated them, then they hid it graciously and guided us well. We might have been lucky in our first jobs, but the school didn't do too badly from their latest recruits. Suddenly Mytchett had two new sporty additions to the staff . . . two new teachers willing to get stuck in to the various extra-curricular sporting activities. I have to add, though, that we weren't pitching in through a desire to show our altruistic side; no, the more we did for the various school clubs, the more food we were entitled to. Wages weren't great – £54 a month – and by the time a young man had budgeted for life's essentials (beer, petrol, clothes) there was little left for food. We discovered quite early in our tenure at Mytchett that we could subsidise our meagre food intake from Monday to Friday by eating a large hearty school dinner with extra helpings thrown in for taking soccer, cricket or gymnastic club. Extra grub eased the difficulties normally associated with self-sufficiency. Not that we lived like slobs at home (my mother would never have brought up a slovenly boy), but it was helpful to have some kind of daily balanced diet served up for us that wasn't readily available from the local chip shop. Cooking aside, life in a large shared flat was perfectly pleasant except that I – the tallest member of our party – had to share a double bed with Colin, whilst my other three smaller flatmates bagged single beds to themselves. Maybe I should have used my height advantage to better my lot? But somehow I was convinced that sharing the biggest bed in the flat was the best option for the biggest chap – even if it meant having Colin kick lumps out of me night after night.

One of the first tasks when I arrived in Guildford was to get down to the local rugby club and introduce myself to the members. It is something I recommend to any outsider coming into a new area, because sport can open the door to an instant – and very active –

social life. There may be a little frostiness to begin with, a kind of outsider aversion, but a shared love of rugby, football, cricket, hockey, etc. will always take away the chill. I had great hopes for myself at Old Guildfordians and felt ready to commit my heart and soul to their cause. Unfortunately, my enthusiasm waned after one game in their black shirts.

It wasn't the people or the place that turned me off the club; they all extended the hand of friendship, which I received gratefully. What turned me off was the rugby. I don't want to be viewed as arrogant; after all, the rugby I had experienced at school and college wasn't exactly rugby to write home about. But I can recall having an overwhelming feeling that I could do better. I wasn't looking to play the game for laughs, or seeking a bawdy bash about with a field full of wheezing, big-bellied boys who'd seen better days. My Saturdays were precious to me – a small window of time free of timetables and deadlines, a time to be me. I wanted to use that precious time to push myself to the limit against an opposition who would do the same. Even at Penlan when we faced Bishop Gore, or at college against teams from the hardened Carmarthenshire League, we met sides that would stamp on us or scintillate their way past us. But Old Guildfordians, with its fixture list against an eclectic mix of the young and the old, seemed a step back to a jokier, softer rugby. I have no wish to denigrate the club because they, and their merry counterparts dotted around the rugby world, are fantastic rugby folk that play an important part in the fabric of the game, but I needed something with more bite. Old Guildfordians and their ilk are clubs where players come young to be blooded, or to which they return when their playing careers are winding down. They are great gathering grounds for rugby lovers, but not the place for a 21 year old looking for a way to test his ability to the utmost.

I made good friends there, though, and those friendships have endured. They included boys like Ed Ram. Ed was someone I can only describe as your typical amateur English rugger player. Short – and a little bit tubby – he knew everyone and had an opinion on everything. He was the consummate social animal and a major factor for making life in Guildford feel so good – although there was one occasion in the infancy of our friendship when Ed might have happily disowned me. It was during the autumn of 1968 and Guildford – with its water-heavy topography – suffered a flash flood. Now I am sure that if we had wanted to, Chris and I could have put a bit more effort into avoiding the floodwater of central Guildford and making our way to work at Frimley Green. However, we didn't need much convincing that my little Mini couldn't survive a dunking. After a quick dash to the nearest phone box and an apologetic call to the school secretary, we did what any other respectable young schoolteacher would have done in similar circumstances . . . we went to the pub.

It was quickly apparent that we weren't the only ones who had chosen to seek refuge from the rain in the local watering holes, and soon a sizeable party had joined us on our mission to drown the day in alcohol (well, you know how animated these all-day sessions can get). After a substantial crawl, we splashed into one of Guildford's more select hostelries and started carousing in voices that were a little more excitable than usual. Like many of my countrymen in similar circumstances, I fell into that strange 'Welshman-in-exile' mood and began eulogising about my homeland. Then a Welsh voice (Chris or me, allegedly) was supposed to have proclaimed with the conviction of a true believer, that 'All Englishmen are bastards . . . except Ed Ram.' I can't imagine any Englishman getting away with that kind of comment in a Welsh pub and, quite understandably, one of the regulars decided to defend his country's honour. My recollection of the ensuing fracas is a little hazy, but I am sure it was Chris who instigated the brawl. Whenever he had a beer inside him he became a cantankerous little bugger despite his rather diminutive size. He used to wear thick-rimmed bottle-bottom spectacles, which I think he believed made him look like Michael Caine. They didn't. Chris had perfected the knack of removing his specs and placing them in his top pocket with his right hand whilst simultaneously throwing a mean hook with his left. But on this occasion, he wasn't fast enough. After a bit of a brawl, our drunken band dispersed and fled to the four corners of Guildford. I ended the night in casualty having 20 stitches put in my back for a glass wound. Chris resembled a panda; his glasses were gone but their imprint had left two perfect shiners. The next morning we heroically convinced our headmaster, Mr Wise, that our injuries were caused by our car skimming across the floodwater and crashing into a hedge. I'd like to think that Ed appreciated our regard for him as being a cut above his countrymen, but then again, he probably wished we had kept our big Welsh mouths shut.

When I reflected on my disappointment at Old Guildfordians, I realised that for any young Welshman in the south-east keen to test his rugby mettle, there was only one club to try out for, so I headed some 30 miles up the A3 to Old Deer Park – the home of London Welsh RFC. At that time, London Welsh was in a truly sparkling era of rugby excellence. In the book *Heart and Soul: The Character of Welsh Rugby* (University of Wales Press, 1998), writer and broadcaster Peter Stead contributed a fine essay on my old friend and back-row colleague John Taylor. No story about 'Baz' could ignore the effect playing for London Welsh had on him. Likewise, London Welsh would have been a poorer place without the acerbic, spiky presence of that flyaway flanker. It was a very special time to be involved with such a special club, as Peter Stead revealed:

> For eight years between 1965 and 1973 the prosperity and educational dynamic of Wales ensured a flow of talented Welsh people to London and the Home Counties, and the Old Deer Park club house, superbly placed between Kew Gardens and the pubs of Richmond, became the place to be seen whether you were a student, a teacher, an MP, an opera singer or just Richard Burton or Hywel Bennett. Here as much as anywhere one sensed that everything was flowing the Welsh way.
>
> This was a famous old club that in its first hundred years was to provide 170 international players, but they were never to be so thick on the ground as in this eight-year period when eleven of the team played for the national side. When John Taylor went to South Africa with the 1968 Lions he was the only London Welsh player selected: when he went to Australia and New Zealand in 1971 he was one of six. The captain of that Lions side was John Dawes, the centre whose appointment as captain of London Welsh in 1965 had been

the vital step in their emergence as possibly the best club rugby side in the world.

'The best club rugby side in the world.' Now there's a claim – but one, when the evidence is examined, that can be upheld. During that period, long before the days of premiership play-offs, national leagues or European competitions, London Welsh consistently won merit tables (*Sunday Telegraph*, *Western Mail*, Whitbread) in both England and Wales, and often won the Middlesex Sevens too.

London Welsh might have been affiliated to the RFU and played the majority of its fixtures against English club sides, but it remained a little oasis of Welshness in a foreign land. It didn't matter where in Wales you came from, what your background was, or what you did; solicitors, doctors, bricklayers, milkmen, railworkers, teachers from the north, south, east, west and middle . . . at London Welsh we were united by our nationality. Being a small-town boy myself, away from home for the first time, it made complete sense to seek out the company of my own kind. I knew I would receive a warm welcome as an ex-pat – another 'Welsh stranger in an English paradise' – but there was no guarantee I would get a game. I had no pedigree or referee, no patron or ex-colleague to vouch for me; all I had to show that I played the game was a letter of introduction from Swansea Rugby Football Club. For the first time in my rugby life it dawned on me that I had no club. I didn't belong to Dunvant, Morriston, Mumbles or one of the other clubs found in the Swansea district. The only club I had played for outside school or college was Swansea and that was a one-off the previous Christmas! I asked the club secretary, Len Davies (who incidentally once played alongside my father, although I didn't know that at the time), if I could come along and train with the squad; he inspected the letter I'd brought, sized me up and told me to bring my kit on Tuesday. It is safe to surmise that my height impressed him more than my credentials.

What did London Welsh have back then that set it apart as a club among clubs? Well, it had a wide player base for a start; one where there was no divided loyalty to valley or town – just being Welsh was enough to fit in. It had good administration and a real rugby pedigree through the active involvement of men like Len, Dick Ellis and the former Wales and Lions player Harry Bowcott. It had a rigorous selection process: all three teams operated under the watchful eye of the committee, which kept the competition for places fierce. It had uncompromising taskmasters like ex-Cambridge Blue Roger Michaelson who would work you until you were literally sick . . . and then still demand that little bit more. Being an ex-international number 8 and a glutton for physical exertion, Roger paid me special attention and would push me hardest of all if he felt I lacked commitment in those horrendous sprints along Kew Road. It had its success; like Manchester United of recent years, London Welsh relied on an 'us against the world' mentality. We were always the side to beat for English and Welsh alike. No one liked us. The English felt we didn't belong in their country and the Welsh thought we had sold our souls to the *Saes* devil. Wherever we went, the crowds would bay for our blood and this open hostility inspired us to turn on the style and stuff the catcalls back down the throats from whence they came.

What else did we have? Well, a tasty array of players from number 1 to number 15 that was the envy of almost any club in the land: look at this for a roll-call – J.P.R. Williams, Jim Shanklin, Keith Hughes, Bill Hullin, Tony Gray, John Taylor, Mike Roberts, Geoff Evans, Jeff Young, Bob Phillips. In that group alone there are Lions and Test players. Men like Bob Phillips could have made it into almost any national side . . . the reason he only achieved Wales B status was the presence of Barry John and Phil Bennett. London Welsh also had an excellent pitch that drained quickly of rainwater and encouraged fast, running rugby. But more than anything else, the factor that truly set London Welsh apart and allowed the club to have such a profound effect on the domestic game, on Wales and ultimately on the British Lions, was one man who played, captained and coached with nothing less than brilliance: John Dawes.

Without doubt, John Dawes is the single biggest influence upon my rugby career. He was my mentor. He remains one of my dearest friends. No story of my rugby life can be told without referring to the massive presence of John Dawes. He is a softly spoken man, someone who thinks deeply and feels passionately. The place he has secured in the annals of the game is as a great, great captain and coach. That word 'great' has been cheapened through the years in the way it has so easily been applied to any old Tom, Dick and Harry. But Dawes is truly worthy of the adjective: greatness as a coach and captain drips from him to such an extent that I believe his ability as a player is often overlooked. As a centre three-quarter, John never had the explosive thrust of a Ray Gravell or the all-round ball skills of a Mike Gibson, but he did have the sweetest pass I have ever seen on a rugby pitch. What he lacked in pace or niftiness he compensated for with sublime timing and quickness of mind. It was amazing how John's hands responded to his rugby brain. Call it instinct, incisiveness or a cool, calculating thought process . . . in my view, John Dawes simply had the best rugby brain ever taken onto the pitch. It is a pity that the people of these islands – people who doubted his playing ability when the captaincy was bestowed upon him for the Lions in '71 – never had a chance to witness his play first-hand in that Test series. Gareth Edwards, Barry John, David Duckham, Mike Gibson, Gerald Davies, J.P.R. Williams . . . they are as close as one can get to an all-time British dream back division. But John, who was slotted in between Gibson and Davies, earned his place on merit and did so much to secure that Test series. He played the game with lots of guile and no panic. His philosophy was simple: move the ball, move the ball, move the ball. And at London Welsh, that's exactly what we did.

As soon as I arrived at the club I made my presence felt in training and got a game for the Dragons (the thirds). It was easy . . . too easy. I scored a hat-trick of tries – and I had never scored tries! Next week I was pitched into the Druids (the seconds) and, again, I did well. The rugby wasn't giving me quite what I wanted, but I was enjoying being at the club . . . although the drives from Frimley Green, Richmond and Guildford weren't ideal, especially during rush hour. But everything changed for me when flanker Tony Gray, who'd been capped against England and Scotland the previous season (and would go on to coach Wales to the last Triple Crown in 1988), was injured. As the Firsts looked to re-jig the back row in Tony's absence, Roger Walkie, who was the incumbent number 8, was shifted to flanker. Suddenly, there was an opening. I believe the comment from Colin Bosley went something like, 'There's a guy playing number 8 for the seconds, he's not much good but he'll guarantee you some ball at the back of the lineout' – although knowing Colin, he probably peppered his assessment with a few expletives. I am minded to disagree with the 'not much good' part of that quote, but Colin had a point. London Welsh had terrific backs and a decent mobile pack. They had a team designed to play quick, open rugby. But an adventurous spirit is about as much use as chocolate boots if you can't get your hands on the ball. And London Welsh hadn't been winning decent lineout ball. Therefore I was brought in to fill a deficiency in the pack.

I heard about my elevation into the big time whilst at home in Swansea for half-term holiday. A telegram arrived at my parents' home saying I had been selected to face Moseley that Saturday and would be required back in Richmond. It knocked me out of my stride; a mere six weeks earlier I had been looking for a club to join, and suddenly there I was, about to start for one of the best sides in the country. If I was shocked, Dai was even more so . . . it took that telegram to convince him that his eldest son wasn't that bad a player. It took that telegram to convince me that I wasn't that bad a player! Partly out of curiosity but largely out of pride, my family all joined me on the journey east to watch me play my second game of first-class rugby.

I am a great believer that if an opportunity comes your way you should grab hold of it with both hands. And when that number 8 shirt landed on my back, I wasn't going to let it go. I knew little about my new teammates and if I felt that I was going to get a kind word or a helpful tap of encouragement to ease my transition, then I was mistaken. You had to earn the respect of your colleagues on the pitch. John Taylor – an established Wales international and British Lion – left me in little doubt about what was expected. He drummed into me that this level of rugby was far higher than any I had experienced before, and new standards were required of me. He also insisted on calling me 'Vernon', which pissed me off no end. John went on to loom large in my rugby story as both player and friend, but he wasn't an easy man to get to know or like . . . and I think he enjoyed his confrontational reputation. Little did I imagine back then that this would be the chap I would go on to share a house with, go on tour with and go shopping with up the West End for the most outrageous flared trousers we could find.

My role was set out for me from that first training session: win the ball and pass it on. We had to play the game differently from other teams because of the relative smallness of our pack. The lawmakers also unwittingly helped us out. When the rule was changed so that you could only kick directly into touch from behind your own 25-yard line, rugby became a more exciting and fluid game. Before that it was often static and predictable, with sides happy to belt the ball over the touchline at every opportunity. Some games must have seen close to a hundred lineouts . . . not quite the free-flowing rugby that brings the crowds in. What Dawes wanted to do was use the new law to our advantage and bring a 7-a-side ethos into our 15-man game. We went out onto the field with a commitment to keep the ball alive. This commitment also played to our strengths . . . and one of our greatest strengths was a young buck student doctor in at full-back called J.P.R. Williams. My bread and butter rugby at number 8 had always been to cover the corner flags, but playing with J.P.R. behind me, and with John's desire to 'move the ball' lodged within my brain, transformed the way I approached the game. If a team was foolish enough to kick possession away to J.P.R., then they were likely to receive the full force of this fearsome rugby animal come hurtling back at them. My job was simple: I had to be there at the breakdown – usually preceded by Tony Gray or John Taylor – and then secure possession. J.P.R. was the most predictable player I have ever played with or against: you knew he would run through the opposition, you knew he wouldn't let anyone pass him, you knew he would always raise his game against England and you knew he demanded nothing but your total commitment to the collective cause. Who says predictability is a bad thing? J.P.R. set standards of toughness and intensity that we all had to match . . . and he set them wherever he played, from Tondu to Twickenham.

Those first few games for the London Welsh 1st XV asked difficult questions of my playing talents . . . questions that I hoped I answered. This was the rugby I had been yearning for. The big old English packs we came up against took some breaking down and I thoroughly enjoyed the mental and physical exertion competing against the best. Everything we did was executed at breakneck speed. I was lucky to be naturally fit but being thrust into this vibrant rugby environment caused my rugby reflexes to come crackling into life. So much of our game was built around space . . . our training sessions placed as much emphasis on playing touch rugby, of getting rid of the ball before going into contact, as it did on scrums and lineouts. My role was being redefined too . . . away from the traditional defensive duties to a more attacking role. Today, number 8s like Lawrence Dallaglio and Imanol Harinordoquy are seen as the men who run the hard yards, the prime ball carriers used to get over the gain line. For the first time, in that 1968–69 season I was actively encouraged to put the ball in my hands and use those basketball skills. But I still saw myself primarily as part of a unit, working with my flankers and adapting *my* game to their game. John Taylor was fast, and Tony Gray was faster, so I let those two fly whilst I mopped up behind. Dawes saw the back row as the pivotal link between the guts and the glory. The rugby we played, rugby that was full of panache, incisiveness and verve, was unlike the rugby being played by other teams. However, Carwyn James was following a similar route down at Stradey Park, home of Llanelli RFC, and the combination of Carwyn and John as Lions' coach and captain respectively reached wonderful fruition in New Zealand in 1971.

Another aspect of my game that set me apart from my contemporaries was my love of tackling. It was unusual for a man as big as me to get so low in the tackle. I rarely took men high, preferring to get down around the legs. I saw the tackle as a play in itself, and an area where intent could be shown to the opposition. And the contribution my tackling made was further increased by having men like Taylor and Gray beside me to snap up any spilt ball and fire it off to the backs. Sometimes I found myself bemused by the speed of it all, captivated by the dash and derring-do as the ball zipped this way and that. Then Taylor would bark at me to get my mind on the game and I'd be off in support once more. Those first few weeks presented a steep, steep learning curve and I had to adapt to the players around me and how we played the game. My height might have got me my start but I was keen to show my teammates that there was more to big Merv than feet and inches. I think the best testament to my burgeoning talents as a number 8 is the way Taylor and Gray accepted me and acknowledged how much better we soon became as a unit. Not that the miserable blighters ever said such a thing to my face! They worked me hard but they recognised that my presence improved their game. We went hunting as a threesome and we nearly always came away with the spoils.

What startles me still about my time at Old Deer Park is the speed with which it all happened. Within a few short months I went from the thirds to a Welsh trial. I certainly grabbed hold of the opportunity, but if it hadn't been for the presence of Messrs Dawes, Taylor, Gray, Michaelson et al., that opportunity might have been short-lived. I know I was in the right place at the right time in terms of where my association with London Welsh would lead . . . but that is another chapter. The years I spent in Richmond were some of the happiest of my life. I am proud to say I played my part in a terrific side that set a marker for playing distinctive, exciting, crowd-pleasing rugby. Not that we pleased everyone, however. I remember one ice-cold winter we went to Wales to play Newbridge (John Dawes' old club) in the days when London Welsh always drew in a big crowd and guaranteed a bumper pay day for the home club. The team met in Reading, got on the train to Newport, had a bite to eat and was then bussed up the valley to the ground. Upon arrival, Dawes took one look at the pitch, saw that it was frozen solid and said we were not going to play on it. He took a fearful ear-bashing from the Newbridge contingent but would not relent. So we got back on the bus and headed down the valley to the train station. A few beers later . . . and then a few more . . . followed by a few more for good measure, and the next thing I remember is waking up in the early hours of Sunday morning in a deserted carriage just outside Portsmouth!

Few clubs have the determination to persevere with a vision, but we did. Few clubs can match what we achieved in the early '70s. In 1970–71 when Wales won a Grand Slam, I don't think I was on a losing side the entire season. Well, if I was, it was only once or twice. How many players can say that when they look back upon their playing days?

I played at London Welsh when Wales was very much on the top of the rugby pile. Even when some of us left Richmond we kept the playing ideals and spirit of Old Deer Park with us, and when we ran out in our national colours we did so with the intention of letting the ball do the work. Let it never be forgotten how big a part the exiles played in the mother country's extraordinary success.

V

Mervyn Who?

One of the most enjoyable times of year to be a London Welsh player was over the festive period, when we would saddle up and head off west to tour the rugby heartland of Wales. The games were hard, with all comers lining up to knock the city slickers down, but the experience itself was marvellous. The single boys in our party could retreat to a hotel in Penard to recuperate and drink the night away, whilst boys like me with families to see, could enjoy freshly laundered kit and big steaming platefuls of home cooking. Great, I thought, the perfect way to combine rugby and family commitments. But away from the aromas of roasts and the baying of the hostile home crowds, something else was afoot . . . we were being closely scrutinised by the Big Five themselves.

The London Welsh Christmas tour was 'shop window' rugby – a chance to show the Welsh rugby fans and press what we were capable of. John Taylor used the tour in December 1967 to propel him into the national team. Funnily enough, he wore a headband too . . . perhaps it had helped us both stand out on occasion? Baz was proof of where a good few games on the road could lead to, but I gave the matter little thought. I was more excited about playing my hometown club at St Helens and then – for the first time in my life – visiting Stradey Park. That match against Llanelli was seen as a meeting of the best of east and west and seemed, on paper, a mouth-watering rugby feast. Both

Llanelli and London Welsh, under the inspirational stewardship of Carwyn James and John Dawes respectively, were committed to playing a fast, open game. However, my recollection is of a very different affair: a dour shunt and shove in the Carmarthenshire mud. All in all, the '68 tour was a success. I performed well enough – and maybe even gave my father something to smile about over a beer with his mates. Many of my club colleagues returned to England with high hopes of being involved in the forthcoming Five Nations campaign, and of showing the Welsh contingent of the Big Five that their London-based member, Harry Bowcott, did indeed have something to shout about. But not me . . . I was unknown and therefore uninvolved. At that juncture, international rugby seemed about as likely as me walking on the moon.

In the run-up to a new Five Nations Championship, it was the practice back then for the Welsh selectors to stage a 'Probables versus Possibles' trial match. Dennis Hughes, that fine Newbridge man, was the incumbent number 8 after playing twice against Argentina the previous September. Wales hardly covered themselves in glory during those unofficial tests, going down to a defeat and a draw, but Dennis was widely considered a dead cert for selection against Scotland. Problem was, he was injured. Dennis was the latest in a long line vying to fill the role vacated by Alun Pask – a good stock of players that included Bob Wanbon, Ron Jones, Stuart Gallacher, John Jeffery and even Dai Morris. With Dennis struggling for fitness, one man's misfortune would be another man's opportunity. Mine. To my surprise, I was invited up to the trial.

Trial matches are universally awful games to play in, often disjointed and scrappy, with teams chopping and changing and players thinking more about themselves than the role they were picked to perform. I played as well as circumstance would allow: took my lineout ball, put in some decent tackles, let a few passes go and then trudged off back to the dingy dressing-room behind the old Arms Park. As I changed, someone said to me, 'Well played, son,' and I replied, 'Thank you very much. Who are you?' The guffaws from my fellow trialists revealed it was a gentleman I should have recognised.

'Rees Stephens,' he said, 'selector.' Nice one, Merv . . . an example of how not to make a good impression.

I put the trial behind me and got on with my life. The following Friday I was en route to school with Chris and we stopped at a Guildford newsagent to pick up his morning paper. He came crashing out of the shop waving it in the air like a lunatic, shouting, 'Merv, you're in!' My first reaction was, 'In what?', and then I saw it in black and white, hidden away at the foot of one of the inside sports pages under the heading Wales XV:

'T.M. Davies (London Welsh).'

'Bloody hell,' I thought, 'I need a drink'.

From a twenty-first century perspective it is difficult to imagine life without a mobile phone, but at that time I wasn't even living in a house with a telephone. So I was almost the last person to know that I had been picked to play for my country. When I did eventually phone home, my father told me that he had heard the news the previous night. People and press back in Wales were left scratching their heads wondering who the hell Mervyn Davies was. What had he done to warrant selection? Some even surmised I must be Harry Bowcott's chief dog-walker! If only selection were that easy. Seriously, I was equally bemused by this startling turn of events; bear in mind, four months earlier I had been playing for Old Guildfordians. The inside back page of the *Daily Mirror* is an odd way to learn that your life is about to change. I went up to London Welsh that evening, partly to receive the congratulations of my club but mainly to seek verification of my selection. I also needed to know what to do next. It was only on the following day, when I received official word from the WRU via telegram, that the news seemed true:

> You have been selected to play for Wales against Scotland next Saturday 1 February. Please delete as necessary and return this card within five days. I can/cannot play.

It took me five seconds to open, answer and post my acceptance.

When Dai Davies played for a Wales XV at Murrayfield just after the war, he took the overnight sleeper train from Swansea on Friday, which got him into Waverley Station early the next morning. From the train station he made his way to an Edinburgh hotel and met up with his teammates – some, it has to be said, for the very first time. From the hotel he was bussed to Murrayfield, changed, played, changed, bussed back, ate and was on the train back home to Wales that same night. A far cry from the professional players of today who appear to spend more time with their fellow internationals than they do with their own families. Off they go into training camps to be poked and prodded and primed to physical perfection. When it goes well, like it did with Clive Woodward and England when he helped turn them from under-achievers into world champions, the indulgence is worth it. When it doesn't, when players get homesick – or resent being treated like children – it can cause a considerable backlash. I like to think, in my day, we struck a happy medium.

My Wales itinerary was straightforward enough (and the amateur laws we operated within prohibited too much squad time together): training at the South Wales Police Ground in Bridgend the following Thursday, a night in Cardiff's Angel Hotel, a Friday flight up to Edinburgh, the match on Saturday and then a flight back on Sunday. What made the whole adventure easier was the company of my fellow London Welsh boys: John Taylor, John Dawes and fellow debutant, J.P.R. Williams.

From the moment I received word of my selection up to the second the referee blew his whistle for kick-off, I was consumed by two thoughts: don't get injured – for you don't get a cap unless you start the match – and don't do a John Jeffery and repeat his infamous blunder. I have thought a lot about John Jeffery in the subsequent years. In some ways I had the career he should have had. John was the young Newport number 8 destined for great things who took the field for his one and only cap against New Zealand in November 1967. Any international sportsman will say that the first time you run out to represent your country is one of the most nerve-shredding experiences you can endure. But to do it at home, in front of an expectant crowd, and to do it for Wales against New Zealand – well, the pressure must build and build. The history between these great rugby nations is a fierce one and it was only in 1987 at the inaugural World Cup when a real gulf in class started to show. The last time Wales beat the All Blacks was in 1953 when a team inspired by Bleddyn Williams, Ken Jones, Cliff Morgan and Clem Thomas gave the watching Welsh a quite awesome day. It must have been a memorable experience because New Zealand has won every Test match since, twisting a thorn further into the Welsh rugby psyche with each defeat. I do not have that many regrets in my life, but one is I never beat the All Blacks in a Wales shirt. And that hurts. But I am not the only player whose international career is blighted with that particular stat. I am sure the men of 1967 feel it too . . . especially John Jeffery. He wasn't the first – and won't be the last – to panic in the shadow of his own posts, but as Bill Davis made the most of his error and set New Zealand on the way to a 13–6 win, I wonder if John Jeffery guessed then he would never get a sniff of a Wales game again? However, that is rugby: cruel, quixotic and unforgiving.

I have never been one to suffer with nerves, but I was a wreck in the run-up to my debut. The press didn't help, openly questioning my ability to step up to the level required for international rugby. I had to remind myself that the selectors had seen something that warranted my inclusion: my ability as a ball-winner perhaps, or my appetite for the physical side of the game. Scotland had big men in their side – lock Peter Stagg was an impressive 6 ft 10 in. tall – so I knew that could be one reason. It might be my first cap, it might turn out to be my last, but I was determined to prove a few people wrong. And besides, nothing inspires a player more than a slating in the press. With my head full of criticism and my gut full of worry I didn't get much sleep that Friday night. It helped having a wise old head like Baz on hand to trap the butterflies.

Everywhere I turned I encountered something new, from flying on a plane to staying in a first-class hotel. But nothing hit me more than seeing the Welsh fans flock in their thousands to Edinburgh . . . and the massive expectations they put on us. And then, of course, being with my new colleagues, that was a buzz in itself, with players who would go on to blaze such a glorious trail across the international stage that they would be known universally by their first names: Gareth, Barry, Gerald. And there were others too, Keith Jarrett, Maurice Richards, Jeff Young and the immense lock pairing of the two granite Brians – Thomas and Price. Characters one and all, but none quite as animated and as effervescent as that barrelling blast of fire and fag ash, Clive Rowlands.

If the WRU ever needed to define what exactly Welsh rugby is then it could do so in two words: Clive Rowlands. Scrum-half, captain, manager, WRU president . . . there is very little that Clive hasn't done – or wouldn't do – for his country. But my first experience of him was in a guise where Wales was actually leading the way: coaching. The groundwork of Ray Williams, David Nash and Clive Rowlands was instrumental in bringing Wales to the fore as a rugby power in the subsequent decade, and the idea of having a dedicated national coaching structure would eventually be adopted by all the rugby-playing nations. Not that Clive was the world's greatest coach (and in all honesty, how much coaching did men of the calibre I mentioned earlier need?) but what he could do, what he was better at than anyone I have ever met, was motivation. His team talks were legendary: scowling and prowling around, beating his fists, dropping fag ash everywhere, ramming home the duty we had to our family, friends, neighbours, countrymen. Clive's rhetoric was so vivid, so passionate he often unwittingly increased the burden we carried onto the field. But it was all done out of pure desire, for few men had a bigger heart than Clive Rowlands and none beat so rhythmically Welsh.

The step up to international rugby is the single biggest step a player can take. It transcends anything else he experiences in youth or club rugby and it is only in the doing of it that he can discover if he is good enough to cope. Teammates and opponents on the international field are considered to be the best players available in their positions; they present a true test of ability, courage and nerve. I noticed the difference from the outset: everything on the international arena was magnified to the nth degree. There was a speed of thought, an increase in pace, greater intensity, smoother skills . . . and all in that chaotic, untamed Murrayfield of old: a vast cauldron of boiling emotions. I loved every second.

The match itself went by in a blur . . . Barry, John, Gareth Edwards and Maurice Richards scored tries, Keith Jarrett kicked the rest of our points, and we finished 17–3 to the good. It was a surprisingly easy win. I did what I had set out to do and played a restrained game with little error. My job was made simpler by the presence of Dai Morris and John Taylor flanking beside me. It was the beginning of a wonderful back-row partnership, one many have considered the best Wales has ever produced. They were both quick, strong men with an eye for the ball. There was a considerable amount of competition between the two and it often inspired their play. Their backgrounds (one working-class, one middle-class) couldn't have been more different, but they did complement one another terrifically on the field. My role was very much to mop up what they missed and on the 16 occasions we took to the field together, we didn't miss much. Dai – or 'The Shadow' as Gareth christened him – was a truly terrific player. Whether he was playing for Wales or his village side, Rhigos, he would approach each game in the same way. He was a godsend to have in your corner and his omission from the 1971 Lions team caused quite a controversy . . . especially in Neath, where he played his club rugby. Some said Dai was snubbed because he didn't like flying, but he did make the New Zealand trip with Wales two years before the Lions, which challenges that particular assumption. I felt his omission owed more to the number of other Wales players in the party and he was, unfortunately, the odd man out. In all the time we played together, I think he only ever spoke to me once during a game. We were heading to a defeat against England in 1974 at Twickenham and were defending a scrum on our goal-line. Andy Ripley picked up the ball from the base and went round the pack. Dai was meant to be first up to tackle him, but he barely moved a muscle. By the time I got my hands on Ripley it was too late and he powered over for the score. As we waited for the conversion attempt, Dai wandered over and said, 'Merv, you missed your man.'

'What do you mean, Dai? First man round the scrum is yours, second one is mine.'

'What number's on his back, Merv?'

'Eight.'

'What number's on your back, Merv?'

'Eight.'

'Your fucking man, then.'

My first experience of international rugby was a memorable one – and to be on a winning side crowned it. The sense of relief I felt was immense, and I was confident my place was secure to face the

Irish a month or so later. Dennis Hughes might have been on his way to full fitness, but it is hard for the selectors to tamper with a winning team. But selection thoughts were put on hold and we enjoyed a monumental night amongst the celebrating Welsh fans. I merrily signed autographs and made a promise to myself never to decline a request for one. After all, a day would come when my signature might not mean anything. My only disappointment was not receiving my cap after the game; it crept through the post, wrapped up in brown paper a few days later. I was a callow chap then, asking Gerald Davies what pâté was and wearing a ridiculous velvet dinner jacket that looked more suited to Tom Jones than it did on Wales' newest international forward. But what exciting times they were . . . times that would only get better.

Wales hadn't beaten Ireland since 1965 and we knew if we were to reverse recent results then we had to come up with a new plan. The only way any team could beat that Ireland side was to stop them from killing the ball – in particular Noel Murphy, the flank-forward. When it came to ball-killing, he was a master. Murphy was a wily character who would go on to coach Ireland and the 1980 Lions. His prime skill as a player was his ability to spoil possession . . . and he didn't mind taking a few whacks in the process. Clive or Brian or one of the senior players came up with a devastatingly simple plan: if Noel Murphy wasn't on the pitch, then he wouldn't be a problem. Ireland weren't about to drop him so we had to take responsibility for his absence.

The 'Murphy Plan' was honed during Sunday training sessions in the run-up to the match. We didn't have the warm-weather facilities of Lanzarote, or access to a purpose-built indoor complex; no, all we had was the endless sand of Aberavon beach, and I reckon we covered every inch of it. Trust me, there are better pastimes for a wet and cold Sunday than running up and down Aberavon beach. That was possibly the one downside of playing for London Welsh: the 5.30 a.m. start to get up to Aberavon for squad training sessions. This was in the days before the M4 motorway – and often after a night on the beers – but the London Welsh players would crawl westward along interminable A-roads, arriving cramped, bad-tempered and early. My mind shudders now when I recall the endless running we did. 'How far, Clive?' came the call . . . 'till I bloody well tell you to stop,' was his response. So we'd run and run and run . . . and then run some more, too far away to hear Clive call us back.

'The Murphy Plan' was fiendishly simple: from the very first scrum, Gareth would take the ball and run straight into him. When Murphy hauled Gareth down, every member of the Welsh pack would run over the Irishman and, with luck, put him out of the match. 'Jeez,' I thought, 'here I am playing international rugby with the best against the best and we're planning to do *this*.' I went along with it because I was the new boy and unwilling to break ranks, but my heart wasn't in it. I had to show my commitment though; training sessions at that level are like trial matches and the man who wants your shirt isn't shy about letting you know of his intentions. John Hickie – a real tough lad from Cardiff – became our Murphy and time after time, week after week, Gareth picked the ball up and ran into him followed by the clomping Welsh pack. If ever there was an unsung hero it was John Hickie, and he certainly spilt blood for his country on the coal-flecked Aberavon sands. Never got a cap, though.

Noise is a physical force: it can knock you off your feet and it nearly did when I had my first taste of the Arms Park experience. Because of rebuilding, the ground was reduced to half capacity but still the noise generated in that rattling old cathedral was enough to induce a dose of the heebie-jeebies. And then there was the anthem. Now, this may seem a controversial suggestion, but I would happily ban the singing of 'Mae Hen Wlad Fy Nhadau' at international matches. After an hour or so of Clive Rowlands ranting away, and then the roar of the crowd as you stepped onto the pitch, to have to sing the anthem, well, I'm surprised no player ever cried off with stage fright. The emotion and the fear can actually become too big a burden to bear, and I think that is why we have often been poor starters in Cardiff. All a player wants to do is get on with playing.

As for the 'Murphy Plan' – well, try as we might, we couldn't get our hands on the ball, and certainly didn't get a sniff of a put-in. Some of the Welsh pack had been so indoctrinated into 'Get Murphy', you could almost see the steam rising from their ears. A maul formed on the halfway line, right in front of the young Prince of Wales. Brian Price (our captain), a class act and superb player, saw Murphy's head pop out of the side of the maul and went for him with a haymaker. Brian always protested that he was retaliating after someone went for his eyes, but he wasn't entirely convincing. It was a poor shot, but one that made contact. However, Mr Murphy must have had a plan of his own because he thought about it for a few seconds, then clutched his face and fell dramatically to the floor. Tom Kiernan, the Irish captain, came running up, shouting, 'That's the Murphy Plan, that's the Murphy Plan, we've heard all about it . . . we're going off.' The Irish must have had spies burrowing beneath Aberavon beach. It did, for a heart-stopping moment, seem that Brian Price would be the first Welsh international player to be sent off, and at one stage we thought Kiernan might get his team to walk in protest, but the referee, Mr McMahon, restored order and the game continued. His comment afterwards raised understatement to an art form when he said, 'Some players got excited.' They did. It was a hard match, but Noel Murphy remained on the pitch throughout and we won 24–11.

There have always been players happy to put it about on the field, but not me. I can't condone pre-meditated, violent action. When I started to play international rugby, I thought, perhaps naively, that foul play would not be an issue. But I soon learned that in places like South Africa, Wellington and Dublin the blood seemed to be perennially on the boil. Experiences in South Africa have been well documented, and I will go into further detail later, but my assessment is that punching, kicking, gouging, stamping and biting is usually the last resort of a desperate team. By way of example, 'the Murphy Plan' didn't work . . . but the four tries we scored made it rather redundant.

For me, the result of the season that year was drawing 8–8 against the French at Stade Colombes. Throughout the entire time that I played in the Five Nations, Wales always appeared to be jockeying with the French for northern hemisphere supremacy. Sometimes brilliant beyond words, often reckless beyond thought, the French are a magnificent rugby breed. Whenever we faced them we had to be mentally – and physically – on the ball. The atmosphere alone was insane: brass bands, cockerels, baying crowd . . . just mayhem and madness, especially at Stade Colombes. Another small piece of my ongoing education was completed when I went looking for a toilet in the changing-rooms only to be pointed towards a pole and a hole in the floor. Readers can get a good impression of what the changing-room interior of Stade Colombes looked like from that ropey Sylvester Stallone and Michael Caine football film *Escape to Victory*.

We should have won the French game, especially after going in to the turn 8–0 up, but we were a little sloppy and the French too determined. Keith and Barry missed kicks, while Pierre Villepreux's boot was too accurate, and that made the difference. But you can't be too downhearted for long in Paris when the wine starts flowing and the after-match dinner gets into full swing. The memory of Brian Thomas and Denzil Williams singing, and of Jo Maso, the French playmaker, strumming his guitar, always brings a smile to my face. We'd knock lumps out of each other for 80 minutes and then sit down next to our opposite number, unable to speak each other's language, only able to communicate via drinking, sign language, a few badly pronounced phrases and music. The French always gave us a tough, tough time . . . but they also threw one almighty party afterwards.

Three matches down: two wins, one draw and the Triple Crown was looming for the 11th time in Wales' history. Many have pointed to that England game in 1969 as the start of our Golden Era, but I think we are getting a little ahead of ourselves. England that year, it has to be said, were poor. Maurice Richards rightly took the plaudits with his four tries, but we were not embracing the open ideals that would eventually make us something special. Barry John's confidence grew during that match and you could see what a force he was becoming on the end of a steady supply of good ball. His antics on the field have passed into legend, but he was a bloody nightmare to play in front of because none of us had the slightest idea what he would do next. People compare players from different eras, but if a modern stand-off tried to play off-the-cuff rugby the way Barry did, then they'd be out on their ear in a second. He relied purely on his instincts. Myth would have you believe he made a break every five minutes, but he didn't. Sometimes he only made one or two in a game, but when he did it was usually to devastating effect. Both he and Gareth Edwards were exceptional readers of the game, and it would have been fruitless for any coach to try to tamper with their talents. We had to tailor our game to fit theirs, but as long as we accepted that we didn't know what they were going to do, then that was fine; we could prepare for the unexpected. It is said that Barry John never tackled; well, he had better things to do. I would happily do his tackling for him if it gave him time to do what he was best at: winning matches. If I were Jonny Wilkinson's captain or coach, I would be sorely tempted to pull him out of the front-line tackling; his particular talents are more useful elsewhere. Barry was a puzzle: he had a mean arrogance on the pitch but a really laidback nature off it. He would sneer at opponents, 'Don't touch me, I'm Barry John.' Not that many could. He wrote a book in 1974 and it lists all his appearances for Wales and the Lions. Doesn't mention the results, just what Barry John contributed to the games. But that's Barry . . . he could get away with almost anything because he possessed that extra ingredient that turns great into greatest.

After one season in the red jersey I went from 'Mervyn who?' to 'Mervyn Davies – Triple Crown winner'. 'This is easy,' I thought, 'let's do it every year.' It took illness and hindsight to appreciate what I was part of in 1969. Being based in Guildford – where the locals had little time for Welsh rugby – distanced me from the obsessive attention of the Welsh public. The Triple Crown was in the bag, but there was an even bigger cherry there for the taking that summer: a trip to New Zealand.

I felt no trepidation when I boarded the plane for the southern hemisphere. I was too happy to worry; there I was, 22 years old and about to fly off for three weeks of rugby in the most fervent rugby country on earth. I had no family commitments, no cares, and I had adapted to Test rugby with relative ease. I showed a complete lack of respect for our All Black hosts – not from malice, but ignorance – I didn't know any better.

The tour schedule alone should have set the alarm bells ringing: flying to the other side of the world with your knees around your neck, turning up in Taranaki at 2 a.m. to be welcomed by the whole town. The reception was well intentioned but the last thing we wanted was to sing 'Sospan Fach' from our hotel balcony. Forty-eight hours later – with an earthquake in between and still full of jet lag – we faced our first game against the Ranfurly Shield holders, Taranaki . . . and it took every ounce of nous and guts to hang on for our win.

All Black rugby at that time was based on forward dominance. They were a huge bunch of men, hard too . . . and the mix of Maori and European genes that had filtered through the bloodline had created giants. They prided themselves on their toughness, on how hard they ran, the ferocity of their tackling, the aggressiveness of their tight game. Five days after our arrival, we met the All Blacks in Christchurch. It was rugby GBH. It was the end of innocence. We were stuffed 19–0 and even that scoreline flattered us. Behind the scrum we might have had parity, but up front they beat us out of sight.

We got our act together in the next two games and put two fine wins on the board against Otago and Wellington. The Wellington match erupted into a brawl but by then we had been kicked, raked, penalised and beaten into action. There is only so much a team can take and going toe-to-toe did wonders for our morale; we genuinely felt we could level the series at Eden Park, Auckland. We didn't and succumbed 33–12. Maurice Richards scored a wonderful solo try, but Fergie McCormick set a then record of 24 points. McCormick enjoyed his moment of glory, but he'd get his comeuppance another day, flummoxed by the magic of Barry John's boot.

The two Test defeats shattered us. We had gone to New Zealand as European champions and expected to do what no other team had done: to win a Test series in the All Black's backyard. Lesser teams would have imploded, but that experience, in a strange way, made us stronger. There was no shame in losing to a team that contained men like Meads, Lister, Gray, Smith, Going, Lochore and Kirkpatrick. What a shock I got when I set eyes on Ian Kirkpatrick; I thought he was a lock forward until he turned away and I saw a number 6 on his back. They bred fear in their opponents and were a magnificent sight in their black strip. Big men wearing one colour only emphasises their size. Bill Shankly did the same with Liverpool in the '60s; he told Ron Yeats, his talismanic centre-half, to forego the usual white shorts and go out onto the pitch dressed in red. The rest is history.

I had nothing but admiration for New Zealand. Even though the Test rugby left us demoralised, we gained so much from being there and spent many an hour skeet shooting, white-water rafting or meeting the locals at their village rugby club. I was particularly impressed by the way our hosts treated Ivor Jones, the WRU president. Ivor toured New Zealand with the 1930 Lions and remained a great favourite. His achievements were fondly remembered and he was afforded a kind and affectionate reception wherever we went. New Zealand treasured rugby and celebrated its heroes.

The real shame of that series is not the defeat itself, but in the manner that we lost. I felt we were beaten before we left the UK. An era was ending in Welsh rugby and it was obvious in the attitude of some of the senior players that this would be their last hurrah. Some sat out training, others lost heart once they appreciated how much effort would be required; but there was a definite sense of a changing of the guard. The younger players, on the whole, stood up and were counted, and I remember on the plane home a group getting together and swearing no team would ever humiliate Wales again. We couldn't live with New Zealand up front so we had to play the game a different way. A Welsh way. A way that utilised our key strength: the ability of our backs. Wales has always struggled to produce genuine world-class forwards: I can name Bryn Meredith, R.H. Williams, Graham Price and Scott Quinnell . . . but there aren't too many more. If we were to avoid such a thumping again then Welsh rugby needed to reinvent itself . . . and quickly.

Back then, certain individuals from the 1969 touring party took some positives from disaster: a need for a new style of rugby, a need for improved personal fitness, and an overwhelming desire for vengeance. I came out of that tour well, and it did my game no end of good to hear New Zealand rugby writer Terry McLean say the 'lean bean had done well' (which is real hyperbole for a Kiwi). Personally, I had come a long way in a very short time. I had looked for the challenge and had found it in New Zealand. Now I knew what I had to aspire to.

There was one other development from that tour that would have a profound influence on the future fortunes of Wales and on lovers of rugby across the world: Clive Rowlands' decision to switch Gerald Davies from centre to wing. How much poorer would the game have been if Gerald had not been given the freedom he needed to weave his magic?

Though they are two nations on opposite sides of the planet, Wales and New Zealand share so much more than sheep, rain and rugby. Many of our people live in small communities, hemmed in by hills. Both countries have a proud heritage and a fierce patriotism. Both nations share a love for the poetic and the physical. Nevertheless, in 1969, we did not share what we both craved most: rugby glory. But there was a generation of Welshmen desperate to redress the balance. We would not rest until we had reclaimed our honour.

VI

Golden Years

Wales was a different country back in the 1970s. It had great coal and steel industries. It had dockyards that saw ships come in from all parts of the world. It had sustainable farming and a burgeoning tourist trade. It had glamorous sons and daughters like Richard Burton and Shirley Bassey, whose flamboyant lifestyles would put them on front pages across the globe. But above all else, Wales and the Welsh people celebrated their nationalism through *rugby*. When 15 Welshmen took the field, we did so as warriors. We played each game with power, panache and pride. We played to win.

Rugby gave Wales a global identity . . . a genuine reason to crow. Three decades on, the legacy of the 1970s still haunts Wales. Modern players, who have grown up in the shadows of their illustrious rugby fathers, have struggled – and largely failed – to free themselves from what once was. Players from my generation are sometimes vilified for being successful, for creating a burden that is too big for the modern-day player, or fan, to bear. True, we've had our say in the media and we've all expressed our views on where it all went wrong, but, believe me, I would be overjoyed to see a Welsh side eclipse our achievements and consign what we did to the past. Nevertheless, our exploits linger on in the public consciousness because we were, to put it bluntly, very good and highly successful. Some of the comparative stats between now and then beggar belief:

for example, I never lost a Five Nations match played in Cardiff and England did not win there for 28 years. Many current Wales internationals are more familiar with defeat than victory in the capital city. Regrettably, it is the teams wearing white – or blue, green, black or gold – who storm the citadel seemingly at will. Ironically, these invaders who come to bury Welsh rugby, and not to praise it, often cite the great Wales players of the '70s as their heroes, their rugby role models.

And what role models they are: Gareth Edwards, J.P.R. Williams, J.J. Williams, Barry John, Phil Bennett, Gerald Davies, Graham Price, Bobby Windsor, Dai Morris, John Taylor. There are others too, who played their crucial part: Steve Fenwick, Derek Quinnell, Ray Gravell, John Bevan, Maurice Richards, Roy Bergiers, Arthur Lewis, Jeff Young, Allan Martin, Terry Cobner, Charlie Faulkner and Barry Llewellyn, a player who but for injury would have become a world-class prop. I could go on. One only has to look at our playing record in that decade to realise how effective we were: between 24 January 1970 and 17 March 1979, Wales played 46 full Test internationals, winning 32, losing 11 and drawing 3. The only low points came in 1973 (with away defeats against Scotland and France), in 1974 (with consecutive draws against Ireland and France and then a controversial defeat by England) and finally in 1978 when we lost a Test series 2–0 in Australia. During those ten years Wales won Grand Slams and Triple Crowns; but since 1980 onwards the cupboard has been disappointingly bare, with only a third-place finish at the first World Cup in 1987, a Triple Crown in 1988 and a Five Nations Championship in 1994 offering some comfort. Not much to crow about now. No wonder my generation has dined out well on our reminiscences of those heady days.

There is, in all honesty, little new that can be said of the 'Golden Years' of Welsh rugby. If you are a scholar of the game – especially in Wales – you can read a plethora of books written by the players who experienced the glory days first-hand. And not just books; the nostalgia industry now offers videos, DVDs, audio-cassettes, songs, paintings, statuettes and personal appearances commemorating the time of times, the greatest tries, the most glorious of triumphs. I heartily recommend John Billot's *History of Welsh International Rugby*

(Roman Way Books, Provincial Printing & Publishing Co. Ltd, Cardiff) as a worthy addition to any rugby literary collection. Writing this book has shown me that my recollection can be a little hazy, but John's book is an excellent aide–memoire, and I have plundered his meticulous research for statistics when necessary. Looking back, flicking through the pages, analysing the match records, I am left with two conclusions about the 1970s: first, how difficult it was for any team to win a Grand Slam and second, how much more we should have achieved. When I watch the Six Nations Championship of today, I still see a tough tournament to win – a tournament full of pitfalls, surprises and intense confrontations. England – so long the dominant force in British rugby – have come unstuck on many occasions. In fact, each Celtic nation has, at some point, thrown a spanner in the wheel spokes of their chariot. I wonder how much England's World Cup success in 2003 owed to finally securing a Grand Slam earlier that same year?

As I said in the previous chapter, a large part of the steel that was so evident in the Wales of the 1970s was fired in the New Zealand tour of 1969. Tours offer priceless insight into the workings of a squad, and as much as the All Blacks played us off the park, a core of younger players were left with the knowledge of what we had to achieve if we were to be regarded as a real force in world rugby. Tours, in the amateur era, were the only opportunities for squads to bond together. Amateur rules and work commitments prevented regular squad sessions, and it was only when we jetted off to foreign climes that we could give the game our full attention. We learned a lot about the All Blacks, but we learned more about each other as players and men.

We departed New Zealand and headed across the Tasman Sea to Sydney, where we narrowly beat the Wallabies. Victory boosted our morale slightly, but we still felt collectively battered, bruised and a little reluctant to be used as human tackle bags by the big, imposing Fijians. But Wales has always taken its responsibilities as a senior nation in international rugby seriously and going to Fiji was unquestionably the right thing to do. We did not go to recuperate or to holiday, we went there to give Fijian rugby a lift. It is an amazing place: picture-postcard views of golden sands and palm trees, and full of friendly, welcoming people. Until, that is, you put them on the rugby pitch and then those big friendly giants turn into automatons hell-bent on knocking seven bells out of the opposition. The match in Suva was a tougher game than we had anticipated, and perhaps the fallout from New Zealand lay heavily on us, but we did triumph 31–11. I remember it more for my busman's holiday in the second row, a move that allowed Dennis Hughes to come in at number 8 where he bagged three tries.

It is events off the pitch that conjure up the fondest memories of Fiji. I recall the squad training next to a swamp during one of the daily tropical storms, and standing there stunned as we were suddenly invaded by thousands of frogs. There were frogs everywhere – hopping up into the faces of the scrummaging forwards, bouncing around our ankles, climbing up our shorts. Keith Jarrett – who had a real aversion to frogs – put in a dazzling display of sidestepping that session. I don't think anyone – man or amphibian – got near him.

Then there was the unforgettable time we met the King of Fiji himself and Ivor Jones – our tour manager – almost caused an international incident. We were invited for an audience with His Royal Majesty at his residence on a small island out in one of the lagoons. We put on our finest clothes and stepped into the dugout canoes for a very wobbly transference across the bay. In keeping with tradition, we were given garlands of pink paper flowers to hang about our necks. All was well until the heavens opened and drenched us in warm rain. The dye from our garlands didn't react too well to the soaking and soon a pink residue streaked down our pristine white shirts. It was no way to be presented to a mighty King, so upon landing our hosts offered us a garment that resembled a sarong. Well, the surreal sight of Brian Thomas dressed in winkle-picker boots and sarong, clutching a cine camera, remains with me to this day. If one felt David Beckham looked ridiculous dressed in similar attire, at least he had natural good looks on his side . . . can you imagine what a bruising great forward from Neath looked like?

Anyway, in accordance with local custom, we were shown into the King's palace and offered kava juice. Kava juice is the Fijian drink of welcome and it is made from an indigenous grass root. It has the advantage of being alcoholic but unfortunately it is impossible to drink enough of the stuff to enjoy any alcoholic benefits, because it tastes truly revolting. In keeping with his senior position, Ivor was offered the first cup. He took a large glug, turned slightly green and promptly spat it out on the floor. The collective growl from all the King's men gathered around in their tribal finery put us in no doubt of what was expected. We drank our kava quickly and made the appropriate noises of approval but hoped not to receive refills. The King also presented us with a beautifully carved whale's tooth, which is now, I should think, resting on some ex-WRU committee man's mantelpiece. I often wonder where the gifts we received from our various tours ended up!

The 1970s kicked off with a controversial game against South Africa at Cardiff Arms Park. It was the first time in my career that I experienced the difficulties of trying to separate politics and sport. Did I want to play in that match? Of course I did – it was a chance to represent my country on home soil against a nation we had never beaten. John Taylor decided not to put himself up for selection, which is a testament to the man's principles, because he was prepared to sacrifice his entire international career for his beliefs. The selectors were never the most sympathetic of people and for a long while afterwards it did seem that John would never get his jersey back. John had good reason to pull out: he had toured South Africa with the Lions in 1968 and was adamant that any player taking the field against the Boks would only be seen to condone apartheid, and it was something he was not prepared to do. My argument was that I needed to see apartheid for myself, but, in retrospect, I wonder how much my desire to play rugby contributed to my decision. It would not be the last argument John and I had about the pros and cons of playing South Africa, but his decision to risk the thing he loved most only increased the respect I had for him.

The game ended in a 6–6 draw and as the final whistle blew, I was left with mixed emotions that had little to do with the match. On one hand, I was pleased to have measured myself against their superb back row of Greyling, Bedford and Ellis, but on the other hand the demonstrations, the catcalls and the flour-bomb attacks from the stands were very unsettling. I did enjoy the dinner afterwards because the South African players were pleasant fellows off the park, especially Tommy Bedford. They did not speak about the protests that followed them across Wales, but one could not help sense that they were living in a kind of detached reality. Unlike other touring sides that managed to go out into the community, South Africa trained in isolation and the players were often left holed up in their hotel rooms after dark.

The Five Nations campaign came and went and we followed the Triple Crown success of the previous season with a share of the Championship. 'Champions' did not have the same mystique as 'Grand Slam' or 'Triple Crown' winners, so there was a sense of disappointment throughout the squad. The key games that year were the final two against Ireland and France respectively.

In Dublin, we were comprehensively dismantled 19–0 and I think, for the first and last time in my career, I was thoroughly outplayed by my opposite number. It was with some relief that I noted Ken Goodall's departure to rugby league at the end of that season, otherwise the British Lions' number 8 jersey in New Zealand might have adorned his back instead of mine.

The press and the fans treated the defeat with disbelief. There were all kinds of conspiracy theories doing the rounds, including tales of a dressing-room bust-up between Gareth and Barry. The simple truth was that we were complacent, and no team, no matter how good, could afford to go to Lansdowne Road without being totally focused on the job in hand. I don't think Dai Morris was particularly focused in the changing-room. We thought he was, sitting there with his head in his hands as Clive launched into his spiel, before he let out an anguished cry and threw a small radio ear-piece away in disgust: his horse had let him down. But the biggest effect the walloping we took at the hands of the Irish had on Wales was a change in captaincy.

On Brian Price's retirement, Gareth Edwards inherited the captain's mantle. It was the second time he had assumed the leadership, the first being briefly in 1968 when, at 20, he became the youngest player ever to captain Wales. Two years later, he was back in charge; the selectors thought Gareth had matured and was ready to lead again. It made sense; Gareth had the respect of his peers and the opposition and was viewed as the ideal candidate. His ability meant he was an automatic first choice in the team, his position ensured he was right in the thick of the action and everything was set for him to enjoy a long run in the captaincy. However, captaincy is a strange art; it can inspire some and weigh heavily on the shoulders of others. Being captain certainly affected Gareth's game; the added responsibility meant that he played within himself. And if Gareth, our most potent attacking force, didn't play to the limit of his abilities, then it affected our whole performance. It must have hurt him to concede the captaincy to John Dawes for the second time in his career before the France game, but he never let his disappointment affect his performance. There were so many attributes that set Gareth apart from us mere mortals: his instinctive ability, the way he could read the game, his strength, his low centre of gravity, his speed off the mark, his aura of invincibility. He wasn't tall, but he was strong, and I believe he held all kinds of sporting records at that school of sporting excellence, Millfield. Gareth could have been a runner, a gymnast, a soccer player – but we were all thankful that he chose rugby.

He had to be a scrum-half because he needed total immersion in the game. Anywhere else in the back line would have held little interest for him because it would have involved periods of inactivity. Unless one counts standing in a river after salmon or putting out on the 18th, I do not think Gareth was ever happier – or more relaxed – than when he had the rugby ball in his hands and a few forwards breathing down his neck. He was quite dictatorial too . . . bossing his pack about where he expected the ball to be delivered from the scrum. The quick ball is 'channel one' ball, which is hooked to the blindside flanker's feet, but Gareth insisted it came out between my feet or preferably at the feet of the openside flanker. And what Gareth wanted, Gareth got. We operated according to a simple rule: we were the ball winners, he was the ball user. And he used it superbly. He was always thinking about the game too, looking for ways to flummox the opposition. We might spin it wide four or five times then, when the defence had spread out to block us, we would sit on it or go down the blind side. Gareth never allowed the opposition the luxury of settling or second-guessing us; he made them work hard both physically and mentally.

For all his instinctive abilities, one has to commend Gareth for the amount of work he put into his rugby. It is common knowledge how many hours top-class kickers put into their particular art, but Gareth was equally dedicated to the demands of his role. He may have been born with an abundance of the essential ingredients for greatness, but hard work turned him into the player of legend that we all know and respect. His pass was a prime example. In his younger days, Gareth had a tendency to rely on the dive pass, but it was pointed out to him that as soon as he hit the deck he was out of the game. He spent hour after hour perfecting long, arrow-straight passes off both left and right hands; precision passes that would buy Barry John and Phil Bennett precious extra seconds and space.

There are countless moments of rugby action that illustrate the playing magnificence of Gareth Edwards. 'That try' he scored for the Barbarians against New Zealand in January 1973 certainly ranks as one of the best, but to me, if someone wants conclusive proof as to why Gareth Edwards was such a formidable playing talent, one only has to watch the try he scored against Scotland in February 1972. True, he only had 75 yards to run, but he showed every facet of his skill set: speed, aggression, side-step, bravery, kicking, balance, eye for a gap . . . and I gave him the scoring pass. I remember seeing him blaze off on his epic run, and wondering what the hell he was up to. Seconds later, the crowd told me . . . and the sight of him slowly walking back with his face covered in red ash from the old dog track remains one of my enduring images from that era. They used to run greyhound races at the Arms Park back then . . . and I doubt any beast on two – or four – legs would have caught him that day. Gareth did go onto a third term as captain in 1974, before I took over, but I doubt he'll be regarded as the greatest of Welsh captains. Instead, he'll have to make do with being widely regarded as the greatest player the game has seen.

With his experience of leading London Welsh, John Dawes seemed the perfect choice for the captaincy. His tenure in charge set him on the path to becoming one of the true greats of the modern game, and he formed the perfect leadership partnership with Clive Rowlands. They were fire and ice, heart and head, passion and precision. John had the game plan and Clive had the enthusiasm.

Clive would spur us on by appealing to all things Welsh, whilst John would coolly evaluate what needed to be done. He had ice in his veins and would never allow us to panic. What made John such a great captain to play for was his complete belief in the players around him and a total commitment to the fast, open rugby we were schooled to play. Wales would often fall behind at the start of matches – especially at the Arms Park – or concede soft tries, but John knew we were capable of outscoring any opposition we faced. His belief in us – and what we were capable of – was vindicated in 1971.

The competition for places in that 1971 team was extremely fierce – so fierce, in fact, that I believe we could have fielded two international teams. The starting XV was effectively built around club combinations, with Gareth, Barry and John Bevan playing week-in, week-out together for Cardiff; J.P.R., Gerald Davies, Dawes, Mike Roberts, John Taylor and myself playing for London Welsh, and other players from Neath, Ebbw Vale, Llanelli, etc. The team combined artful three-quarters and mobile forwards. No team had decided on the definitive way to play rugby union and the game had developed in different ways in different countries. The All Blacks relied on aggressive forward power, and one could often literally have thrown a blanket (albeit a large one) over their entire pack because of the cohesive way they worked as a unit. Other nations were categorised in other ways: the spoiling Scots, the battling Irish, the flamboyant French and the big, bulldozing English. Wales was never a nation to produce big men so we had to rely on speed, intuition and a willingness to back our talented three-quarters.

After a relatively easy win against England, we headed north for the great game of that season, a game that has since been cited as one of the most thrilling matches of rugby ever seen. The memories from the Murrayfield clash are vivid ones: the massive crowd spilling onto the pitch, Delme Thomas with his sleeves pulled up over his bulging biceps, John Dawes demonstrating the art of taking and giving a pass in the tackle, Barry John and Peter Brown missing easy conversions – and, of course, John Taylor. John's conversion has rightly passed into rugby folklore, but people forget that he scored a superb try, taking the ball from J.P.R. and thundering through the retreating Scots to finish with a spectacular dive. But his kick, well . . . that was something else, something quite extraordinary. Popular legend would have us believe it was the first time John had ever kicked the ball, but he had done so consistently for London Welsh and Wales. But fair play, it was one of the true great pressure kicks. I could not watch because we needed the two points to win the match, and I did feel responsible for our predicament after giving away two soft penalties. The London Welsh boys knew what John was capable of with his left boot, but I could see the bemused looks on the faces of the praying Welsh fans around us. I think only one man had total confidence in John's ability to bisect the posts and that was John himself. From a mile out on the left-hand touchline, he launched the kick that would give us a 19–18 win. One point. That was the difference between keeping the Grand Slam in our sights, and watching it disappear. One point . . . one piece of inspiration . . . one bit of good fortune. Years later, Gerald Davies captured what we felt when he said:

> The whole year was a magical year . . . but the one [game] I probably have the fondest memory of is the Scottish game because it typified so much of what Wales were trying to do at that time. We wanted to play some rugby, to utilise the gifts of all 15 players that were there. We wanted to develop some character and character is important in any sport because without it, you give up.
>
> *Welsh Rugby's Six of the Best: The Seventies,*
> Green Umbrella Video.

With England and Scotland beaten, we could concentrate on Ireland and the title we all badly wanted to win: the Triple Crown. It was a convincing victory and it helped lay the ghosts of the previous year to rest. Denzil Williams became the most-capped Welsh forward, with 35 caps . . . a record I would eventually go on to beat. For the second time in three seasons I had been part of a Triple Crown-winning side and we had one more match left for the ultimate prize: the Grand Slam.

I always felt sorry for the French in terms of the Five Nations because they only had the Grand Slam to go for. At least the Home Nations had two bites at glory: if they went down to Les Bleus then they could always seek some solace from the Triple Crown. However, I don't pity them that much, because in the era when I played international rugby (between 1969 and 1976), we could always count on the French to give us the toughest of times. Sure, other countries could – and sometimes did – surprise us. I experienced defeat away to Scotland, Ireland and England. But there was always something particularly challenging about playing France, especially away from home.

We went into that match in March 1971 buoyed by our recent successes and the news that 11 Welshmen had been selected for the Lions tour later that year. But any over-confident thoughts were soon dispelled when we saw the French line up opposite us. I only had to look at the giants around me and the sight of men like the Spangheros in the second row and Benoit Dauga at number 8 soon tempered any expectations I might have had of an easy time. They played a similar type of game to us but with far more abrasiveness up front. One of the French forwards' favourite tactics was to employ a 'Murphy Plan' on some hapless individual; you didn't quite know when the boots would come flying in, but you knew they would. I got my dose in 1976. Our apparently off-the-cuff rugby was in fact quite structured, but the French really did it without thought. The French used their backs and forwards in unison to create a smooth, fluid style . . . but a style that had teeth.

We won that game by nine points to five through tries by Gareth and Barry. I remember Gareth's try quite well. I'd taken a heavy knock in the midfield after tackling Carrere, I think, and I was trying to shake it off. I glanced back to our try line to see Bourgarel twisting and turning his way forward with support either side. 'Try' I thought. The next thing I knew, J.P.R. came tearing down the wing on his own. I tried to run but I could not shake the injury so I embarked on a kind of Long John Silver-esque hobble. I picked up a little speed, but it was not my desire to support J.P.R. spurring me on; it was the prospect of being beaten in a foot race by our prop Denzil Williams. Poor old Denzil, he made a beautiful support run, the full length of the field, and still found enough space to give himself a clear canter in under the posts. All he needed was the ball, but I don't think J.P.R. believed in passing to props. Denzil was the obvious recipient until Gareth came haring up on the wing and took the score. Denzil could have played himself into myth – much in the way that Graham Price did in 1975 – but J.P.R. probably chose the correct option.

The French game is also remembered for 'Barry John's only tackle', when he busted his nose in the process of stopping Dauga. That's a little bit unfair, as I did see Barry put in a couple more tackles in the matches we shared. But, as I said earlier, he wasn't there to tackle people – he was there to win games. After taking such a knock, we were surprised to see him come back onto the pitch (though with his nostrils stuffed full of cotton wool), but none of us were then surprised when he ghosted through the French midfield to score the decisive points that secured us our first Grand Slam since 1952.

Gareth has since said about that day at Stade Colombes:

> It had everything. It typified what international rugby should be all about: commitment, skill, controlled aggression. French flair was at its best because the tackling was immense. The score that day could have been anything. The Welsh side was in its infancy but I think it matured that day in Paris because it was truly a great match.
>
> *Welsh Rugby's Six of the Best: The Seventies*,
> Green Umbrella Video.

We all contributed to our splendid series win and not just through our point-scoring exploits. Our defence was strong, our forwards delivered good ball and our backs executed their plays with precision. Rugby is a team game for individuals who come together to provide a united front. We all enjoyed playing the running game and worked damn hard to achieve our aims. The entire squad bought into the Dawes' philosophy: it was not about winning, it was about winning with style. There were many unsung heroes in that team including Arthur Lewis, Jeff Young and my old mate from

London Welsh, Mike Roberts. Mike was a big man to have in your pack, 18 st. plus, and what's more, when he pushed, he pushed 18 st. plus. Mike was a north-Walian by birth and a real gentle giant off the pitch. But shackle him and Delme together in the second row and we had an explosive pairing. I rated Mike as one of the best second-row players of that era. He used his weight – and his aggression – to devastating effect in the scrum. It was a testament to Mike's fitness and desire for the game that he was drafted back into the Wales team in 1979 after a four-year hiatus. In many ways Mike was the complete opposite to Geoff Evans, his London Welsh teammate who came into the national side the following season. According to Geoff, he owed his rugby rise to beer. His consumption of bitter had transformed him from an 11 st. university student into an 18 st. monster. He was one hell of a player and terrific company after a match.

With Grand Slams come expectations, and the following season the anticipation about what we would do next was intense. On matchday in Cardiff, that expectation would reach fever pitch. The mayhem would begin in the morning, and the players brooding away inside the Angel Hotel were only too aware of what was happening beneath their windows. I'd take a late breakfast and wait till we were called together to listen to Clive's talk. After a light lunch (honey and toast for some, steak and chips for others, or a raw egg and a glass of sherry for Delme!), we would leave the Angel in small groups and walk the 300 yards or so to the ground. Passing through the assembled crowds was always an interesting experience. The smell of beer was everywhere and the reception we received verged on hysteria. We'd sign autographs, take endless hearty slaps on our backs and grab a few kisses from the girls. There would be touts loitering on the street corners pleading for tickets and makeshift stalls selling pictures of the team; someone, somewhere was making a lot of money out of merchandise but the players never saw a penny. Baz and I had a pre-match routine that saw us go into a little sports shop opposite the stadium to buy a new jockstrap each. Then, away from the riot of colour and noise, there would be cold deliverance into the bowels of the ground and a chance to collect our thoughts.

I always loathed the 90 or so minutes before kick-off and would desperately seek tasks to take my mind off the coming storm. I would eventually find solace in the mundane: checking my boots, strapping my ankles, taping my fingers, having a cigarette. There was little chance to get a rubdown because Gerry Lewis, our physio, appeared to be solely in the employ of Gareth Edwards. Gareth is very proud of the fact that he never suffered from any serious injuries when playing for Wales, but I am hardly surprised because he received more attention from Gerry than all the other 14 players put together.

'Come on, Gar . . . let someone else have a go?'

'I can't . . . my knees are bad, I need to get them sorted.'

Like the true thoroughbred he was, he expected – and got – preferential treatment.

With 25 minutes to go before kick-off, I'd put on my new jockstrap, then my right sock, left sock and shorts before Gerry presented me with my jersey. It became a little ritual that we all appreciated – especially Gerry himself. He was amongst us as kit man and physio, but he worked far harder in that changing-room than we did during the match. The effort it took for a rather slight 8 st. man to throw around blokes often double his size earned him the right to present the team shirts.

Before we left the changing-room, I would find a quiet corner with Dai and John and go through our signals and our objectives as a back-row unit. The last routine I had to attend to was wrapping the four-inch Elastoplast around my head. My headband was no gimmick; it was there to stop me getting cauliflower ears. Believe me, when your head is being ground and pummelled between the buttocks of two huge locks you need as much protection as possible. If scrumcaps had been a bit more fashionable then I would have worn one. I am a firm believer in taking as much padding onto the pitch as allowable; after all, rugby hurts. All I had was a bit of tape – and that almost put me in hospital, thanks to Geoff Wheel who once tried to rip my headband off; it felt as if he was taking my head with it.

Then the knock on the door would come and we would leave the sanctity of the changing-room. There are many great tales of incidents before the teams reached the pitch, and two of my favourites involve Bill Beaumont. Apparently, Bill was leading his team out in Cardiff when someone shouted down the tunnel, 'May the best team win, Bill', to which he replied, 'I fucking hope not.' The other anecdote comes from Twickenham. On one occasion, Bill was supposed to have said:

'Right boys, this Welsh team has had it. The Pontypool front row are past it. Allan Martin and Geoff Wheel? They're no good. Terry Cobner? He's too slow.'

A voice was heard to respond: 'Hang on, Bill . . . what about J.P.R. Williams, Phil Bennett, Gareth Edwards, Gerald Davies?'

To which the immortal reply came: 'Fuck me, boys, surely even we can beat four men.'

We should have won a second consecutive Grand Slam in 1972 and if the tournament had been contested on the pitch then I am confident we would have. We beat England 12–3, Scotland 35–12 and France 20–6. An IRA bomb attack in Aldershot had increased tension on the mainland. The WRU requested a neutral venue for the Ireland match, but Irish officials insisted that Dublin was the only offer on the table. Bomb threats were made, some probably hoaxes, but others alarmingly real, and the decision was put to the players. Once it became obvious that some players did not want to risk their safety then the IRA had won. The WRU was not prepared to allow a Wales team to travel to Dublin with anything less than a full-strength contingent so we pulled out of the game. I wanted to go, and I felt that we had the players in support that could have done an excellent job replacing those who resisted. But one of the greatest assets that the Welsh squad of the early '70s had was its togetherness and harmony. I don't remember frayed tempers or any cross words; it may be boring to read about, because I have no tales of intrigue or in-fighting, but we all got on well. Sure, we tended to stay within our little club cliques and people like Gareth and Barry were terrific friends off the field, but, on the whole, we were a tight, loyal unit. We stuck together and respected the decisions of our colleagues who didn't want to travel. We live as much in a world of terrorist threat today as we did then, and we must take account of people's genuine fears. But I still think that we missed a golden opportunity to achieve something remarkable in 1972: back-to-back Grand Slams.

The biggest shock of that particular 1972 Championship was Barry John's decision to retire from the game. One cannot underestimate the draw 'The King' had on the public around him, especially after his exploits with the 1971 British Lions. He was rugby's first superstar and living life under such intense scrutiny obviously didn't appeal to him. True, Barry walked away when his celebrity status grew out of all proportion, but he was also canny enough to see that it was the optimum time to cash in on his fame. Barry John has been accused of many things: arrogance, bloody-mindedness and selfishness, to list only three. But that was Barry John the player. Barry John the man was – and is – a charmer, very easy company and a good bloke to be around. He was also very shrewd. By retiring at the relatively young age of 28, he opened up enough business and financial opportunities to secure his family finances for years to come – something that few other amateur sportsmen achieved. I wish he had played on, however. I am sure that he does too, although he might never admit as much.

When Dai Watkins went north, many Welsh fans thought Wales had lost its cutting edge. Then Barry John came along. When Barry John retired there was even more teeth gnashing and hand wringing. Then Phil Bennett came along. When a player retires, he usually wishes his replacement well, but perhaps he secretly hopes that the replacement isn't quite up to the same standard. I don't know if Barry might have wished that of Phil, but my view is that in 'Benny', Wales had a replacement of equal ability – and one who had already been around the squad for a couple of years. But they were very different: whereas Barry was cool and aloof, Phil was a little firebrand. As a back-row forward, I saw them both close up, and both were unpredictable, inspired and blessed with match-winning talents. If I had to split them, then I can only do so on aesthetic grounds: Barry was a smooth, wafting glider whose pace was deceptive and whose manner was effortless. Phil was more jittery and staccato in his running and he possessed a quite brilliant sidestep. But what do aesthetics matter if the end result is the same? Wales and the Lions should be thankful that two such players came along in one generation.

Phil almost made a dream start to his life in that most famous of rugby jerseys – the red number 10 – when he so nearly orchestrated a memorable defeat of the All Blacks in December 1972. The joy of winning a Test series with the Lions the year before dissipated with yet another defeat at the hands of New Zealand. The Lions' win had obviously galvanised the All Blacks to develop their backs and I could tell then that New Zealand rugby was on the rise once more. The game itself was close and controversial, with obstructions, missed kicks and disallowed tries. We should have won, but we did not, failing by 16 points to 19. It remains one of my bitterest experiences on the rugby field.

In some ways, we stagnated over the next two seasons. We won only our home matches in 1973, and in 1974 we probably had our most dismal run. I did not play well in 1974 and genuinely felt I had risked my place on my second Lions tour to South Africa. Drawing with France and Ireland was bad, but losing to England – well that was considered a disaster. The RFU refused to let our anthem be played – decreeing that 'God Save The Queen' should suffice for England, Scotland and Wales – and it threw most of the boys, though not me. I did score a try in that match, a thundering charge from all of two yards out. My opposite number Andy Ripley also scored and although he did not tuck me up in the way that Ken Goodall once did, he certainly made an impression. That 16–12 defeat still sticks in my craw. I do not like losing, but I can accept defeat if a team deserves it. I think that day was marred by sloppy refereeing which certainly cost J.J. Williams a legitimate try and prevented us from playing the advantage we were due. The hardest part about that defeat was the aftermath: it was Clive Rowlands' last game as coach, and the injustice he felt about the result wrecked what should have been a memorable send-off. But that's Clive all over: he never could switch off.

By 1975 the new national coach and natural successor to Clive, John Dawes, had made an important decision: he wanted to appoint the ungainly youngster he had first met at Richmond as his captain. Before I captained Wales in 1975, I captained my college XV. I never captained London Welsh nor did I ever captain a Lions tour game. When the call came to captain my country, it was a great honour and one I dared not turn down. I then had to think about what kind of captain I might be by looking at the example set by the finest captains I had played under – Willie John McBride and John Dawes himself. I decided it fell into two categories. One option was to be like Dawes, a calculating thinker whose brain constantly worked over the nuances of what was happening around him. The other option was to be like McBride and lead from the front by wholeheartedly throwing myself into the action. It felt easier for me to follow my instincts and copy the big man McBride.

A captain needs three things in his armoury:

1. Respect.
2. The ability to lead by example.
3. Good instinctive qualities.

John believed I had all three.

There were other men in the Wales team of my era who could have filled the captaincy role, men who possessed the qualities I mentioned above, like Gareth Edwards, J.P.R. Williams, Gerald Davies and Phil Bennett. But luck was on my side; my position on the field made my selection ideal and I am a great believer that a forward should captain a side. It is up front where the rhythm and tempo of the game can best be ascertained – and more easily influenced. The other main candidates came from the backs and it would have been difficult for a wing, or a full-back, to lead. John recognised that none would quibble with the decision to appoint me whereas the others might not have been so readily accepted. I was one of the boys and my easy-going nature put me on good terms with everyone in the squad. In fact, I assumed my affability would work against me and deliberately set about distancing myself from the rest of the squad (another Willie John tactic).

Since taking the number 8 jersey for London Welsh in late 1968, I had never been dropped by Wales, the Lions or my club teams. I was confident that, barring injury, I would be selected for each game and never felt seriously – or consistently – threatened by any would-be challenger. I respected my fellow number 8s, but I did not fear them.

Leading by example was second nature. A number 8 had to be conspicuous and put himself about the pitch. I didn't know any other way to play the game and I loved the big bruising tackles and the relentless struggle for the ball. If my team was flagging, I found it easy to lead the charge. By the time John asked me to take over from Gareth, I felt ready, willing and able. When I told my father he looked up from his paper and said, 'About time, too.'

That '75 season fills me with a sense of immense pride and extreme frustration. I was proud to captain my country . . . I was certainly a long way away from the schoolboy who could not get into the Swansea youth side. I was proud of the rugby we played. As I led my team onto the Parc des Princes I knew, for the first time in my international career, that we had a devastating set of forwards in Price, Windsor, Faulkner, Wheel, Martin, Evans, Cobner and, dare I say, me. I was proud of the win in Paris with six new caps including Graham Price, who scored a monumental try. I was proud of the havoc we wreaked on England, led from the back by an inspired J.P.R. Williams, who played perhaps his greatest match. I was proud of the way we beat Ireland 32–4 – a beating so comprehensive that it forced three Irish heroes (Willie John McBride, Ken Kennedy and Ray McLoughlin) to hang up their boots. I was proud of the tries we scored through Gareth, Gerald, J.J., Roy Bergiers and the unlikeliest scorer of all, Charlie Faulkner. It was a display that gave us the Championship. But it wasn't enough.

The 1975 season was sullied by a silly defeat up at Murrayfield. A defeat I must shoulder the blame for. A defeat that cost us yet another Grand Slam. An incredible 104,000 people crammed into Murrayfield to watch a match that the Scots won by 12 points to 10. John Bevan started at fly-half but had to leave the field due to an injury. Phil came on, but he wasn't 100 per cent fit. Steve Fenwick suffered a knock and was replaced in the centre by my Swansea colleague, Roger Blyth, who was a full-back by trade and not in the same international class as Fenwick. However, injuries happen, they are part of the game. If there was blame to be apportioned for that defeat, some must lie with the captain: I made some very poor judgement calls. The worst was when I asked a jittery Phil to take a penalty kick – a kick he was completely unprepared for. Phil told me he did not fancy it, but I ignored him. As captain I should have respected his wish, recognised his doubts, and asked someone else to step up. In the end, he missed and we gifted victory to the Scots. Phil endured a torrid time in the press when we got back to Wales. But that season was a watershed for us: the pack was bedding down nicely and the free-flowing rugby we endorsed behind the scrum was leading to more tries being scored. The captain would grow in confidence over the summer tour to Japan, and I set my heart on 1976. I knew it would be a year that I would never forget.

I am blessed to belong to such a golden era of rugby, to play with – and against – some of the greatest names in the game. I can close my eyes and the memories swarm over me like an Irish pack. I think about the men I jousted with: Fran Cotton, Mike Gibson, Gordon Brown, Pierre Villepreux . . . and I see true giants of rugby. Then I think of the men in red surrounding me, men who can claim to be amongst the best to have picked up a rugby ball. If I had to choose one, and since it is my book I feel I can, there is one player who had it all: ability, skill, physical courage, mental toughness . . . and he had it in bucket-loads. My choice is easy. The greatest player I have ever seen was at his very best during the Golden Years of Welsh rugby – and his name is Gerald Davies.

VII

Being a Lion – Part One

It is not uncommon for British Lions tours to be the subject of controversy before they depart these shores. The choice of manager, coach and captain incites much debate in the press and pub alike, and, more often than not, one particular part of our island race feels snubbed or slighted. This is not a new phenomenon, for there has been grumbling and griping about who is picked to tour with the Lions for the last 30 plus years. We are well within the era of the dominant English and therefore, nowadays, it is the Celts who grumble most. I don't think the Welsh, Irish or Scots complained too much in 1971, since they contributed 25 players to the original touring party, plus captain, coach and manager. Sometimes we Celts have tunnel vision when viewing the British Lions, especially when the Lions come dressed in white.

I was never a great student of rugby and therefore before 1971 I lacked familiarity with, and deference to, the heritage of the Lions (although John Taylor had altered my perception with his stories from South Africa in 1968), but my understanding of – and my fondness for – this great rugby institution grew on tour. My desire to go with the Lions was two-fold: one, I wanted to test myself at the very highest level; and two, I wanted to dish out some cold revenge against New Zealand for what they did to Wales in 1969. Despite a Triple Crown, a Grand Slam and 16 consecutive Wales caps under my belt, I still felt undernourished as a player. The only way that I could sate my hunger was by confronting – and beating – the All Blacks. Not that we were given the slightest hope of doing so.

For the record, there were six Englishmen, six Irishmen, six Scots and twelve Welshmen in the party. Six of the chosen Welshmen came from London Welsh – seven once Geoff Evans joined us as a replacement. Yet, the key to any successful Lions' side is to break down club and international barriers; to put away the partisan nature of the four disparate countries and come together under one banner. Whereas one's instinct as a player is to mill around the boys you know best, the answer for the squad has to be to put all thoughts of tribal loyalty aside. Touring the far side of the world for three and a half months is no easy undertaking; it requires fortitude and brotherhood and it is certainly no place for cliques.

Ironically, the biggest controversy that surrounded the '71 tour was, in many ways, the reason it eventually succeeded: the choices of captain, coach and manager. It was highly unusual to select three Celts to run the show, but in John Dawes, Carwyn James and Doug Smith, the Home Unions' committee took a calculated – and profitable – gamble. The main perceived weakness in this trinity of leadership was the choice of John as captain. The Welsh had long been regarded as difficult tourists, finding it hard to mix with other nationalities, suffering more from homesickness, so to have a Welshman in charge of a large contingent of other Welshmen was deemed risky. Nevertheless, as a captain, John was without equal – as he had shown for club and country over the previous seasons. Yet many people – especially the gentlemen of the press – wondered whether he could hold his place in the starting line-up and ride the legitimate playing claims of John Spencer, Chris Rea and Mike Gibson. New Zealand was no place to carry a passenger and when former captain Michael Campbell-Lamerton dropped himself in favour of Delme Thomas in 1966, a precedent was set: captains had to play as well as lead. Lions tours were changing. The age of the affable, sociable leader – more ambassador than action man – was consigned to the past. Doug took a lot of the press commitments from John, leaving him to clear his mind and concentrate on leadership. It must be said that John held his own on the field; in fact, he went on to feature in more games than any other tourist and played the best rugby of his vastly underrated career. The British public back home, free from in-depth analysis and TV coverage, never saw John Dawes at his playing peak and are the poorer for it. Doug Smith, writing in his end of tour report, aptly sums up John's contribution:

> The appointment of John Dawes was probably one of the main reasons for the success of the tour. A charming and knowledgeable man who held the respect of everyone in the team, not only for his own outstanding ability as a player, but for his friendliness.
>
> *The History of the British & Irish Lions*, by Clem Thomas.

Whilst John was at the sharp end on the pitch, the two other men in charge shaped events through their very different, but equally engaging, personalities. Doug Smith was an old Lion, a Scot living in exile in England, who knew full well what was needed to survive New Zealand. He was a natural manager of men: he was also a superb problem-fixer. He was tough, loyal, ultra-confident, charismatic (when he had to be) and a real 'players' man'. It was joked that the only thing that rivalled the growing expectation heaped upon the Lions was Doug's expanding waistline. The threat of having to carry Doug the length of the pitch for a training misdemeanour helped focus our collective minds. But his gruff Scottish manner and professional background (he was a doctor by calling) afforded him the air of an out-of-hours headmaster: the respect was still there but so was an approachability; being let into his confidence felt like a special privilege. Doug was also the man who made the most famous prediction in rugby history when he said the Lions would win the series two to one with one match drawn.

Working in tandem with Doug was Carwyn James. The Home Unions' committee predicted correctly that Carwyn would fail in his attempt to become Plaid Cymru MP for Llanelli, and when he wasn't elected they offered him solace with the premier coaching job in the northern hemisphere. Carwyn was a complicated, passionate man, one who loved his country and his rugby. He was a purist in many ways, classically minded, idealistic and proud. He was also an individual who wanted to do things on his terms. Should he have succeeded Clive Rowlands as coach of Wales? In place of John Dawes? Well, in my view, the jury is out on that matter. Carwyn was undoubtedly the most gifted coach I ever played under, (and don't forget, out of five encounters with the All Blacks his teams only lost one), but he was a maverick too. He would have wanted the WRU (and the Big Five) to relinquish control over selection, and back then radical thinking and conservative committees did not bode well together. Besides, John didn't do a bad job, did he?

I did not quite know what to make of Carwyn at first. I knew him by the reputation he had built as coach of Llanelli. I knew he had played for Wales in the late '50s but without great distinction because his era coincided with the legendary Cliff Morgan. But the men who knew him best were devoted to him. To Barry John he was a boyhood hero and the mutual respect they had for one another was evident to all. Barry summed up Carwyn's influence on the Lions in his autobiography:

> Carwyn never undermined his position as coach by trying to be 'one of the boys'. He retained his authority always but never became aloof or authoritarian. He knew how to handle us – when to push this player, when to hold back with that player. When he got up to speak to us we always concentrated . . . because we knew he was telling us how to win the matches. His approach was quiet and reasoned. He regarded us as inflammable fuel and was anxious not to throw in the spark prematurely.
>
> *The Barry John Story*, by Barry John

I have always felt slightly detached from the coaches' words. Clive Rowlands was a scrum-half, John Dawes a centre, Carwyn a fly-half . . . none had played number 8, none truly understood what went on 'in there' in the maelstrom of the scrum. My memories of our initial coaching sessions were of Carwyn talking about 'individual skills'. I was mystified at first; we were perceived to be the best 30 players in the country, proven as individuals. Surely the aim of squad coaching would be the forming of a team ethic? But here Carwyn excelled. He invited us to take personal responsibility for our role but without ever telling us what to do. He questioned us constantly about how we would deal with a specific situation should it arise. He had a persuasive knack with players that led us to believe that his suggestions were ours, not his. If Carwyn coached me, he never coached me . . . if that makes sense. One of his greatest strengths as a coach was an ability to listen to his players – and that is a skill a few modern-day coaches could do with learning. Carwyn was also a great forward-planner and believed in using the depth of the full squad to keep everybody fit and involved. He might have known his preferred team before we left the UK but everybody trained – and played – with a belief that they could make the Test side. He and Doug complemented one another perfectly as manager and coach and utilised the vast experience of men like Willie John McBride and Ray McLoughlin. Doug and Carwyn knew the tour would succeed or fail in the hands of the players, and by giving us a direct voice they softened the lines between team and management. We went to New Zealand united. We went as one. Never had a squad left these shores so committed to winning. The New Zealand players and public may have been expecting us to roll over, but the whole mentality of British rugby had changed: we were a tough bunch who knew how to play with the ball in hand. Getting hold of the bugger would be the problem.

Regarding player selection, the shock omission from the party was that of Dai Morris. I thought it odd not to pick such an integral part of a Grand Slam back-row unit . . . such a seasoned forager. I felt for Dai, but I had to trust in the selection process and accept that his exclusion had solid reasoning behind it. Again, hindsight proves that indeed it did. Another disappointing part of Dai's absence was missing his friendship. I felt comfortable in his presence; being with him was easy, making new friends wasn't. I was never the most vociferous person off the pitch, and I felt nervous about meeting the men who had been my opponents. Despite some initial reservations, it was a good experience to finally see a different side to those I had been jousting with over the last three seasons. You can gain a smattering of knowledge about an opponent when you come up against him on the field, but when you pack down together you soon grow to understand what makes him tick. One only had to look at the tour party to see that this was a squad selected for a purpose. The key was upfront and big men were needed to find parity with the fearsome New Zealand pack. The backs were as good as any ever sent from these islands: Bob Hiller, J.P.R., John Bevan, Ali Biggar, Gerald, John, David Duckham, Arthur Lewis, Chris Rea, John Spencer, Gareth, Chico Hopkins, Barry and Mike Gibson. Barry memorably said: 'I had Gareth Edwards on one side of me, Mike Gibson on the other. I could have played in a duffel coat.'

The backs would be fine . . . but the forwards would require some deft handling.

From the moment I received the invite to tour, I was adamant that it would be T.M. Davies of London Welsh and Wales who would be wearing the Test jersey come 26 June. Without wishing to sound arrogant, I knew I was a better player than Peter Dixon, the other specialist number 8 in the party. Pete was a quiet boy. Bright too, studying up at Oxford. He had been selected to play for England just the once but, at 6 ft 3 in. tall and 15 st., he added considerable bulk to the party. I sized him up at Eastbourne and felt he lacked the 'dog' to face Messrs. Kirkpatrick, Wyllie, McNaughton and co. However, the thinking behind his selection was not to use him at number 8 but to put him on the flank next to me. This may also have been influenced by injuries to Mike Hipwell and Fergus Slattery, but his ultimate inclusion meant there would be two lumbering forwards at the back of the scrum and just one flier in John Taylor, meaning the whole dynamic of my game would have to change.

The tour began in Eastbourne: not the liveliest place for a pack of Lions to sharpen their claws. It reminded me of the old saying: 'Dover for the continent and Eastbourne for the incontinent.' Training was an insipid affair because no one dared risk injury before getting on the plane. The only positive aspect to come from our time at the seaside was meeting kit suppliers and picking up new boots. We should have been preparing in New Zealand, but the NZRFU did not want to pick up the tab for that extra week's stay.

Besides, New Zealand was not our first destination; we headed for

Australia to boost interest in the game over there. The 15-man code held very little attraction for the Aussie public, but if anything could raise its profile then it would be the arrival of the British Lions. Our defeat against Queensland followed by a narrow win over New South Wales probably did Australian rugby a world of good, but it didn't exactly help our reputation across the Tasman Sea. Or did it? Whilst the New Zealand press prepared the obituaries, we knew that jet lag was the root cause of our sluggishness during those first two games, not the opposition.

I was under no illusions about what lay ahead. The experience of 1969 stayed with the Welshmen who had lost there. The Irish, too, had suffered the ignominy of defeat in 'the land of the long white cloud'. We were a squad who were fit, full of self-belief and driven by retribution. There was no false expectation about this tour; we went as underdogs but with a hard, inner belief that we could be the first touring side ever to win a series against the All Blacks on their home soil. I knew that the ferocity of the games, the hostile nature of the crowd, the press and the weather would put us under the gravest pressure. The scrutiny would be intense . . . we were big news. The thousands who turned up at Auckland to greet our arrival left us in little doubt that we were embarking on a titanic struggle.

As a squad, it was fortunate that we gelled well together. Full-grown men possessed of ego and machismo can make tense travelling companions, but we kept what could be a mundane day-to-day existence interesting. We were received extremely well by our hosts – except on matchday. The crowds would swell to watch us train, and we did things on the training paddock that perplexed our audience, such as undertaking whole sessions without the ball, or playing soccer. The squad quickly fell into a routine, training at 9 or 9.30 every morning with plenty of emphasis on running, sprinting and stretching. After lunch, if we had some free time, we could go off on a specially arranged activity, sleep or hit the hotel bar a little earlier than usual. When you are living and breathing rugby, travelling in a bubble, it can become quite tiresome. I was feeling fit and well fed, but was occasionally bored and isolated. I did enjoy meeting the locals, taking sojourns down to the local rugby club and soaking up the atmosphere. New Zealand – like Wales – treated rugby in a quasi-religious manner, and, in some ways, it was a new experience for me because as a young boy I didn't spend time in a local Swansea club. But you could see it in the eyes of the young Kiwi lads, drinking in the spectacle of the Lions arriving on their doorstep, each one sizing us up, fancying their chances even at a tender age. The schools also treated us well. We might be beating their local heroes on the park, but the children we visited kept scrapbooks of our exploits across their nation.

I do pity the boys of today who touch down in a country, play their matches and then leave. I can only compare what we did to an expedition or a grand adventure. Tours need time and space to develop, to find their identity. A squad becomes a mini-society of its own making, with its own rules, rhythms and guidelines. Every squad has its characters, and we certainly had our fair share. Two of the biggest jokers were Ray Hopkins and Bob Hiller. They might have been as different as coal dust and cut glass, but they kept us permanently amused. Their friendship grew so close that Ray, with Bob's blessing, was made an ''onorary 'arlequin' . . . and not many from Maesteg can claim that distinction. It is a testament, too, to their attitude as tourists that they remained so good humoured. Both were trying to shift immovable objects in Gareth and J.P.R., but they never let their understudy status affect their commitment to the wider cause. Bob had a particularly fine time, scoring over 100 points and earning the deserved nickname 'Boss'. Much is made of the 'dirt tracker' (or reserve player), but I believe no player ever resigns himself to being second-best. The midweek team has a tremendous impact on the Test side: by winning matches, they keep the pressure on the boys in the Test shirt.

Singing – as well as tomfoolery, cards and liar-dice – helped keep morale up. The lads all had their favourite songs: John Taylor liked 'Big Rock Candy Mountain', Derek Quinnell loved 'My Way' and the Irish boys had a song for every mood from 'Wild Rover' to 'Danny Boy'. I was more of a mumbler at the back and never a willing soloist, but I did contribute 'Sloop John B'. I cannot over-estimate how important our tour choir was to creating togetherness and harmony. There was always a fair bit of jostling about who would claim the revered post of choirmaster. Baz seized it in 1971 and guarded it as jealously as he did his Test place. Music followed us up and down the islands. We even mastered a fairly decent rendition of that wonderful Maori song 'Po Karekare Ana', which endeared us to our hosts. Peter Dixon travelled everywhere with his guitar, although I never saw him strum it. The boys would use song to rouse the spirits and channel the emotion as we flew across the islands or bussed our way toward the Tests. On both my Lions tours, singing was deemed crucial to our success.

The worst part of touring, apart from the soaking wet kit, was being Duty Boy. The only bearable part of this essential role was that we all had to do it and God help you if your turn fell on a matchday. Duty Boy took charge of all non-playing affairs: from the breakfast menu and kit allocation to making sure the Liaison Officers had a full and interesting itinerary for us. Luckily, in a land as diverse as New Zealand, where the terrain ranged from sub-tropical rainforests to snow-capped mountains, there was always plenty to do. There was one excursion, however, that I will never forget for as long as I live.

Being 6 ft 4½ in. tall – or 6 ft 5 in. depending on how much bounce my hair had – made flying an uncomfortable experience. I did not particularly relish those flights but I learnt to grin and bear it. At least I felt safe, cramped but safe, on those big passenger jets, and I would readily endure a 40-hour flight in a BA bird rather than two minutes in a prop plane with Sean Lynch.

I first got to know Sean – or John as he was officially known – en route to Heathrow from Eastbourne. We were on the coach chatting away and I asked him what he did for a living, to which he replied 'vintner'. Being Irish and in the alcohol trade I assumed he liked a drink but Sean said 'no', it didn't go well with the job. Well, he played me for a fool because I have never known a 'teetotaller' to consume so much booze! He was like most Irishmen I had had the pleasure to befriend: they were either yelling or whispering, full speed or stationary, teetotallers or skilled boozers. He could sing too, and quickly became a firm tour favourite. He was a terrific prop, tough as teak but terrified of creepy crawlies. Some malicious little so-and-so found a dead bird and decided it would be a laugh to hide it in the bottom of Sean's kitbag. Well, he picked up his bag and took it to his room and we waited for the screams but nothing, not a sound. This went on for days. Every time he walked past with his bag, someone would whisper, 'Has he found it yet?' He hadn't, he kept foraging around in the top part of the bag, oblivious to the smell, without finding his gruesome guest. It got so bad that none of us wanted to share a room with him and then it happened: he picked up his bag and the bottom fell out spilling a revolting mess of bird carcass and wet kit all over the floor. Sean's reaction was priceless: 'Where did that come from?' he said looking overhead, oblivious to the end.

Back to the excursion I cannot shake from my mind. It was decided that the Lions needed to get away and unwind between Tests, and we were flown to Queenstown on the South Island for mountain rest and recuperation. The party was split into small groups for transfer because the plane could only take nine or ten people on one run. We took off in this tiny plane and proceeded on a near-suicidal journey swooping down valleys, banking over dead volcanoes, skimming across the top of snow-capped peaks. Suddenly, Sean completely lost the plot and all hell broke loose. It only takes one nervous flier to create a plane full of nervous fliers and Sean was adamant he wanted to get out . . . even at 10,000 feet. We pleaded, cajoled, threatened and eventually sat on him until we landed. None of us flew with him on the flight back.

The Lions stormed their way through the first part of the tour, beating Thames Valley Counties, Wanganui King Country, Waikato and the New Zealand Maoris. The Wanganui match resonates still, not just because of the try I scored and the way I played at the back of the lineout but also because that was the day I felled the Pine Tree.

No player encapsulates a nation's attitude to sport like Colin Meads does for New Zealand. In a land of rugby giants he still rules supreme and is regarded by many as the greatest ever All Black. He epitomised the natural strength and hardness that New Zealanders like to identify with and tales of him training on his farm with a sheep under one arm and a fence post under the other are legendary. He may not quite have been at his best in 1971 but even sub-standard Meads ranked higher than most. He was the flag-bearer of New Zealand manhood and King Country was his particular domain.

In *The Roaring Lions*, JBG Thomas's in-depth tour account, Bryn writes in a matter-of-fact way of the encounter that felled Meads: 'Colin Meads got up from a maul slowly, after being on top of the ball, and rubbed his side.' I think it was yours truly who put him down on the deck. I can recall a ball being hoisted into the air and racing after it. Just as it was about to be claimed I remember thinking, 'If I hit this guy right, I'll clean him out.' And I did. I caught the catcher right under the ribs and I heard a cracking sound followed by the breath being thumped out of his body. It was only when I got up and looked around that I saw it was Meads. He went off but came back on bandaged up to finish the match. I do not think he knew it was me who hit him because I am sure I would have felt his fist if he had. I thought, 'Christ, of all the people to do over, why him?' and I was a little bit wary for the rest of the game because Pine Tree wasn't shy about making his presence felt. The seriousness of Meads' injury became a national talking point and the authorities were keen to play it down. The official verdict was 'torn rib-cartilages', although I've never known cartilage to 'crack'. From that point on in the series, carrying his damaged ribs, Meads was a little more subdued. It may have been a combination of age – he was 35 – and injury, but the great talisman of New Zealand rugby was visibly dented. A chink in the All Blacks' armour had appeared.

Two other games in the run-up to the First Test, against Wellington and Canterbury, proved crucial to our chances . . . and for entirely different reasons. Against Wellington, we played scintillating rugby, rugby that caused our hosts to sit up and take notice that we were a very real threat to their position as top dogs in the world game. This was where the tour truly came to life, and our backs – in particular the young, dynamic left-wing John Bevan who ran in four tries – had an absolute field day. Suddenly, Gareth, Barry and Mike burst into action giving the wide men time and space to operate, and we ran home comfortable winners 47 points to 9. The watching press universally agreed that the Lions had seldom played with such all-round excellence and ingenuity. The first stage of the tour in the North Island was over; in the South we would have to rely more on guts than ingenuity.

I missed the Canterbury game and for the first, and only, time in my career I can safely say I was glad to be out of reach. A groin injury forced me to sit out training and my place in the First Test was in serious jeopardy. If I had been selected to play on that grim June day, then I might have followed a few of my colleagues on a flight home. It was one of those matches when you felt your blood boil to see what was happening. We suspected that this was a pre-planned assault to scupper us before the First Test a week later. In terms of injuries it did, because we lost both our first-choice props in Ray McLoughlin and Sandy Carmichael. Ray broke his thumb when retaliating and Sandy had his cheekbone staved in. There were other casualties too: Mike Hipwell hurt his knee and was out of the tour, Fergus Slattery lost two teeth and suffered concussion, and both John Pullin and Gareth Edwards were floored by sneaky punches. The Canterbury players kicked, punched and trampled all over us, but still they could not win. The New Zealand press themselves were outraged by their countrymen's antics and dubbed it 'the game of shame', and one paper, *The Truth*, went further, writing 'New Zealand rugby has become as grotesque as a wounded bull.'

Certain players were regarded as the main instigators of the foul play, but we suspected it was pre-planned by the Canterbury coaches. The first salvo in a face-saving campaign was fired when it was claimed that we were merely victims of rough justice. They said if the Lions insisted upon lying all over the ruck then we would have to deal with the consequences. Ridiculous. Why hadn't this been the case in any of the previous matches, which had all been relatively clean games? We didn't change our game plan; it was our good form and unbeaten record that had set alarm bells ringing. When the New Zealand coach, Ivan Vodanovich, came out with his infamous 'Battle of Passchendaele' quote, we knew we had the upper hand. Vodanovich's rhetoric and Canterbury's punches did more to prepare us for the First Test than any training session could have done. New Zealand rugby was worried; they were resorting to the lowest form of intimidation. Jack Sullivan, chairman of the New Zealand council, deserved credit for defusing the situation when he slapped down Vodanovich by saying, 'There will be no battle at Carisbrook next Saturday.' Some perspective was needed; it was, after all, just a game. But in case it happened again, Carwyn schooled us to get our retaliation in first.

Losing Ray (who was a damn fine pack leader) and Sandy was a bitter body blow to the party, but, as is often the case, one man's bad luck is another man's golden opportunity. They were replaced by another Irish–Scottish combination in the guise of Sean Lynch and 'Ian' McLauchlan who came in to prop either side of John Pullin. We were lucky to have such outstanding tourists as these unsung heroes from the front line. McLauchlan was raised into Lions folklore when Doug Smith christened him 'Mighty Mouse'. Sean Lynch, well . . . as I hinted at earlier, he caused us to scratch our heads and wonder about his sanity on quite a few occasions.

The First Test at Carisbrook Park, Dunedin, was the single most important point of the whole tour. Success and failure hinged on one result. The mood in the dressing-room was one of grim determination. Carwyn did not go in for the drama of a Clive Rowlands address, preferring to remind us quietly of what we had to do. When we walked out onto the pitch in front of 45,000 partisan fans, the atmosphere and the expectation was electric.

I can honestly say that First Test was the most remarkable match that I ever played in, and a few of my colleagues will echo that. To be in Dunedin on a greasy day in June 1971 was to put a marker down for British, nay, for world rugby . . . for that was the day when the All Blacks were made to seem human. I still don't know how it happened. I have never worked so hard in a game without touching the ball. We seemed to be constantly on the back foot and what ball we got, Barry kicked. The desire for running rugby was jettisoned; pragmatism replaced playfulness. I wondered if we lacked the courage of our convictions to use the ball; it was the game we had been playing – and mastering – all tour. But the skiddish conditions and Barry's deadeye positional kicking saved our energy so we could concentrate on defence. Tackles won that game, not tries. But I'll hold my hand up and say New Zealand contrived to lose it too. They had one game: bash, bash, bash straight up the middle, and we did not let them pass. Barry finished off full-back Fergie McCormick and had him scrabbling around in the mud all afternoon; it was sweet revenge for what he did to Wales in '69. It was a day for heroes. None more so than Ray 'Chico' Hopkins. Forever in Gareth's shadow, he stepped into the light after Gareth departed with a dodgy hamstring early in the first half, and played a blinder.

We won 9–3 through fortitude and good fortune. Ian McLauchlan charged down Sutherland's kick for a try and Barry kicked two penalties. There was no dash from the three-quarters, no searing blindside breaks: it was guts that got us the glory. Afterwards, Willie John said what we all thought, 'How the hell did we win that one?' Unbelievably, that was Willie John's first Test win in Lions colours in nine appearances; no wonder he looked shocked. But to answer the big Ulsterman's question, we were outplayed but not outfought. The All Blacks lacked the flexibility to adapt their game. Would they change? Could they? I got the distinct feeling that they had stagnated since 1969. Meads was magnanimous in defeat and said, 'We can do better next time.' They did, but the damage to All Black domination had already been done.

We knew that the Second Test at Lancaster Park, Christchurch, would be a struggle. Everything had been geared to winning the First Test and it would prove difficult to lift ourselves up to that same demanding level again. The Lions made just one change, with the tall, powerfully built David Duckham coming in on the left-wing for John Bevan. 'Dai', as an army of appreciative Welsh fans would know him, was always going to feature in the Test side. When he ran in six tries against the West Coast at Greymouth, his claim could no longer be ignored. The All Blacks were more adventurous in their selection, replacing the hapless McCormick at full-back with Laurie Mains, shunting Brian Williams out onto the wing and bringing in two men from the Canterbury encounter: Howard Joseph at centre and my 'old friend' Alex Wyllie in the back row.

The match will be remembered for Ian Kirkpatrick's barnstorming 60-yard try: a try which should have barred him from any back-row union because of 'unwarranted athleticism'. He put in a devastating display, as did Sid Going at scrum-half. New Zealand fought back at us in the way we knew they could and ran out comfortable winners 22–12. But something happened in that game which suddenly gave us the conviction that we could win the series.

We started playing expansive rugby for the first time, which allowed Gerald Davies to run in two tries. Whether the All Blacks eased off (which seemed unlikely) or the forwards started winning quality ball, parity had been found at last. We won one match without playing well and lost another after improving significantly. Anything could happen next, and Carwyn told us when we left the field that he had seen enough to convince him that we would win the next Test. It didn't wash at first, but in the days that followed the Lions collectively believed that Carwyn – thoughtful, enigmatic seer that he was – might be right.

Despite the feeling of buoyancy pervading the squad before we headed back across the Cook Strait for the Third Test in Wellington, changes were made in the pack. Young Gordon Brown came in for Delme Thomas and set himself on the road to becoming a great Lions legend. In the back row, Peter Dixon was ousted in favour of Derek Quinnell, who joined the small handful of players to win a Lions cap before playing for their country. I sympathised with Peter because he had given his all in an unfamiliar position but, after a long and gruelling tour, when the outcome would come down to the wire, fresh impetus is often required. My groin strain lay-off meant I was a little fresher than some of the boys in the party, and I think it was reflected in my performances. One of New Zealand's great attacking ploys was the peel from the back of the lineout and I was charged with the task of nullifying the threat. Carwyn was good at that, assigning individual tasks. Derek was brought in to thwart Sid Going, and I remember listening to Carwyn telling him not to concern himself with anything else except Going. I thought, 'You lucky bugger, what about the other 14 players!' It was pointless looking for sympathy from John Taylor; he was down to be dropped in favour of Fergus Slattery, but Fergus fell ill and John came back in. John was furious that he had been left out and thundered onto the pitch determined to show Doug, Carwyn and John Dawes that they had been wrong. He did.

New Zealand made a very bizarre selection choice by bringing back former captain Brian Lochore for Whiting. He was undoubtedly a terrific player in his day, but 31 July 1971 would not be his, or New Zealand's, day.

By the half-time whistle we had used the wind to our advantage and were ahead by 13–3, thanks to two tries from Gerald and Barry and a few other kicks from 'The King'. New Zealand could not breach our line in the second half. From the back of the lineout I could sense the frustration and angst felt by my opponents. We won more ball in that match than the previous two combined and should have pulled away. The tendency was again to play it safe and only when I captained Wales did I realise that these restrictive tactics were, in fact, correct. Big Gordon Brown bossed Lochore that day and we successfully defended our lead. As the final whistle approached, the mighty Meads was heard to say, 'Give us a break, Ref!' New Zealand hearts were shattered.

The subsequent two weeks felt like the longest of my rugby life. The tour went on and on and we faced Manawatu, North Auckland and Bay of Plenty. The big fear was injury and every player was sometimes literally down on his knees begging for a safe passage through to the decider. Although we couldn't lose the series, we could draw it by losing the Fourth Test and that would have felt like nothing less than catastrophe. Since we had touched down in New Zealand in mid-May we had played 23 matches, losing just 1. We had scored 541 points and conceded just 190. It was a rout. But a rout that had cost us blood, teeth and broken bones. Now it all came down to the last 80 minutes . . . 80 minutes that would change our lives.

The Fourth Test in Eden Park, Auckland, was probably the worst of the series because of what was at stake; the All Blacks showed their desperation in a first-half lineout. Cool heads were needed in a match like that, but they lost theirs completely. As the ball sailed in, every member of the New Zealand pack turned and smacked his opposite number. Luckily, Ian Kirkpatrick stood opposite me and he wasn't a dirty player so his punch was deliberately ineffective. Gordon took a terrific wallop from Whiting that left him needing five stitches across his eye. As I said in an earlier chapter, a team that resorts to violence is a team on its last legs. At this point, I must add that John Pring – the referee who adjudicated the whole series – kept control of a potentially explosive situation and avoided another 'Canterbury' erupting. Neutral refs were not used back then, but we felt Pring was a far fairer referee than Pat Murphy, the All Blacks' preferred official.

New Zealand led 8–0 but we clawed our way back to a 14–14 draw thanks to the boot of Barry, an unlikely try by a fully restored Peter Dixon and J.P.R.'s near legendary drop goal. Bob Hiller teased J.P.R. by telling him he would only be considered a true all-round full-back if he kicked a drop goal in a Test match. I'm sure he did it to prove a point to an Englishman. The whistle went and I felt more tired than elated. Fourteen weeks of slog had come down to this, but it was worth it. We won the series 2 to 1 with one Test drawn. Doug Smith was a prophetic genius.

On our arrival back at Heathrow, we were greeted by the most amazing reception imaginable. Our only inkling of what our achievements had meant back home came from pressmen like Cliff Morgan. Few in the party believed that we were front-page news, but the thousands who waited for us at the airport convinced us that we were part of sporting history. It didn't end there; my parents and brother were present to shepherd me, the conquering hero, home to another all-night party.

Of my own performance, I felt justifiably proud. Many believed I had firmly established myself as a world-class player. The challenge I had always sought had been met and the revenge I badly wanted had been taken. And I liked it . . . I liked the feeling of beating the best in the world and I wanted more. There weren't too many brickbats flying in my direction; instead, a genuine respect had emerged for the man once known as 'Mervyn who?' Without question, the Lions made my reputation. Perhaps the greatest compliment about my part in this story comes from the great man Meads himself who said: 'If one of the 1971 Lions more than any other spelled out from the start the trouble the All Blacks would have in the series, it was Mervyn.' Now there is a rugby epitaph to be proud of.

My, how I look back on those days with a tremendous sense of pride. The players and staff of that tour were lucky to be part of something extremely important and we have dined out on our achievements until this day. More achievements were to come my way, but nothing gave me quite the same buzz as being the bloke who played number 8 when we beat the All Blacks. Delme Thomas once said: 'Unless you have been to New Zealand, you don't know what physical rugby is all about.'

Too bloody true, Delme boy . . . too bloody true.

VIII

Coming Home

My return to London from the 1971 Lions tour was to bring about a new turning point in my life. I wasn't aware of it then, but internal cogs had been set into motion and ideas about moving back home to South Wales had rapidly taken shape. Being a successful Lion was just the start. Suddenly, the overlong bloke with the bushy black hair popped up into the public eye. It was a new, and not entirely unpleasant, feeling. I enjoyed the attention, the friendly nods from passers-by and the pints of beer put over the bar for my consumption. Winning for Wales but living in England had previously protected me from such exposure. I didn't experience the same level of interest that swooped and swirled around my more illustrious Wales-based colleagues. But being a Lion – a Lion that had done the impossible and won in New Zealand – put me squarely on the map. And I thought, perhaps, I had found an escape route out of teaching.

I am hard on teaching but not hard on teachers. The men and women who stand up at the front of a classroom, who articulate and advise, guide and coax their charges through an ever-changing curriculum, deserve society's wholehearted support. The best contribution I ever made to the teaching profession was leaving it. Teaching isn't for the half-hearted: there is far too much at stake. It took me a while to figure out my inadequacies, but I got there in the end. Ironically, my sporting exploits could have guaranteed me a teaching job for as long as I wanted one . . . but my success in rugby hid my failings as a schoolmaster. I could have lived a happy, comfortable school life, but I would have been duping my students and myself. I needed a change of direction.

Before I get ahead of myself, I should explain what kind of life I was returning to from the Lions. I left Mytchett Junior in 1970 and took up a post at the Emanuel School, just off Clapham Junction in London. Emanuel was a voluntary grammar school with great designs on being a 'sporting school'. By the time I left Mytchett I knew I was no blackboard specialist, so I needed somewhere that could exploit what meagre teaching talents I possessed. What was I good at? Sport. Therefore, what kind of subject was I best qualified to teach? Physical Education. It helped having my London Welsh colleague Tony Phillips on the staff, and I am sure his influence went some way to persuading the school to employ me.

The boys from Emanuel were encouraged to excel in, and express themselves through, sport – particularly rowing, cricket and rugby. Tony and I took over the running of the rugby and we put together a decent team. I wasn't a natural coach, so I relied on the drills and words of the men who had coached me, men like Roger Michaelson, Clive Rowlands and Carwyn James.

I landed on my feet at Emanuel. I was given time off to play for Wales, and the school enjoyed the kudos of having an established international player on the teaching staff. When I was selected for the New Zealand tour, they paid me a full wage and brought in a supply teacher to cover my lessons until I returned. For the first year and a half, I very much enjoyed my life there. The boys worked diligently at their sport and were a good bunch of lads to be with. On the rugby field, Tony and I pushed them hard and they responded keenly to instruction. It helped not having parental interference from the touchline – a common intrusion today – which often has a detrimental effect on a boy's sporting development. If 'Dad' stands there, screaming from the sidelines, doing the 'three bs' (bullying, bragging and bollocking), he risks taking all the fun out of his boy's game. Different times, different culture – back then, few fathers influenced what we did. The Emanuel pupils respected Tony and me because we were out there playing high-profile rugby every Saturday. It didn't stop the boys shoeing us over whenever they got us trapped at the bottom of a ruck. I have fond memories – and a few stud marks – from my first serious foray into coaching, and it gave me great pleasure to meet up with a few of the old boys from Emanuel before the Wales–Italy game in the 2004 Six Nations. However, there was a downside to our brief reunion: seeing skinny young lads like Andy Roberts and Mike Hawker (as they remained in my memory) with grey hair and beer bellies made me feel rather decrepit.

My other duty at Emanuel was teaching English, but I spent more time outside the classroom than inside it. And that is when frustration set in. My tracksuit kept me prisoner, and soon my work and my hobby became inexorably bound. A regular winter week consisted of coaching the boys on Monday, Wednesday and Friday, training with London Welsh on Tuesday and Thursday evenings, school matches on Saturday morning and London Welsh games on Saturday afternoon. Before and during the Five Nations there would also be national squad training in Wales on Sunday. Come rain or shine, barely a day went by when I wasn't outside in my boots. All my life, rugby had been about release from reality on a Saturday afternoon. Suddenly, rugby *was* my reality – and it grew tiresome.

My decision to leave teaching was taken before my decision to leave London Welsh. I envied Gareth and Barry back in Wales because they had qualified as teachers but never actually taught. Gareth worked with the Hamers, a family firm from Neath involved in light industry, and Barry worked for a financial services company based in Cardiff. I fancied doing something similar, but all I was qualified to do was teach and play rugby. Teaching had rapidly lost its appeal, so what could I do? If I was a marketable commodity, if I had a name that could gain me alternative employment, then I needed to go where it was valued most. I had to go home. And with my wedding fast approaching, a new start in South Wales seemed perfect.

In terms of geographical distance it isn't that far from London to Swansea, but psychologically the gulf is huge. Leaving London

Welsh was a terrible wrench. The club had propelled me to rugby's top table. Without men like Michaelson, Bowcott, Bosley, Richards, Dawes, Gray and Taylor, I would still have been playing in some rugby backwater. The men I played, drank and shared stories with were my friends and my family, and I looked on Old Deer Park as my spiritual home. When I had first arrived there, I was selected purely as the man who could win some lineout ball for our backs. When other big men like Mike Roberts and Geoff Evans joined, I was free to concentrate on other aspects of my game and I evolved into an all-round player. It was such a wonderfully cosmopolitan place too, a little idealised version of Wales where what you did didn't matter: belonging was what mattered. The boys at London Welsh – especially the two Johns and Tony – worked hard to keep me in Richmond, but the time had come to move on. Theoretically, I could have had my choice of clubs in Wales, but, realistically, there was only one: Swansea.

My father was delighted that I was going to join the team that he had played for and captained with such distinction. My enthusiasm, however, wasn't so great. Swansea was not a club with the playing pedigree of Cardiff, Newport, Llanelli or Pontypool. It was rumoured that I could have had my pick of any – although my father would have disowned me if I had joined the dreaded Scarlets. But I went home, because Swansea was my hometown, I liked living there, and – most crucially of all – I could earn a crust there. I knew in 1972 when I contemplated my move that it was pointless to seek a teaching post. The Lions tour to South Africa was my next great sporting goal but no Labour-controlled education authority would pay me if I went to play in a country that embraced apartheid. Besides, teaching was off the agenda. The prospect of paying a mortgage is a great leveller and I said I would play for Swansea if they could find me a job. They were as good as their word and they did.

The Blyths are a big-name family in my area of Wales. Norman and Len ran a successful firm that supplied industry with safety wear and protective equipment. It was agreed that I would go and work for them as a sales representative. My appointment benefited both parties: the Blyths got a bloke on their sales force that people wanted to meet, and I worked for a family who were passionate about their rugby – and, in particular, Swansea Rugby Football Club. I owe a lot to Len and Norman; both were acquaintances of my father, and Len had played flanker for Wales, so they were the perfect bosses. After I fell ill, they were marvellous and they made sure my family was looked after and my job was safe. Both men knew how much rugby meant to the Welsh public and someone with my playing profile could be readily used to their commercial advantage. It wasn't unusual for sales to increase the Monday after an international, especially if Wales won. And if Llanelli beat Swansea then business way down west was even better. I would be dispatched across the Loughor to take a fair bit of stick and pick up a few sympathetic orders from triumphant Scarlets fans. I enjoyed my new work, being out on the road, meeting clients and building long-lasting relationships.

If I had entertained any thoughts that my acceptance as a Swansea player would be a foregone conclusion, I would have been staggeringly naive. I wasn't. I knew I had to prove myself all over again . . . and the prospect did not frighten or bother me. If I could win over a sceptical and cantankerous old so-and-so like John Taylor, then I could win anybody over. But I had to bide my time. After all, how would I have felt if an established international and successful British Lion had decided to grace my club with his presence? I would have done what my new colleagues tried to do to me: dump him on his backside and force him to earn my respect. I knew it would be hard, and there would be much antagonism, but I did not expect most of it to come from the top; I thought my coach would back me up.

In a career crammed full of encounters with tough-minded individuals, few battles felt tougher than those with Ieuan Evans. Ieuan had been the main man at Swansea for a few years; he dictated the style of rugby the club embraced and was very much in charge of team affairs. It was quite obvious that Ieuan did not want me getting in the way of his grand Swansea scheme. He told me my presence 'messed up all his lineout calls' but his eyes and his body language revealed a lot more resentment than niggles over set-piece plays. Perhaps he saw me as a prima donna . . . a Fancy Dan coming from London full of London ways. Out of respect for him and my new colleagues I acquiesced and said I would play as instructed; it was up to me to fit in with them and not vice versa. But we didn't hit it off from day one, and by the time Ieuan left to take up a post with the WRU, I was glad to see him go. Personality clashes are part of the game, part of any work culture, but you just have to grit your teeth and get on with it for the good of everyone else. However, despite our differences, I recognised that Ieuan was a very good coach . . . much more than the forwards-obsessed grinder that I initially thought he was. His work with the Wales Youth XV in later years was of the highest order, and even back in the mid-'70s, I remember him drilling us in the importance of warm-ups and warm-downs; ideas that are now universally accepted in all sports.

When I did venture an opinion to Ieuan, I was usually shot a withering look and ignored. I remember we played Fiji to mark Swansea's centenary and Ieuan told us that we would show them how to play rugby by spinning the ball around. 'Hang on,' I said, 'this is Fiji.' The sun was beating down outside and the ground was rock solid. I had been to Fiji, and I had some understanding of what Fijian rugby was about. I said that we had to keep the ball with the forwards if we were going to win. But Ieuan got his way and they thrashed us by 30 points. I also enquired why the clubhouse was full of soft drinks and was told the Fijians 'don't drink alcohol'. I had to stifle a laugh: our guests proceeded to drain the bar that night . . . leaving the squash and crisps blissfully untouched.

So my new coach didn't want me, but what about my teammates? It didn't look promising there, either. At my very first lineout practice I took up my customary place at the back only to feel the wrath of Roger Hyndman: 'What are you doing standing there? I stand there, you fuck off!'

'All right, Rog, no problem . . .' I still caught his ball, though. Roger became a good mate, although he did have a tendency to drone on and on and on about his playing credentials. I remember one training run from St Helens down to the university when I got stuck with Roger. From first to last stride he badgered me to put a good word in with Clive Rowlands about why he should be playing for Wales. Onlookers must have thought I was putting in some serious legwork, but I was only trying to get away from Roger. Another time he cornered Baz after a game against London Welsh and lectured him on why *he* should be playing for Wales and not John: 'Taylor, I'm faster, I'm fitter, I'm better than you.' I gave up reasoning with Roger fairly early in our acquaintance. The best way to cope with a Hyndman outburst was to roll the eyes and let him go on.

Compared with London Welsh, Swansea was a more dogmatic and political club. There were factions looking after the interests of the rugby, cricket and hockey teams, and much heated debate spilt over into the bar after AGMs and EGMs. I felt uncomfortable with some of the decisions made or mooted and thought it best to stay out of it and concentrate on playing. There was an aggressive undercurrent there, too, but then that's a Swansea thing . . . you're only one ill-chosen word away from being punched.

I learnt a fair bit about 'the Swansea punch' during my three and a half years there, my first lesson coming before I played my first real game. It was decided that the squad needed some bonding time together, so in the summer of 1972 we were flown out to Rome for a pre-season tour. Great, a chance to get away to the sunshine with the boys . . . what better way could there be to break the ice. Everything went well at first, although there was some disappointment when we learnt we were being billeted out at Aqua Sentosa, part of the old Olympic village, five miles out in the sticks. Being a cosmopolitan type who had worked in London and seen a bit of the world, I thought I'd like to leave the endless games of cards behind and head into Rome for a spot of sightseeing, so Roger Blyth, Alan Majors, Arwel Rees and I jumped into a cab and off we went. We had an enjoyable evening seeing the Trevi Fountain, the Spanish Steps and taking in a few bars along the way. The night was moseying along nicely when a car came speeding down a narrow alley and forced us to flatten ourselves up against the wall. A few derogatory shouts coupled with some choice Anglo-Saxon expressions echoed out into the night at the driver, and we thought little more of it. Suddenly, the car stopped and then reversed. An altercation took place, but the sight of these big Welsh boys meant nothing serious happened. The incident was over before it began and we continued on our way to the next bar. As we sat inside, soaking up the Roman atmosphere, our peace was shattered by the screeching brakes of a police car. The next thing I knew I was staring down the barrel of a gun. Within seconds a paddy wagon arrived and we were bundled inside. Without any explanation we found ourselves locked up in the Queen of Heaven Gaol – one of Rome's most notorious penitentiary centres and home to a wretched band of bombers, murderers and rapists. I didn't realise squaring up to a motorist carried such a severe sentence. There had to be another reason to explain what was happening. There was . . . but it took another seven or eight hours until we discovered what it was.

What complicated our situation was our inability to communicate with our captors. We couldn't speak Italian and they couldn't speak English. I think Roger Blyth managed to make headway with someone who could speak French and at 3 or 4 a.m. I was sent – under police escort – to retrieve our passports. I didn't know where we were staying and I couldn't explain my ignorance to my guards, but eventually, more through luck than judgement, we found our way back to Aqua Sentosa.

Our small party was eventually released when the police realised we were victims of mistaken identity. Our Swansea blazers had put a bounty sign on our heads, and we soon discovered why. Apparently, a large party of the boys decided that they, too, would go and see the sights of Rome. Being typical Swansea boys they quaffed a few drinks, then a few more, and then the inevitable argument began. When 20 or so Italian lads turned up on Vespas, the Swansea boys decided to heal the internal rifts and concentrate their aggression on the locals. A big fight broke out and one of the Italians – who happened to be the son of a high-ranking police official – hurt his leg. Within moments the sirens started blaring and the Swansea men fled into the night. They were all eventually rounded up and brought in. Some remained incarcerated for ten days. As we left, Roger Hyndman was heard to shout out through the bars to Neil Webb, 'Give the missus a call if you get the chance.'

It was a nightmare beginning to my Swansea career, and it intensified when I saw a copy of the *Daily Mirror* on the flight home: 'Mervyn Davies Locked Up in Italy'. No one else was mentioned by name . . . just me. What the hell had I done to deserve this? I could picture heads being shaken in disapproval up at Old Deer Park and more than one ex-colleague murmuring, 'I told him so.'

As one would expect – and hope – it got better. I did earn my spurs as a Swansea man, and I would like to think my presence in the All Whites helped galvanise the team and bring more players to the attention of the national selectors. The lone international in the team when I arrived, I was soon joined by young men that Ieuan had nurtured like Roger Blyth, Geoff Wheel, David Richards and Trevor Evans – who started getting the recognition they deserved. My game had changed once more, and I was heavily involved as a ball carrier and defensive number 8. At one point, the entire Swansea back row played international rugby – Trevor and me for Wales and Mark Keyworth for England. I enjoyed being a key player and slowly my influence grew on those around me. It helped when Stan Addicott took over from Ieuan as coach, because we developed a close working relationship.

Stan couldn't help me deal with the toughest opponent I ever encountered in South Wales, however. Nor could experiences I had enjoyed in New Zealand or South Africa; the midwife who stood guard over my wife on 27 April 1975 proved absolutely insurmountable. I was keen to be present at my boy's birth but I was told that expectant fathers were a nuisance beyond compare and was sent outside, out of the way. I paced and prayed and smoked what felt like a thousand cigarettes, but my wife delivered a healthy, lovely baby boy. I have talked about changing clubs or playing certain games as being life-changing events, but becoming a father put everything else in its correct place. Rugby was a game, that's all . . . a game. It had given me a comfortable life. And it would help build a secure future for my family, but it was no longer my number-one priority. They were.

I was offered the captaincy of Swansea before the 1975–76 season, after I had already captained Wales. Whereas I had no hesitation accepting the offer to lead my country, I was a little more reticent about taking the reins at my club. Being a day-to-day captain is a thankless task and one that demands 100 per cent commitment. I was a father, I had international duties to uphold, and I wasn't entirely comfortable with the archaic committee structure favoured by Swansea. But I agreed; I felt I should share my experience with the players around me. And it was, after all, another challenge. Maintaining the gap between captain and player wasn't as difficult as it had been for Wales because I was already considered to be slightly aloof – my closest friends were probably Neil Webb (who I wanted and got as my vice-captain) and Mike Yandle, largely because we all lived near one another in Pontlliw and would travel to training and to matches together. I didn't care a jot what people thought about me . . . I was happy to play my rugby, have a jar and then leave early to go home to my family. I never felt the need – or necessity – to socialise with the Swansea players in the same way that I had at London Welsh. My life no longer revolved around the rugby club . . . I was a family man.

The biggest gripe I had about playing rugby in Wales at that time – and it is a gripe that modern players still air – was the number of games on the domestic fixture list. At London Welsh we played once a week on Saturday, and that was enough. One game kept us fresh, focused and eager for more. In Wales we had to play on Wednesday evenings and Saturday afternoons, which meant a season could contain up to 60 or more games for a leading international player. You cannot do that with rugby . . . the body cannot cope with that amount of physical punishment. I soon got a reputation as someone who 'chose' his games, and I will not refute that claim. But look at the games I chose. I never refused matches against the toughest opposition – and believe me, the prospect of playing Pontypool on a wintry Wednesday night did not always fill me with glee. The chance to face Stuart Lane of Cardiff or Hefin Jenkins of Llanelli always appealed because I was the best number 8 in Wales, and I wanted to maintain that position. The matches I tried to avoid were games against lesser clubs where I was seen as a target, a scalp to take. Some of my opponents from these clubs were not interested in playing better rugby than me, they just wanted to leave their mark all over my body. I was punched, kicked and stamped on because I was Mervyn Davies. Even then, I resolved to retire at the top. When I captained Swansea, my prime rugby commitment was to Wales and that is why I lobbied hard for fewer matches for senior players.

Initial critics of this ploy, like Geoff Wheel, were soon won round to my way of thinking when they became regular internationals. To play the best at your very best requires rest and conditioning.

They were good days though, and I was lucky to see two sides of the club experience with two vastly different teams. I might have won the ball for London Welsh, but I felt my influence on Swansea was greater because they needed a leader, a target, and a man who could make a difference. We slowly improved as a team and a good Cup run in 1976 was the culmination of three or four seasons' development. All we had to do was get past Ray Prosser's Pontypool and we would be heading for the final and a big day out for club and city in Cardiff. One big effort was required from Mervyn Davies. Would I be up to the task?

IX

Being a Lion – Part Two

The story of the 1974 Lions in South Africa has passed into rugby folklore. In my mind, images and phrases connected with the tour shimmer like mirages in the African sun: Willie John, '99', the battered Boks, high jinks on the high veldt, the free running of J.J. Williams, dumping Boland Coetzee on his backside, Dr Danie Craven's despair and our squad earning the title of 'the Invincibles'. We were nigh on invincible: played 22 matches, won 21 and drew the very last game, the fourth and final Test. Our African trek took us from the depths of political controversy to the heights of a truly great sporting achievement. We became the first team to beat the Springboks in a four-game series for 78 years. Hannes Marais – the beleaguered South African captain – rated us better than Brian Lochore's 1970 All Blacks: fine praise, indeed. But were we the best Lions? Perhaps. Was it our greatest achievement? I think not. The record books insist that it is, but ask the men who toured in '71 and '74 to compare both feats and I am sure they will say winning in New Zealand was the pinnacle of their rugby careers.

But perhaps to consign the '74 Lions to second place so quickly is to do it a grave disservice. To begin with, we had to deal with something the '71 squad never encountered: expectation. Winning in New Zealand had broken the mould for British rugby and we left these shores with a victorious legacy to uphold. There is something wildly romantic about going to play rugby in South Africa . . . and Willie John's Lions followed a romantic – and sometime anarchic – African dream. I don't think I have ever enjoyed a tour as much: the weather was good, the camaraderie superb, the itinerary varied and the rugby surprisingly easy. Being a British rugby player travelling the length and breadth of South Africa in the 1970s was to travel like royalty. We stayed in the best hotels, we were introduced to the wealthiest families, we were taken to the most wondrous places . . . but it was all a façade. Scratch the surface of this carefully presented image and the real South Africa was revealed as a raw, angry and downtrodden nation. And it was this sense of injustice felt on behalf of the majority black population that politicised so many people. It wasn't only the politicians and the media who stood in opposition to us going: grandmothers, schoolchildren, professional people, students, academics, factory workers and fellow sportsmen felt the same way. Whether or not the British Lions should go stimulated fierce argument and we became the big issue of the day: if we went, we supported a most heinous regime; but if we stayed, we allowed politics to interfere with sport. Each man invited to tour was asked whether they could commit body, spirit and principles to such a venture. We had to search deep within our souls and be ready to stand by our decision.

The closer the tour moved to reality, the more the political pressure intensified. I was prepared for the worst because I had been anticipating it for three years. Since my return from New Zealand in 1971, if an invite for another Lions tour came my way, nothing – or no one – could stop me. I even (willingly) sacrificed my teaching career to ensure I had a clear run at South Africa. In the early '70s I lived with John Taylor in London for a while, and, as previously mentioned, he was vehemently against the idea of going back. In his view, apartheid was a barbaric system that would be ratified by the appearance of a high-profile sporting institution like the Lions. I shared his thoughts on apartheid but was still determined to go, and I window-dressed my willingness to tour by telling him that I wanted to see what he had seen for myself. That is not entirely true; I didn't need to see apartheid to know how morally reprehensible it was. I just wanted to play against the national team from a country who regarded themselves as the best rugby men on the planet. Same old story, same old Mervyn . . . looking for the challenge.

Anyone who claims that sport and politics do not mix is sadly naive. They do. How can they not? From the day money was made from watching people chase a ball around a patch of grass, to the moment when a group of individuals were called up to play for their nation, sport and politics have been completely entwined. It was argued that the Lions supported apartheid by going to play out there but that besmirches every member of our party. There is a counter-argument: we gave the dominant Afrikaner race an almighty shock by beating them in the one place where their sporting masculinity was most precious – the rugby field. Our core support on tour did not come from a Barmy Army troop of British fans; it came from the black and coloured South Africans, shunted behind the goal posts, staring into the sun. Revisionist views might claim that we did it for them. But that is not strictly true. We did it for ourselves – but we were glad that so many people got so much from seeing their so-called superiors smashed. To the people who organised demos and marches against us, who bombarded us with abusive letters, to the Labour-controlled education authorities who refused to pay teachers like J.J. Williams a wage, rest assured . . . we damaged the self-image of the South African ruling classes as much as any sanction did. We did, however, receive criticism from a small section of the black population, and I remember a very uncomfortable afternoon spent facing pro-apartheid accusations during a question-and-answer session at a Johannesburg university. Accusations which, I must add, we all strenuously denied.

There was one instant benefit to the pre-tour political furore: a decision was made to get the Lions out of the UK as quickly as possible. There would be no pointless parading up and down the sands of Eastbourne, we were despatched from Heathrow post haste and whisked away from the ongoing controversy. It was a blessed relief to leave the lobbying behind and start concentrating on the rugby.

There were a few familiar faces and well-established names missing from the squad. Stalwarts of 1971 like John Taylor, David Duckham, Gerald Davies, Mike Gibson, Bob Hiller, Sean Lynch,

John Pullin, Delme Thomas, Mike Roberts, Ray Hopkins, Peter Dixon, Derek Quinnell and, of course, Barry John were absent. Mike Gibson would eventually fly out and join us, but Gerald – like John Taylor a tourist from '68 – refused our pleas to take part. His conscience would not allow him to return. He may not regret his decision, but the sight of Gerald Davies skimming across the surface of those hard South African pitches would have been something to behold. The absence of Gerald and the other Wales boys meant there wouldn't be such a pronounced Welsh feel to this particular squad. Wales had struggled in the Five Nations over the preceding seasons and therefore only contributed nine Lions – as did England – with eight and six chosen from Ireland and Scotland respectively. And as Wales had stuttered, so had I: it was largely felt by the press and pundits that I arrived at Jan Smuts airport as second-choice number 8. Andy Ripley from Rosslyn Park had made a terrific impact upon the international scene, but I knew, once the tour began, I would go full tilt at that Test shirt.

On paper, the '74 squad lacked the creativity, flair and zip of the '71 party, but one area where they bettered their earlier counterparts was the quality of the forwards. The '74 vintage was the toughest bunch of boys I ever packed down with. They included uncompromising characters like Gordon Brown, Mike Burton, Sandy Carmichael, Fran Cotton, Tommy David, Ken Kennedy, Stuart McKinney, Ian McLauchlan, Tony Neary, Chris Ralston, Andy Ripley, Fergus Slattery, Roger Uttley, Bobby Windsor and the captain, Willie John McBride. Just as John Dawes left his mark all over the '71 Lions, Willie John did likewise with his team. It was on African soil that the big man from Ballymena cemented his status as, arguably, the greatest Lion of them all.

Willie John McBride remains a mightily impressive character. He was a ferocious opponent, a steadfast colleague and an inspired leader. He was, and I'm delighted to say still is, a true and trusted friend. In a career that often saw Irish rugby veer from delirium to despair, Willie John was a rock through good times and bad. But it is the Lions that define him and his contribution to the game. He toured five times in total and managed the New Zealand party in 1983. Yet it was in South Africa that Willie John enjoyed his finest hour.

Something changed in Willie John after the First Test victory in New Zealand in 1971. For a man on his fourth Lions tour, Dunedin was incredibly his first taste of victory in that fabled red shirt. By all accounts, on previous tours Willie John rather enjoyed the social side of touring and was known to be a little bit rowdy. But winning in New Zealand opened his eyes: he saw what feats the Lions were capable of and it inspired his play. He discovered that Lions rugby did not have to be a hopeless cause and with the wise words and encouragement of Carwyn James ringing in his ears, he was re-energised as a player. Three years later, his experience, ability and aura made him the obvious choice for the captaincy, although there was an element of 'poacher turned gamekeeper' about his appointment. I thought long and hard about Willie John when I was given the Wales captaincy a year later: making the transition from being one of the boys to leader isn't easy, but I knew if I used Willie John as my role model and, like him, led by example, I would soon be on the right road.

As in 1971, the choice of captain, coach and manager was crucial to the Lions' chances of enjoying a successful tour. And as in '71, the Home Unions' committee was spot on because Willie John, Syd Millar and Alun Thomas all shared one thing in common: they had been to, and been soundly beaten in, South Africa. It was no place for pushovers and a tough mental attitude coupled with unflinching physical bravery was required of one and all. Our squad would need steel and stamina and our leaders had to be men of the very highest calibre.

I knew Willie John well from past encounters; in fact, I knew him better than Alun Thomas – which is strange because Alun was a Swansea man and even worked for the Blyths, like me. It is a testament to the generosity of the Blyths that they allowed two men from their workforce to decamp to South Africa for a few months of rugby. Alun was a no-nonsense manager who had played in the centre for Wales with distinction in the '50s and toured with the Lions in 1955. He knew South Africa and South Africans . . . he also appreciated how easily our attention could wander and kept a watchful eye over his charges throughout the entire campaign. Syd Millar, the coach, hailed from the same Ballymena club as his captain, and it was their symbiotic thinking and instinctive pairing that formed the core of our squad. We joked that as soon as the appointments were made, Syd and Willie John locked themselves away in a shed with a bottle of the finest Irish to plot our opponents' demise. And when Millar – a former prop constructed from pure Irish granite – came out with the line 'we have a plan' early in the tour, we knew we were right.

Plan or no plan, the first factor we had to deal with upon arrival was the altitude. I had heard plenty of scare stories about playing rugby at altitude so I was a little bit nervous of what to expect. My previous experience of high-altitude rugby was up at Eugene Cross Park, Ebbw Vale . . . which isn't quite in the same league as Potchefstroom, venue of our first training session and some 5,000 feet above sea level. Syd told us to do a couple of circuits followed by a few sprints and I thought, 'Great, no problem.' I was fine for ten minutes and then I felt like my body was cracking in half and I dropped, doubled up, desperately trying to suck air into my burning lungs. Gareth Edwards assured me, with a huge grin on his face, that it would get easier. It did, but it seemed to take a murderously long time to train my wretched lungs to survive in such a thin atmosphere. Andy Ripley appeared to have no problem adjusting to the thinner air, and his sprightliness only soured my mood. By the time I played in my first tour game against South-West Africa at Windhoek, I was in better shape – but the last 20 minutes were probably the most gruelling physical test I ever put my body through as a player.

In the first few weeks of the tour, Andy Ripley was the man leading the charge for the number 8 shirt. I have nothing but the utmost respect for Andy: he proved his worth as a fantastic athlete and an all-round nice guy. Without doubt, he presented me with the stiffest and most prolonged one-on-one playing challenge I ever encountered. He bested me in a meeting at Twickenham when he powered past Dai Morris for a try (he was your man, Dai) and possessed certain elements in his game that I could not match. His loping stride, speed and delight at running with the ball in his hands made him the antithesis to the kind of player I was. In squad terms, we complemented one another because we offered the team different options. The 1973–74 season saw the worst rugby I ever played for my country and the knives were out for my reputation. Andy was in the ascendancy and even Carwyn James said I would have trouble keeping him out of the Test team. The fast South African pitches were perfect for his mobile game but having Andy in my sights was just the boost I required. Perhaps I had rested on my laurels for too long, safe in the knowledge that I, Mervyn Davies, could see off all challengers. Traditional number 8s, yes, no problem . . . but Andy was different; he was an athlete first and foremost, and then a rugby player. He admitted as much when he told me that he came to rugby late when he was an 18 year old and actually still preferred track and field. To him, rugby was just running but with a ball in his hands. If he had been schooled in the game from an earlier age and had the tactical game that I had, he would have been an unstoppable force in the world game. I must credit him for improving my play at a crucial time in my career; he certainly made me push myself to the limit of my ability.

Andy was also one of the true individuals in our party. He was quiet – a little enigmatic – but interesting company. It is easy to settle into a mob mentality when on tour, but Andy prized his individuality. Whilst the boys would laze around in the sun on the beach, Andy would be off surfboarding, oblivious to the shark warnings. On another occasion, I remember watching bemused as Andy and John Moloney ignored the searing temperatures and raced one another around a 400m athletics track. Extra running? I'd never heard of a forward who actually derived pleasure from extra running! Andy also deliberately set out to wind up Alun Thomas, who could be a little officious to say the least. He adopted two stray kittens and put an advert in the local paper to find new owners for them. I don't think Alun was at all pleased when the hotel was suddenly besieged with people, keen to adopt these little 'lion cubs'. But the most amusing of Andy's many antics was when he committed the cardinal Lions sin: he broke the dress code. Each member of the Lions party was instructed what to wear and when to wear it. We were issued with our clothing before departure and were told it was our responsibility to ensure that we adhered to the tour dress code. It served two purposes: one, it made us look good and two, it presented a united, cohesive front. The dress code was rigorously enforced, especially when we attended one of the countless receptions laid on for us. Functions and drinks receptions are often the bane of a player's life when you have to answer the same questions time after time after time. Many we were subject to were tedious beyond belief, but we had to smile and chat and engage with our hosts. Andy, enjoying his outsider status, probably felt the boredom factor more than most and when Alun instructed him to wear, 'number-two blazer, grey slacks and tie' that is exactly what he turned up in: no shoes, no socks and no shirt. Alun turned a spectacular shade of red and immediately expelled him from the function, and Andy left with a big smile on his face.

As a number 8, Andy Ripley was arguably a more dynamic back-row forward than I was, and he excelled in the early round of easy provincial games; but I knew my forte was the physical stuff. The Test matches would be harder, rougher affairs where a player had to put tackles in and be prepared to dive in when the studs were flying. That was my game, that is what I brought to the table. The Lions would win or lose up front and Syd's great plan was to obliterate the South African pack at the set piece. In the early provincial games we destroyed scrum after scrum after scrum and we could tell that our forward power was having a huge psychological effect upon our hosts. This spreading panic gave Syd the incentive to push on in training and seek total forward domination. The training sessions became harder and harder, and Millar was transformed into a single-minded taskmaster. I don't think the backs saw a coach during their time out there because all the attention was focused on scrummaging. The Springboks prided themselves on the power of their forwards and we knew, irrespective of what was happening in the provincial matches, that was where they would try and damage us. But South Africa had been in isolation for too long. They held onto the old story that British rugby wasn't renowned for producing packs of the same fearsome calibre as the giants of the southern hemisphere. They were wrong. Times had changed. Underestimating what British rugby had become would cost them dear.

I recently read a piece of research that stated a number 8

contributes very little, in terms of power, to the scrum. Apparently, all the grunt comes from the front row and the locks with the flankers chipping in slightly. The number 8 might as well be elsewhere for all the effect his shoving has on the men in front of him. I wish I'd known this 30 years ago because it might have excused me from the countless hours I spent bending my back and heaving behind some second row's vast backside. Syd would have undoubtedly dismissed it as tosh. I can still hear his Irish brogue saying, 'Let's have 20 scrums . . . now let's have 20 more.' And just when we had pushed until our sinews had popped and our muscles melted, Syd would snarl, 'And now 20 more for luck.' They were gruelling, punishing training sessions that still make me wince to think of.

The provincial games had gone like a dream and we'd breezed past Western Transvaal, South West Africa, Boland, Eastern Province, South Western Districts, Western Province and a Federation XV, accumulating 294 points against a mere 63. The Lions were going into overdrive and the startling 97–0 win over South Western was the biggest victory by any touring side ever in South Africa. In that match alone J.J. crossed six times and Alan Old slotted a record-breaking 37 points. But that points record was scant consolation for Alan – or E.N.T. as he was known because of the size of both his nose and his ears and his incessant chatter. Alan sustained a very bad knee injury in Cape Town and was forced out of the tour. If he had stayed fit, I think the affable Yorkshireman might have pushed Phil Bennett close for the Test stand-off place.

The match against Eastern Province introduced the Lions to another favoured tactic of our hosts: violent play. Many of our opponents appeared to be little more than institutionalised bullies, and if a match didn't go their way then they would resort to foul play like kicking, stamping and kidney-punching. Gareth – who was acting captain in that particular match – asked the referee to intervene after the attacks got too much, but the official seemed reluctant to get involved. So the Lions, not for the last time on tour, had to protect themselves. Much has been made of the physicality of the Lions squad, of our willingness to use our fists, but it was purely for self-preservation. We never instigated the fighting, but we were adamant that we would stop any nonsense quickly and brutally. This was where the infamous '99' call was first used. Willie John decreed that this would be the call where each and every Lion would turn and hit his nearest opponent. Willie John wagered that the referee could not send all 15 men off. I did not feel comfortable with this approach, but I have to grudgingly accept that it did serve a useful purpose. Many people still believe that we punched our way to victory but that is untrue; '99' was used sparingly, but the threat of its implementation certainly put the Springboks on the back foot.

It was a nervous bunch of men corralled into our Cape Town hotel to hear Syd Millar announce the team for the First Test. Everything on tour – collectively and individually – is geared to this moment. Being in the starting XV is all that occupies a player's mind from the instant they are selected and once that First Test XV is picked, the tour changes. Players are then either fighting to keep their place or fighting to replace another man. No squad actually talks about a hierarchy forming but one does as soon as those chosen names are aired. Some players feel more aggrieved than others by their omission and Tony Neary – that excellent England flanker – voiced his displeasure later in the tour. His place in the back row had been taken by Roger Uttley, who was a lock by trade, but on Lions tours players can be drafted in to cover unfamiliar positions because a specific skill or attribute can be utilised. In Roger's case, it was his physical presence, and although Tony was unlucky not to get the nod, the selection decision would eventually prove sound.

Syd went through the names: Williams, Steele, McGeechan, Milliken, Williams, Bennett, Edwards, McLauchlan, Windsor, Cotton, Brown, McBride, Slattery, Uttley and Davies. I barely heard who else had been selected because I was concentrating on the 15th and last name on Syd's starting roll call. I was in. I had done it. I had claimed the jersey for my fifth successive Lions start . . . but now I had to earn it. As I breathed out a big sigh of relief I noticed that the first person to congratulate me was Andy Ripley. I had weathered his challenge, and now it was time to step up and face another.

Despite our barnstorming run through the provinces we knew that a Test match would require something extra. For once, as 8 June dawned in Cape Town, the weather was on our side. Continuous rain had fallen in the days prior to the game, coupled with two games before the main event, and the Newlands pitch had been reduced to a quagmire. It would indeed be a forwards' confrontation.

I don't think I can recall a better-prepared team before a Test match. The men who had already toured in '71 knew how vital it was to win the first rubber. Little was said, but it was understood that little had to be said. Willie John's pre-match speech was a masterclass in understatement: he merely puffed away on his pipe and after minutes of heavy silence just said, 'We're ready.' Syd was equally succinct, saying, 'We shall go forward. We shall go on. We shall overcome . . .' and then, echoing what Carwyn had said three years earlier, 'We shall take no prisoners.'

The forwards played like heroes that day, each one setting down a marker for his teammates and his opposite number. Bobby Windsor had a storming match. He was rapidly becoming one of the stars of the tour with his caustic one-liners and eye for a scam. Ken Kennedy was the more experienced hooker, but Bobby played himself into the Test reckoning and set about dismantling his opposing number. Every scrum was its own mini-war and I could hear Bobby snarling and snapping away, getting right in the faces of the Bok front row. The pressure our pack exerted on theirs had Bobby almost hooking the ball with his head. He had the right temperament for big-match rugby and, I believe, wrote the patent that day for what good, destructive hooking required.

Bobby might have been a warrior on the pitch, but he wasn't so brave in the air. Touring means flying and one just has to learn to get on with it. Most flights pass without incident but when a bird was sucked into one of our plane engines as we left the coast and headed towards Johannesburg and we had to turn and land, Bob caved in. I was oblivious to all the drama, but Mike Gibson was heard to cry that he wished he'd posted his letters home as we skimmed some 50 feet above the ocean waves. It was too much for Bob: he, Chris Ralston and Stew McKinney decided a five-and-a-half hour drive through the African night was better than another second aloft. Not that Bobby had a peaceful journey; they stopped at a roadside stall to buy melons and he was almost bitten by a snake. Flying and snakes . . . Bobby's two biggest phobias: I bet he thought the whole continent was out to get him.

The moment I set my own marker down came early in the first half when flanker Boland Coetzee took an inside pass from his wing. It was one of those unearthly occasions when time stood still and I unleashed the perfect hit. It was the tackle of my career and it gave me terrific pleasure. You can keep your 50-yard runs and wizard little sidesteps: for me, catching Coetzee right up under his ribs, digging in hard and sending him wheezing ten yards backwards onto his arse was bliss. As soon as he hit the dirt the boys rucked over him and won turnover ball. All around us we heard the South African crowd let out a collective, almost wistful, groan. If the Boks thought they were going to bully the British off the park through their forwards, then they were in trouble. We won the game 12–3 thanks to the kicking of Phil Bennett and Gareth Edwards. I almost went over for a score, but, alas, no tries came that day. It didn't matter. We won the match and we won it without the ball going through the hands of our backs. The Lions were one up in the series with plenty more to come.

South Africa was stunned. Their fans couldn't believe what had happened to their heroes in green. We went on unchecked and marched past Southern Universities, Transvaal and Rhodesia before gearing up for the Second Test in Pretoria. The team we faced there was vastly different, with South Africa making an unprecedented eight changes. None of us could grasp why they had made eight changes: it smacked of desperation, a team in freefall. I would have given those players beaten in the First Test a chance to redeem themselves, but the politics and the expectations of South African rugby were beyond my understanding. Not all was well behind the scenes. There were some dissenters in the South African rugby establishment who stood up against the regime – Tommy Bedford, for one. Towards the end of the tour we played and beat Natal, dressed our wounds and sat down for one of the most charged post-match dinners I had ever experienced. Tommy – a hugely respected figure and a man many believed should have been captaining the Springboks – made an astonishing attack against the South African selectors for ignoring Natal players and then finished his rant by raising two fingers to them. I admit that I sometimes felt a bit frustrated when I was captain of Wales and Swansea – especially with selectors – but I never felt that bad.

The Second Test was a far more satisfying win than the First. South Africa could make all the changes in the world but nothing could stop us from beating them. We won handsomely 28–9 and scored cracking tries through J.J., Dick Milliken and Gordon Brown. The solid conditions underfoot inspired both backs and forwards to blaze into the Boks. Phil Bennett played the game of his life and scored a magical solo try that did much to lay the spectre of Barry John to rest. I was pleased for our backs that day, as their exploits went some way to silencing criticism that the Lions were merely a ten-man team. But I took greater satisfaction from the way Roger, Fergus and I dovetailed as a back-row unit. Uttley was a tremendous competitor, hard too, and Fergus gleefully snaffled anything in green. I had always admired the way he played against us for Ireland but to hear his banshee howl directed at someone else was a pleasant change. 'They haven't got an answer to us, Swerve . . .' he said as we hit the changing-room, and he was right: the series was ours.

With two Tests up and two left to play, the Lions were totally in control of the series. We were allowed a little R&R to burn off some steam and headed to Kruger Park. It felt bizarre to be on a game reserve in a park that was bigger than Wales, but the lads appreciated the time they spent getting back to nature . . . until the beer ran out. Even Alun Thomas underestimated the level of our collective thirst, and we ran dry with 48 hours to spare. But the park itself was incredible and we had a terrific time going off on dusk or dawn expeditions to see lions, wildebeest, giraffes and springboks. At night-time, however, our party of human lions were a little more timid than their cat-like namesakes. An unexpected growl or the sudden sound of snuffling just outside a mud hut caused a few of the boys sleepless nights wrapped in each other's arms. Mike Burton and Stew McKinney were in their element and scared half the lads witless with their after-dark antics replicating the stalking habits of some of the local beasts.

Many of the best memories I have from my time in South Africa are built around the stunning beauty of the interior or the coastline. There was one time when we were staying in Port Elizabeth on the southern tip of the continent and a few of us – Roger Uttley, Mike Burton and Gareth Edwards included – went deep-sea fishing. I thought the whole excursion was marvellous, pitching up and down in the huge ocean swells, but I don't think Gareth and Roger felt likewise for they spent the whole time hurling the contents of their dietary intake into the Indian Ocean. After an hour or so, one of them whimpered he would kill himself unless he was immediately taken back to port. Mike and I hated waste so we strapped ourselves to a mast and started consuming the huge amounts of food and drink we had brought with us to sustain us on our voyage. We didn't catch any fish but remained happily onboard as our shipmates crawled back onto dry land.

We entered the Third Test in Port Elizabeth brimful of confidence. By then we knew the South Africans could only draw the series. Again, they made wholesale changes – 11 for this match alone. Such drastic tinkering cost them the match before we kicked off. I was amazed they dropped their giant lock, John Williams, who was, in our view, a world-class performer. But fear and anxiety are a selector's greatest enemy. They picked a team to hurt the Lions and, by all accounts, the South African minister for sport gave them a rollicking in the changing-room beforehand and told them that they were expected to win at all costs. Their decision to be ultra-physical was reflected in the bizarre decision to pick Gerrie Sonnekus – a number 8 – at scrum-half.

South Africa had nothing to give us that day except their anger and their bitterness. We could hear them squabbling about lineout calls and basic scrummage technique. Marais, who was a decent chap and was probably too nice to lead a team in such disarray, had obviously lost his men. It reached the point of farce and would have been laughable if it had not been for the foul play. This was perhaps the most controversial match I ever played in, because it was the game when Willie John called '99' twice. The first call resulted from a reckless piece of rucking where Moaner van Heerden appeared to be the main culprit, and the second call came in the second half where a few more boots went flying in. There were two important consequences from each incident: first, the Boks retreated and second, we scored. Bizarrely, the South African officials and crowd seemed more aghast at losing face than they did at losing points. I was astounded to hear that Danie Craven publicly announced that he was ashamed of his players later that night. I don't believe I hit anyone, but I made my presence felt.

We emerged victorious 26–9 from the Third Test and secured the series. J.J. scored another two tries to set a series record and established himself as the finest finisher in the game. Gordon Brown also got his second try in as many Tests but put himself out of the final match by injuring his hand. The other points were scored by Phil Bennett and debutant Andy Irvine – who came in for Billy Steele on the wing and had a brilliant game. It was mission accomplished. Willie John was carried shoulder high from the field and the global domination of British rugby was complete.

It was, perhaps, inevitable that we drew the Fourth Test in Johannesburg. The job had been done, the squad was exhausted and we all longed to go home. South Africa, in all fairness, raised their game and we could see the delight they felt when they carried Marais from the field. But how strange to see a team celebrate avoiding a whitewash . . . how far the mighty had fallen. The Lions' appetite had been dulled by an ugly match in Natal when we were pelted by all kinds of objects from the crowd. The '99' was called again and this time the crowd appeared to welcome it. J.P.R. Williams was singled out for much abuse after he stood toe-to-toe with Tommy Bedford. J.P.R. enjoyed a punch-up and would never win a popularity contest in Natal, but he decided to stay on there and work as a doctor. Perhaps he appreciated the weird physical code of honour that seemed indicative of South African rugby.

It was a tough tour, but despite all the punching and kicking that went on, I emerged injury free. I certainly never shirked my physical responsibilities, but I did appear to be protected. The only real injury I received (apart from a few bruises) had nothing to do with rugby. We were on one of our excursions and went up river to see a crocodile farm. Our guides took great delight pointing out which particular crocs were man-eaters. One huge blighter gave us a shock when we watched him devour a 20-gallon drum of flesh in about five seconds flat. Walking on through the reserve, well away from the monsters with the gnashing teeth, I spotted a little baby croc walking along the path. No doubt inspired by the antics of Messrs. Burton and McKinney, I picked him up and was going to throw him at Fergus. Next thing I knew, this little bugger turned around and firmly attached himself to my finger. It was my only real injury of the tour . . . unbelievable, a Lion bitten by a crocodile.

We left Africa undefeated, with 21 wins out of 22 matches under our belts. We had seen both the ugly and lovely sides of this strange, fascinating land. We had also seen the emergence of black rugby when we played the Leopards, and we knew, back then, that if they could unite on the field and bring the players and supporters together, then they would be a force to be reckoned with once more. I still think we are waiting to see that genuine coming-together today.

When we landed back in London, we were treated like conquering heroes. Politicians and public figures who had lined up to condemn us now wanted to be photographed with us, but we took it all in our stride. I went back home to Pontlliw and was treated to a marvellous homecoming. It was all a bit bemusing and it took me quite a while to realise that I was part of a small group of men who had wrestled rugby supremacy back from the southern hemisphere.

As I said at the start of this chapter, in the imagination of modern-day rugby fans, the 1974 Lions have usurped the feats of '71. At the time of writing there is a 30-year reunion planned; another opportunity for 'the Invincibles' to re-live the on- and off-field exploits we all shared. Most will make it but the party will be duller without the presence of the great Gordon Brown who sadly died a few years ago. I'll look at Fran and Bobby, at Fergus and Roger and Ian, and we'll pay quiet homage to what we achieved as forwards and friends. Willie John, captain and gentleman, a man of few words but so wisely eloquent with the ones he chooses, said it best: 'There's a brotherhood in rugby football . . . and there's a bond. The bond of 1974 will never be broken until we die . . . and we might even meet up there.'

I'll wager Gordon is waiting for us . . . with a round of drinks and a funny tale to tell.

X

1976 and All That

In the spring of 2004, an economic think-tank known as the New Economics Foundation decreed that 1976 was the 'best' British year in recent memory. I suppose they looked at it from a socio-economic viewpoint and studied such factors as unemployment levels, interest rates and average household income. They probably assigned a mathematical formula to quantify their results. Their findings provoked much debate in the press and feature articles took the readers on a nostalgic trip back to the past. Ask the British public for their memories of that year and they are likely to mention the summer drought . . . a summer to which all subsequent heatwaves have been compared. Those with an interest in popular culture might cite disco or the rise of punk rock. The big sporting memories might well centre on the first Wimbledon crown for Bjorn Borg, James Hunt winning the Formula One World Championship, David Wilkie's triumph in the Olympic swimming pool or Southampton pulling off one of the great FA Cup shocks by beating Manchester United in the final. However, my memories of 1976 are conflicting ones. I captained my country to a Grand Slam, becoming only the fourth Welshman (after W.J. Trew, John Gwilliam and John Dawes) to do so. I was happily married and the proud father of a bright, lively little boy – and I had been asked to captain the British Lions on a return journey to New Zealand in 1977. So for all these reasons life was good – but 1976 was also the year when I almost died, which is why my memories of it are mixed, to say the least. But, let us look back on the good times of 1976 first.

In the days before the world of international rugby was united in its pursuit of the Webb Ellis trophy, countries measured themselves against opposition from their own hemisphere, with perhaps an additional fixture against the All Blacks every second year or so. To achieve glory in the Five Nations was to reach the very pinnacle of European rugby. To be English, Irish, Scottish or Welsh and to win the Triple Crown was a monumental achievement, but to go one better and beat the French – that was the ultimate challenge. A challenge, in my eyes, that was only bettered by a Lions success in New Zealand. On paper, Wales had three great teams of the 1970s and they came together in '71, '76 and '78. These teams secured the Grand Slam. We could have – should have – won more. But we didn't . . . Grand Slams are damn hard things to win. Therefore, on paper – and by achievement – these three teams must rank above all others.

The team we assembled for the 1976 campaign came of age that previous January day in Paris. Had it not been for my insistence that Phil Bennett attempt a penalty against Scotland, we might well have gone into the '76 tournament as defending champions, looking for an unprecedented back-to-back win. Our reaction to that missed opportunity was exemplified by the way we put Ireland to the sword in 1975. Phil enjoyed a majestic day when he passed, ran and kicked like a dream. We raced away to 32 points, with only Willie Duggan spoiling the party by intercepting Gareth Edwards' poorly conceived reverse pass to run in a score that meant little in terms of the outcome but caused me to tear a strip off the great scrum-half. My anger, however, was tame compared to that of J.P.R., who saw Gareth's part in Duggan's try as something approaching betrayal.

The 1975–76 season kicked off with a September tour to Japan, which helped solidify our game patterns and the plans we were striving to adopt. In November, we played a relatively easy match against Australia at the Arms Park; it must be remembered that Australia was not the force in the '70s that it is today. The only glitch came with the withdrawal of Phil Bennett on the eve of the match, which did unsettle our rhythm. But despite that we enjoyed a comfortable victory (28–3). However, John Dawes – ever the master tactician, ever the perfectionist – was unhappy; he would not allow us to rest on our laurels and in his captain he had a willing on-field enforcer.

I always felt my spirits soar over the festive period. I like Christmas and New Year as much as anyone, but my thoughts always stretched beyond the holiday season and into the murk of January. Many people experience a dip in their spirits at this time of year. The cold and wet weather, coupled with days of gloom and darkness, can have a miserable effect. But a rugby player suddenly comes alive at the prospect of what is to come: the Five Nations . . . the supreme test of his ability. I did miss activities I would have loved to try, like skiing, because the prospect of injury and of absence was too much to bear, but even the most unwilling of trainers (such as I), felt added purpose during those punishing runs.

As a player I had never felt in such good nick. I felt totally at ease in my role as number 8: ball carrier, ball winner, tackler and leader. I believed there was no better number 8 on the planet at that time and I backed my ability 100 per cent. Arrogance? Yes. However, what are we unless we strive to be the best? It is said that form is temporary but class is permanent; I was regarded by my peers, and those watching from afar, as a 'class act', and my playing record shows that indeed I was. Yet it is how a player reacts when he reaches the top that determines how good he is. Getting there is relatively easy: having someone in your sights, like a climber working their way to the summit of a mountain, provides the incentive to succeed. And knowing there are others competing with you adds extra reason to push harder. But staying there, striving to improve your game whilst fending off those who would push you off . . . that is the mark of a great player. I have seen those who did it and who have done it – and for longer and better than me – but I have also seen some who got there, eased off and never became the player they had the potential to be.

As captain, one area that did trouble me was the loss of my stand-off, Phil Bennett, for the England match. Phil had been plagued by injury, but the problem was compounded when he pulled out of the trial match to play for Llanelli, and this opened up a whole can of bad feeling. Whether it was Phil himself, or the club, behind this decision mattered little, but it was the wrong one. Club rugby was there to support the international team. Having a strong national side has a trickledown effect and strengthens the domestic game. It was as true then as it is now that clubs often feel short-changed by the demands a national team puts upon their playing staff, and it can be difficult for them to operate without their best players and their biggest crowd-pullers. But a beaten national side helps no one. Phil was one of the best players in the game and Wales needed him. I think he was ill-advised when, being the good – and loyal – man that he is, he decided to abide by his club's wishes. His position as captain of the Possibles did not give him the incentive to trial; John Bevan (who had deputised against Australia and played well) entered the trial as first-choice number 10. The attitude of the WRU was tough and uncompromising: when Phil pulled out of the trial, they dropped him from the squad. Irrespective of how good a player John Bevan was, or how bright a talent young David Richards of Swansea might have been, Phil Bennett was a proven player for Wales and the Lions – a matchwinner in fact – and merited a place at least on the bench. The whole sorry affair provoked me from irritation into annoyance. It was another unwanted intrusion into our preparation. Instead of spending time talking about the physical and mental condition of the squad, and about what objectives we had for the season, all people wanted to talk or write about was 'the Phil Bennett affair'. Publicly, I toed the line about not concerning myself with selection matters, but privately I was seething. The matter resolved itself in the most unexpected way when both John and David were injured, allowing Phil to take the field at Twickenham. I suppose he could have told the selectors what to do with the shirt, but he didn't (nor do I believe a man like Phil ever would). He went on to have one of his best seasons for Wales.

This relatively trivial matter demonstrates how big a passion rugby is in such a small country. It became the topic of schoolyards, pubs, factories and bus queues. To some it became a matter of east versus west, of Llanelli (seen by many from the west as being at the vanguard of Welsh rugby) once again being shown disrespect. For others it hinted at a changing attitude in sport where the player was growing too self-important. For many, the WRU were perceived as being archaic: an entrenched organisation with little ability to see beyond its own committee room. For me, almost 30 years later, I see it as the Welsh being Welsh. All of the above views are true, but more than anything else the 'Bennett Affair' showed what an unhealthy obsession the Welsh public had – and still have – with the number 10 jersey. No other matter polarises fans like that shirt. The wearer must take on a mantle of Arthurian greatness . . . greatness perceived to have been passed down through the ages. Yet, every outside-half I have seen playing for Wales has, at some point, received the most vociferous criticism. Even men like Barry John, Dai Watkins and Phil Bennett have had scorn poured on their abilities. The debate goes on about who is worthiest, who is best to be the saviour, but it is all utter nonsense: the jersey has been romanticised into farce. Give any number 10 a halo, a set of wings and a pair of boots with booster rockets on and he still will not win a match unless he can get his hands on the ball. I may be a bit of a gnarled old forward, but in my opinion you can't win rugby matches unless the boys up front do their bit, and I wish my fellow Welshmen would put the number 10 debate into its proper context. A great number 10 (and for such a small country we have produced an unreasonable number of truly great ones) is the golden sword in the armoury, the conductor of the symphony . . . but for him to shine and be effective he must rely on the industry and artistry of others.

A recent example of this Welsh obsession with the outside-half was the return of Jonathan Davies to the union code in 1996. Unquestionably, Jonathan is up there as one of the great Welsh players. His speed, instinct, nerve and wonderful touch had him delighting fans wherever he played. When he switched codes, he got even better and proved his playing ability by excelling in two of the toughest arenas in sport: the north of England and Australia. The league game saw the best of him as a player, and the try he scored at Wembley for Great Britain against Australia was as revered in Wales as any he had scored in union. But when he came back to Wales, the romantic mist once more descended over Welsh eyes. Jonathan had his personal reasons for his return and Cardiff enjoyed a coup (and a healthy upturn in gate receipts) by signing him. They threw him back into a game he hadn't played for seven years after a handful of training sessions, in a match that was re-scheduled to achieve a higher television audience, demonstrating the dream-state that can engulf some aspects of Welsh rugby. A bandwagon started rolling and, within a few months, he had the Welsh number 10 shirt on his back again and Wales, once more, sought a saviour. The most ironic part of this story must have been the reaction of Jonathan himself, seeing the unrealistic hope in people's eyes. The game had changed, so had the player and the man . . . but the expectations on that shirt remained just as heavy.

Prior to the England game and away from the Bennett non-selection fiasco, there was one piece of selection news that did bring a smile to my face – Swansea were placed in the privileged position of fielding three back-row players in that game. Trevor Evans joined me in red whilst Mark Keyworth – or 'Cabbage' as we affectionately knew him down at St Helens – was called up for England. When we discovered Mark's promotion to international honours, Trevor and I set about undermining his confidence – and it worked. Mark did not have the best of matches, but that was perhaps more down to the England selectors playing him out of position at number 6 than anything Trevor or I did. I was subsequently pleased to see him get another cap . . . as long as it wasn't against us.

It was an easy win and I revelled in the part I played. In comparison with the 1971 team, I had a far more prominent role, which befitted my position as captain and one of the senior players. Terry Cobner, Tommy David and Trevor Evans were different kinds of flankers to John Taylor and Dai Morris. Dai and John were fliers whereas Trevor, Tommy and Terry played a more defensive and physical game. Ever flexible, I changed my game to reflect theirs and therefore enjoyed more of an attacking role. I was known as 'Merv the Swerve', and if I ever had swerved, it would have been at this juncture in my career. But I didn't – not then, not ever. I did enjoy going forward, though: leading the line, so to speak. England could have been dispatched easily, but there were discrepancies in our performance. As so often, a 'great Welsh team' pulled off a victory without playing well. We beat England largely due to the powerhouse performance of J.P.R. On too many occasions Wales relied on one man excelling . . . and against England, it was usually J.P.R. John Dawes hit the nail on the head when he stated publicly that we 'had to buck up'. We did.

The way the games had been arranged that season meant that, in theory, it was the hardest Triple Crown to win (England and Ireland away) but the easiest Grand Slam (France at home). Against Scotland, we got back on track winning 28–6 with Phil Bennett overtaking Barry John to become Wales' leading points scorer. His performance was a nice rebuttal to those who had tried to de-select him, and I wryly thought to myself that he wasn't playing too badly for the third best outside-half in Wales.

We went to Dublin with more belief than I can remember. I had never won at Lansdowne Road, but this time we flew with a sense of confidence oozing through the team. Ireland may have shipped a few of their greats in the previous year but they still had some cracking players on show. I passed a personal milestone by becoming the most capped Welsh forward of all time, my tally of 37 beating my old friend, Denzil Williams. They were consecutive caps too; my country had never dropped me since my debut in February 1969.

Of all the matches we played that season the Ireland game was probably 'the one' in terms of an attacking performance. We had, in my opinion, been unfairly criticised for playing '35-yard rugby' – boring rugby where the ball was kept largely with the forwards – though with someone like John Dawes coaching a side, I don't see how that was possible.

We scored 102 points in that campaign during days when scores in the 30s would be the equivalent of 50-plus today. I knew I had a set of wonderful backs behind me, but before they were allowed to cut free, I wanted enough points on the board to secure the win. John's mantra was 'win with style' whereas mine was 'win at all costs'. As a captain I believed the game could be divided into three phases: confrontation, consolidation and domination. The first 10 to 20 minutes were crucial. If I won the toss, I elected to kick long so we would get the ball in our hands either at the lineout or from a misdirected punt. During those first ten minutes we would exert pressure and then, once the opposition had felt our presence, we'd try out a few moves through the backs and hopefully, by the start of the second half, we were ready to dominate. It might have been more conservative than the John Dawes way but it proved a successful compromise. Too often Wales had played fast and loose, spreading the ball too readily, and had come unstuck. In 1976, we held onto our creative principles but added a far more ruthless streak. I still believe it is the right way to play winning rugby.

J.J. Williams said of the game: 'For once we clicked, we played some outstanding rugby.' He was right. For those who continued to question our ability I must refer them to Mike Gibson, speaking just after his side went down 34–9, who said we were 'as good as the 1971 Lions'. High praise indeed, from a man whose opinion deserves respect.

And so it came down to the last match, fittingly against the French. Every small boy who dreams of playing rugby for his country dreams of occasions like a Grand Slam decider. Speaking as a man who came into rugby with little expectation of success, to find myself leading out the national team in such a game was almost unbelievable. But reflecting on the enormity of the occasion was for another time; our immediate concern was that we knew the French would give us the biggest test we had faced in over two seasons. I also knew the battle would be won or lost up front, with the key area being Rives, Bastiat and Skrela versus Trevor Evans, Tommy David and myself at the back. For once the anthem did not intrude on my concentration; that day my mind was wholly on the job in hand. I had enjoyed a decent run against the French, winning four, drawing two and losing one but you never knew how it would go. And you also never knew which poor bugger was going to be on the receiving end of some fancy French footwork: on that occasion, it was me.

I had played international rugby all over the world for eight seasons and remained virtually injury free: a groin problem in New Zealand 1971 was the worst setback that I had endured. Sure, I had taken clouts and kicks, but I seemed to emerge from every encounter virtually unscathed. The only time I went off in my career was against France in 1972, but the match was won and I had no objection to going off and allowing Derek Quinnell to win his first cap. The sight of him charging down the tunnel, knocking people out of the way in his anxiety to join the action, is a popular memory from Wales' Five Nations past.

I remember a ruck forming ten minutes or so into the game and the ball flying out into the backs. The next thing I knew, the entire French pack was running over me. Being flattened by a French juggernaut is not one of my fondest memories from my international days. I lay on the turf feeling pretty rotten, with a terrible pain in my leg. A well-aimed stud had punctured my left calf muscle and my leg was starting to swell up at an alarming rate. Gerry Lewis – the physio – raced on, took one look at my wrecked calf and said 'You're off, Merv.' I always had a lot of time for Gerry, but there was no way that I was going to leave the field that day on his say-so. I can't remember what I said to him – and maybe the glare in my eyes rammed home the message – but Gerry left the field alone. I thought about the boys, about not letting them down or leaving them without a leader, but my main reasons for wanting to stay on the field were entirely personal: I did not want to miss this match. I would dearly like to claim some mystical foresight, something that told me to stay on the field in what would be my last match. Truth was, I would have been ashamed to go off, and I was also scared to miss out. Powerful, selfish emotions. A parallel can be drawn with Bobby Windsor. Bobby took a knock in one game, a game we had all but won, and I said, 'Why don't you go off and give Roy Thomas a run out?' I had a soft spot for Roy – the Llanelli hooker – he sat on the bench many times and didn't get one cap. Bobby wouldn't give an inch; his attitude to the shirt, and the pride he felt in wearing it permeated the entire team. I, too, had learnt to treasure it, to push on through the pain. I also thought if I left the field and someone came on and had a storming match in my place, I might never be selected again. From being a man with 100 per cent confidence in his own ability I was reminded, in a spin of studs, how fragile my position was.

The game was an ugly affair, with both teams playing uncompromising rugby. The swelling in my leg increased and my physical capability deteriorated as the match wore on. But mentally, I remained sharp and alert to the demands that are always on the captain's shoulders. Having three front-line kickers helped and Phil, Steve Fenwick and Allan Martin – the lock with the siege gun boot – each contributed two penalties apiece. We did cross to score one try through J.J. Williams but the French scored twice and would have gone over for the win if J.P.R. hadn't pulled off a blockbusting tackle on Jean-Francois Gourdon to seal our win – and the Grand Slam. A modern-day video referee might have judged Gareth Edwards' epic 1972 try against Scotland a little harshly. Well, a modern-day ref might view J.P.R.'s shunt of a shoulder barge illegal, but Mr West of Ireland didn't see it that way in 1976 – and certainly neither did I, nor a large section of the millions watching worldwide. It was a classic, physical piece of rugby intervention, and it won us the match.

Of the 'three great' Welsh teams of the 1970s, I believe the '76 side was the best and we achieved what we did by using only 17 players throughout the entire campaign. Mike Knill – the Cardiff prop – came on for Graham Price against France for a wonderful 40-minute cameo in the front row. But other than Mike, 16 players were selected over 4 games. I view that team of J.P.R. Williams, Gerald Davies, Steve Fenwick, Ray Gravell, J.J. Williams, Phil Bennett, Gareth Edwards, Graham Price, Bobby Windsor, Charlie Faulkner, Geoff Wheel, Allan Martin, Terry Cobner, Tommy David and Trevor Evans as *my* team, *my* boys.

I was asked in the press conference later, 'What next for Wales?' and I confidently predicted 'three Grand Slams in a row'. But that was not to be. Wales won another Grand Slam in 1978 under the captaincy of Phil Bennett, with my friend Derek Quinnell wearing number 8 with distinction. That was a watershed year for Welsh rugby, as both Gareth and Phil called time on their illustrious playing careers. The Grand Slam in 1978 was a marvellous achievement, but I do wonder if the '76 team has been somewhat diminished by the successful Grand Slam sides that flank it in that decade? Perhaps, but in 2003, BBC Sport ran an online poll to determine the greatest-ever sporting team, and we won . . . from a list that included the 1970 Brazil World Cup team. Maybe we are not the forgotten men of rugby after all.

I was carried on the shoulders of the fans off the pitch, exhausted and in agony. The night in Cardiff turned into a mammoth drinking session, where the French – to their eternal credit – joined enthusiastically in our celebrations. One man remained sober longer than his fellow revellers, and that was me, the captain, waiting his turn to speak. But later that night, back at the Angel Hotel, the singing and carousing increased and I absorbed all around me, happy with my lot, feeling content and settled at the summit of the game – and excited about what was to come.

Three weeks later, in that very same city, I was fighting for my life.

XI

Felled

Late March . . . and a spring morning breaks clear across Swansea Bay. The air is fresh . . . as fresh as Swansea air can be when the salt rises and flies continually from the waves. The day begins with a little more urgency than usual for a sleepy, out-of-season Sunday. It's a big day for a town that loves its sport . . . the good times are coming.

A few miles away up the valley at Pontlliw, the bang and clatter of little Christopher Davies sets a house in motion. His mother rises to deal with him whilst his father stretches out his long frame for a few minutes more bed rest. He has been thinking about the coming day, but now that he is fully awake he feels there is little point in dwelling on it. He pulls himself out of bed and enjoys an unlikely Sunday sensation: there is no pain; there is no ache . . . his body does not throb from the previous afternoon's adventure because there was none. His legs and back and arms and shoulders feel fine, although his mind doesn't linger long on his physical actuality. Despite his best intentions not to dwell on it, he cannot escape thoughts of the confrontation that will be played out later that afternoon.

The Sunday-morning routine is a little more hurried than usual; the boy breakfasts first, followed by his parents. Dad eats, dresses, potters around for a while and then collects his kit together. A car horn sounds out in the street; the man ruffles the boy's hair, picks up his kit and leaves the house. He gets into the car and the journey down the road to St Helens begins.

Men gather at the ground. All shapes, all sizes, suited in their Sunday best.

149

The chatter is incessant and typically male: rude jokes and half-hearted insults punctuate the air. As the coach leaves the shadow of St Helens, the atmosphere on board is one of bravado and trepidation. The tall man stares out of the window, people cheer and one small boy raises his hands in salute. A flag is unfurled and flaps against the Mumbles skyline. The coach continues out of Swansea and moves steadily eastward.

The plan is to get on the road early and then decamp a few miles outside the capital. The journey passes and the coach reaches its first destination of the day, a pub called the Bear in the small, well-presented Glamorganshire village of Cowbridge. The Swansea men can relax now, at least they can try. They all huddle down tightly around the dining tables, order lunch and long for a soothing beer . . . but there can be no beer till later. The jokes ease off; the eyes that sparkled and shone in Swansea now deaden with serious intent.

A few look towards the tall man, the captain, the leader; normally so self-assured and so confident. This is a man who has spent his sporting life dealing with days like this. But there is no solace to be found in his sallow face; he is strangely silent, distracted almost. His food lies untouched on the plate before him. Big men have big appetites. But not today.

The clock goes round, creeping ever closer to final departure. The men leave the Bear, get back on the coach and begin the decisive part of their journey into Cardiff. They are sucked through the traffic and then emerge, delivered, outside Cardiff Arms Park.

Time plays tricks: for some the next 90 minutes before kick-off flash by, whilst for others, each second is drawn out to tease and torment. The changing-rooms are unfamiliar but the routines are the same. Some stretch and retch whilst others stare blankly at the wall. The Swansea boys are in a new place in terms of big-match moments. Some are seasoned players, others little more than kids . . . today, they are underdogs, but they are ready. Stan Addicott starts shouting but eyes are not on Stan. They are on the captain. 'What do you reckon, Swerve?' says one voice, but there is no reply. The captain speaks only when he feels the need to speak; he's getting himself ready. He chooses his words carefully. He is ready. Where he goes his men will follow.

The players run onto the field desperate for the game to begin. The crowd is large and partisan, and the supporters from both clubs are primed and ready to roar. Television cameras scan the players, picking up every gesture and every look with its all-seeing eye. There are no formalities, just a few hard stares and then kick-off.

The white headband always made him stand out. It was worn at first for practical reasons – to protect his ears and calm his hair – but soon the headband became his trademark. Crowds from Twickenham to Taranaki used it as a beacon to track the tall man's whereabouts on the field. Whenever bodies came together, there at the bottom of the chaos would be the tall man in the white headband, digging away, wrestling for the ball.

The game is on, and it soon develops into the big forward shunt the pundits from the morning papers said it would be. The firm turf and fine weather cannot drag the ball out of the forwards' claws. There is too much at stake – a Cup final appearance, the honour of west and east.

The tall man in the white headband is covering the pitch in what seems like seven league boots . . . then, with 28 minutes gone, as the ball goes wide, the tall man in the white headband is suddenly conspicuous by his absence. The play pans away, the maul breaks up, and the players fly off in pursuit of the ball. All except one. He has fallen.

There are cheers – and jeers – from the crowd. The try celebrations end sooner than expected. Something has happened. Something is wrong. A hush descends. The trainer runs on. He crouches down and looks anxiously over to the sidelines. A doctor arrives. Then another. The tall man in the white headband has stopped breathing.

Ambulance. Nurses. Tears. Prayers.

An eternal wait. A surgeon's scalpel.

A foggy reawakening.

Then a slow dawning that a life so loved, a life so blessed has gone.

* * *

I have no clear recollection of the events before, during or after my brain haemorrhage. All I retain are a few scrambled images: fighting with the nurses to be free of my bed, scribbling my name on a piece of paper, having my head shaved, J.P.R. Williams smuggling beer into my room. If one can imagine my life as a film, then the film now has a sizable jump cut: from two days before the semi-final encounter against Pontypool, to about ten days afterwards. I have effectively lost a fortnight of my life. Perhaps forgetting was my instinctive way of dealing with the trauma? My knowledge of events is, therefore, second-hand and my memories have been largely pieced together by listening to the people who went through the crisis with me and from reading press reports from that strange, surreal time. I was at death's door and caused a great deal of anxiety to a great many people . . . but I sailed through that lost fortnight in a kind of hazy – yet blissful – oblivion.

I am loath to be defined as the man whose playing career ended when he suffered a brain haemorrhage on a Cardiff rugby field. But I am. I cannot escape what happened in my past, but I can put it into some kind of context. Remember, this happened half a lifetime ago. In fact, I have now almost lived longer with the repercussions – both physical and psychological – of the events of that March day, than I ever did without them. Grand Slam captain of Wales, two-times winning British Lion, a stalwart of a revolutionary London Welsh team . . . great achievements in the game, but my public fall from prominence, at the very height of my playing prowess, has pigeon-holed me as the man who had, and lost, it all. It is not how I see myself. Sure, there were many black days of intense bitterness where I felt I had been unfairly treated by life (which I will come to later). But what I eventually came to realise – and what some people might not know to this day – was how close I was to never having any of it in the first place. Missing out entirely, never reaching the top of the game, not leading my country to glory or being part of the Lions' success . . . now that would have caused me greater lasting damage.

During my playing days I remained relatively injury free. I broke my jaw in college, I strained my groin in New Zealand and the French pack once made mincemeat of my calf, but somehow I got away with it. I never shirked a tackle, I never eased off, I always put my body in the places where it hurt most but I never suffered any real, long-lasting injury. The closest I came to being forced out of the game for a significant period of time was in April 1972 when, in all likelihood, I suffered my first brain haemorrhage. The timing was fortunate because I had a summer break from rugby that year to get myself well. It wasn't diagnosed as a haemorrhage back then, but if it had been, then the Mervyn Davies story would have ended just before it really got going. Surviving two brain haemorrhages . . . now there's another achievement to put on the CV.

I have stronger memories of brain haemorrhage number one than

I do of number two – probably because it was less incapacitating. I was playing for London Welsh in what must have been one of my last games for the club before my move to Swansea. We were up against our big rivals, London Irish, and were determined to show them that we were the dominant team of exiles in the English game. The weather that day wasn't ideal rugby weather (not for us forwards, at least); it was extremely hot and the air was still and arid – conditions best described as lung-busting.

I remember feeling physically sick. My head felt like it had the New Zealand pack doing the haka inside my skull, and the bright sunlight only intensified the pain. It is uncommon to be taken ill whilst playing a match because the adrenalin pumping through the body usually masks any other sensation. At first I thought my headband must have been wound too tightly around my head, but after I removed it, the searing pain remained. It got so bad that I asked if I could leave the field. But this was in the days before substitutes were allowed and we needed the points, so I was politely told to shut up and get on with it. I gritted my teeth and carried on. The game concluded but my condition worsened and, eventually, I collapsed in the showers. Luckily, Bob Phillips and J.P.R. – my London Welsh teammates – were both doctors and recognised the seriousness of the situation; I was rushed into the local hospital in Roehampton. Over the next few days I was put through a rigorous series of tests that culminated in a lumbar puncture – which I regarded as the most painful medical procedure ever inflicted upon a patient. It felt like an eagle's talon had been stabbed into, and then dragged along, the inside of my back. The final prognosis was a form of meningitis – an inflammation of the membrane surrounding the brain. I was told I would be okay and was discharged to get on with my life. There was a week or two of headaches, and I tried to avoid bright sunlight, but soon the problem seemed to go away. Four years later, when my medical history came under closer scrutiny, it was suggested that my case of meningitis was probably a small brain haemorrhage. Had I been diagnosed correctly in 1972 then surgery would have fixed the problem and reduced the chance of it recurring four years later. But, if I had been diagnosed correctly in 1972, I would have packed my boots away there and then. There would have been no second Lions tour, no Swansea rugby, no Wales captaincy and no Grand Slam. If I am being honest with myself, then I am grateful that the original diagnosis was incorrect. The doctors at Roehampton got it wrong, but in doing so they gave me four more years of successful rugby.

I am often asked: did rugby cause the bleed in my brain? Did the continuous build-up of whacks and bumps and impacts mess up the Mervyn Davies grey matter? When asked the very same question, my neurosurgeon, Robert Weekes, told the press that it could have happened 'if he had been sitting at home in his armchair'. Medical opinion remains divided, but there have been other cases in rugby where a causal relationship seemed possible. Bill Beaumont was forced to retire from rugby on the advice of his neurosurgeon after he sought an explanation for a series of blackouts. Keith Jarrett, a good few years earlier than Bill, faced a similar dilemma before he bowed out of rugby league. I am not saying the physical demands of rugby did not play some role in what happened to me, but it was never proven to be the root cause.

Going back to that fateful day in March 1976, my Swansea teammates did note a change in my behaviour before the match: allegedly, I was more subdued than normal. My experience of big-match occasions meant I had plenty to share with my team, but I was strangely reserved. A semi-final is the hardest game for any club to negotiate and my stand-offishness was put down to nerves. Swansea had come a long way that season and the prospect of a Cup final in the national stadium had set the town abuzz. Sure, we all felt the tension but big games need big-game players and there was no one in the All Whites who could match what I had done on the field. So I wasn't that nervous. My distraction was not caused by fear; it must have been my illness.

When I went down at 3.28, some onlookers apparently thought I had been done over by our opponents. The Pontypool forwards had a fairly robust reputation back then (much to coach Ray Prosser's delight) but they were blameless; I am quite sure that nobody touched me. From what I've subsequently seen on tape and been told, a maul formed near the halfway line and I helped secure possession for our backs. My instinct then would have been to run up field in support of the attack and try to anticipate where the breakdown would occur. It was second nature to me . . . reaching the breakdown was the bread and butter of my game. But the move did not break down; I did. I slumped to the turf and lay there, motionless, in the foetal position. Play continued and Roy Woodward – our winger – scored a lovely try and we took the lead. The Swansea boys were jubilant until they turned and saw me slumped 50 or so yards away. Replacement flanker, Baden Evans, was first to reach me. I had stopped breathing and he made a somewhat clumsy attempt to rip the gum shield out of my mouth. He succeeded – and almost took my lips off in the process – but his quick thinking certainly prevented me from swallowing my tongue. Medical attention arrived almost immediately and, once my airways were clear, I was given mouth-to-mouth resuscitation before being stretchered off and taken under the stand for further assessment. I stopped breathing for a second time, and I would have died there and then in the shadows but for the resuscitation equipment on hand, which effectively breathed life back into me. Here I must thank good fortune because I am convinced the weakened blood vessel in my brain was due to bleed that day, and if it had happened anywhere else, then I would have died. It was unusual to play rugby on a Sunday, and if I had been engaged in normal Sunday afternoon pursuits like playing golf or squash, eating lunch, driving along the Mumbles Road or pushing my son around the local park, I would have been finished. Even if I had been playing rugby at any other South Wales club ground, then I doubt I would be here today to tell this tale. But playing in Cardiff, a club which had excellent medical facilities, and playing in front of 15,000 people – which included a dozen or so doctors – undoubtedly saved my life.

Swansea went on to win the tie 22–14 but, at the final whistle, it was the plight of the fallen captain that remained top of the post-match agenda. Swansea chairman, Viv Davies, could only say that I was unconscious and in hospital. Gordon Rowley, honorary surgeon to the WRU, and Jack Matthews, a GP who had played centre with great distinction for Wales, were instrumental in getting me to Cardiff Royal Infirmary (CRI). The Duty Registrar, Dr Bob Leyshon, assessed the paralysis down my left-hand side and was convinced I had had a major brain haemorrhage. He decided that I needed to be moved from the CRI to a specialist unit. If I was to survive the night, then I would require the best possible care . . . and Dr Leyshon knew that would be found under Wales' leading neurosurgeon, Robert Weekes, at the University of Wales Teaching Hospital up at the Heath.

Soon word was out about the seriousness of my illness, and the next day a press scrum gathered outside the Heath Hospital. Over the next few days, as I remained unconscious, Mr Weekes handled his press conferences beautifully: he provided a delicate balance between hope and realism. 'Yes,' he said, 'Mervyn Davies is fighting for his life.' I would need surgery, but first the medical team had to stabilise me in order to give me a fighting chance to survive a highly dangerous procedure.

I wish that I could report back from some kind of dream state, a safe cocoon, where I was a whisper away from my wife, my son and my parents. If I did visit such a place – which I sincerely doubt – the memories are now lost forever. People rallied around: both Swansea and the WRU were splendid in their response and ensured my family had whatever support they needed to ease their burden. After a week of waiting and monitoring and regular updates on the national news, it was decided this was as good as it was going to get and I had no hope of improving further without surgical intervention. On 6 April, Mr Weekes decided the time had come to operate.

An arteriogram, which charts the passage of blood through the brain, and an isotope scan test to show the extent of the damage, revealed the severity of my problem. The bleed from the blood vessel had killed off the brain cells surrounding the tear. Mr Weekes and his team of seven would have to access a point three inches inside my skull, directly behind the bridge of my nose, and repair the damage. They cut along my hairline from the centre of my forehead to the tip of my ear, peeled back my skin, drilled a hole in my skull and got on with the job. Once inside, they had to negotiate a series of smaller arteries before reaching the broken vessel. It is an understatement to say that brain surgery is devilishly intricate work with no room for error, but even by the standards of an experienced team of neurosurgeons, the procedure in my case was unusually difficult. The stakes were high: the slightest mistake could cause irreparable damage or even death. This is work where millimetres matter. Mr Weekes likened the procedure to clipping the neck of an inner tube that had swollen and bulged through the protecting wall of a rubber tyre – but done on a microscopic scale and with my life in the balance. I was under the knife for over three hours, but I came through and the surgical team were pleased with their labours. Now, it was a matter of wait and see.

Apparently, I came round on ward B4 and started swearing at my family. I cringe to think what language I must have used, but the air was no doubt blue. At least my family knew that my speech hadn't been affected by the scalpel, nor had my ability to remember and articulate certain well-known barrack-room phrases. It took days for me to regain full consciousness, and my memories of that initial period of recuperation are no clearer now, but I do know from others what happened and, from knowing what happened, I can imagine what I felt then.

The unbelievable goodwill that came from people all over the world overwhelmed my family. The hospital received over 4,000 messages of good luck. I couldn't possibly reply to them all, so as my strength and my understanding returned, I conveyed my gratitude via the press and the BBC. Men I had played with, and against – like Willie John and New Zealand hooker Tane Norton amongst others – took the time to contact me. Welsh colleagues like Barry John, John Dawes and Derek Quinnell called in with good cheer, threatening to liberate me from my sickbed. I also received supportive words from all the major unions in the game. On one occasion, I apparently saw twenty-three visitors in one hour. No wonder Sister Morris scowled at my guests . . . we were destroying her ward routine. And still, I was news. Cliff Morgan came in with a camera crew to interview me. I looked quite a sight with my shaven head and Paisley-pattern dressing gown but I retained some sense of personal pride in my appearance and insisted Cliff shave me before they started filming. He asked me how I had been filling my time and I said that, when I wasn't giving my nurses grief, I had been playing games made by a company called Invicta. Within a day or two, Invicta sent me a load more, delighted with the exposure I had given their business. If I had been thinking more clearly, I might have promoted something that would have provided a bigger financial kickback! I even had representatives of golfer Arnold Palmer's company contact me, but I could not think for the life of me what possible use a sick rugby player would be to them. The fact that for a few weeks in the spring of 1976 I was one of the highest-profile sportsmen in the world escaped me completely! How naive we were back in the '70s.

Slowly, the interest faded. The camera crews left and the reporters sought out more exciting stories elsewhere. I was glad to see them go. I will always be grateful for the love and kindness shown towards my family and me during that time, but as my self-awareness returned, so did my desire to stop the Mervyn Davies freak show. I felt embarrassed and humiliated by all the attention my illness had created. I did not want any of this. I felt weak, pathetic – lost, even. But I also felt incredibly lucky. The road ahead towards any kind of lasting recovery would be long and arduous, but I had entered hospital physically fit and strong and had a good chance of rediscovering some kind of normality. My doctors told me I might even be able to play rugby again in a year or so. They were dangling a carrot to encourage me (and doing it for the best reasons), but I knew, quite early on, that my rugby days were gone. Unless I could envisage playing for Wales or the British Lions then I wouldn't even try to come back. The prospect of taking the field as a shadow of the player I had once been appalled me. The thought of losing rugby ripped me apart, but they were feelings I had to put aside for now. My only priority was to get well . . . I had a family to support.

The medical team at the Heath under Mr Weekes and the nurses led by Sister Julia Morris did an immense job coaxing me back to life. It couldn't have been easy having a 'celebrity' patient on their hands. Not that my status did me any favours . . . particularly with the nurses. They were fairly brutal in their desire to get me up and mobile, and even removed my bedpan in an effort to make me walk to the lavatory. All I wanted to do was lie down, but I was bullied and badgered into action. They always seemed to get their way.

When I asked Robert Weekes what the future held for me, he was honest enough to say he didn't fully know. I would need rest and intense physiotherapy. I had only been ill for a fortnight or so, but already there was considerable muscle wastage. Inactivity and weakness had caused my left foot to drop so I had to have it put into a plaster cast to prevent permanent damage. I lost my sense of smell and my vision was affected. The biggest problem, however, would be the long-term effects on the left side of my body. The paralysis had lessened, but there was considerable locomotor damage. Mr Weekes said that in a year to 18 months' time I would have recovered all the movement I would ever be likely to have. All I could do was play a waiting game.

Eventually, and to my enormous relief, I was moved from Cardiff and sent closer to home – to the hospital up in Gorseinon. My employers, Len and Norman Blyth, were an enormous help and told me to forget work and concentrate on getting better. They paid me a full wage and said my job was waiting for me whenever I was fit enough to return to full employment. It was just the kind of news that I needed to hear.

The period of time over the glorious summer of 1976 was strangely peaceful. I had a little garden outside my room where I could sit and watch Christopher tottering around chasing insects. He took his first steps when I was in a coma and weeks later it was difficult to tell who was the most unsure on his feet: father or son. We were learning to walk together. Seeing Chris, feeling the strength return to my body a little more each day, gave me a sense of real hope. The door was open and friends and family would call in and say hello and have a chat. One chap, who wasn't exactly the sharpest knife in the drawer, told me he was after my Welsh shirt and would try to impress me with the number of press-ups he could do! It was all good entertainment: I felt relaxed and cared for and safe. I didn't allow myself to brood too long on rugby and besides, it was summer . . . rugby could wait.

I viewed my recovery as another challenge to overcome. Playing sport wasn't the goal on this occasion. My goal was lower, yet somehow greater: my goal was being normal. Being strong, being mobile, being useful . . . that became my focus and I worked hard over those few hot months with Mr Llewellyn, my physio. He was a remarkable man; he had been blinded in the war, and when one sense was taken away from him, it seemed to heighten his remaining senses. The connections between his brain and his sense of touch were quite incredible, and he was a real inspiration. We worked well together. The more he had me lifting weights and squeezing rubber balls, the more I wanted to do. I was driven by my quest for normality.

Whilst I was in Gorseinon, improving, there remained a very good chance that I would lead an active life. Rugby was gone, there would be no Lions captaincy and no three successive Grand Slams, but there might be golf and tennis and squash. There was also Christopher: he'd need his dad to teach him how to ride a bike and kick a ball. There was so much I had to look forward to and as long as I kept getting stronger, anything was possible. Well, that is what I told those who asked me how I was doing. I was bullish, determined and cheerful . . . I would not let a brain haemorrhage beat me. But internally, in the dark hours of loneliness, I was terrified. What would I do when the new season started and Saturday afternoon came along? Where would I go if I couldn't play rugby? Where else could I get that fix, that supreme sense of release that rugby had given me over the years? I didn't play sport for mere enjoyment . . . I played sport to win. I understood winning; I was good at it. But what if I could not win anymore? What if I couldn't play sport well enough to win? So many questions remained unanswered. Time would reveal all but I secretly feared the inevitable: the man I had once been was no more.

XII

Sinking

Saturday afternoons gave me some of the brightest – and some of the bleakest – hours of my life. When I was in the game, I craved the physical and emotional release that came with charging around the pitch in pursuit of a rugby ball. There was something about *playing* that stirred my soul. I never had the same enthusiasm for training or even midweek matches, but waking up early on a Saturday morning, knowing there was a game to be played, was always the highlight of my week. It's nearing 30 years now since I played my last match, but I still occasionally rise on a Saturday morning and experience those same pre-match sensations. Part of my brain and some of my memories were scrambled by events . . . but I often receive a tantalising glimpse of what I lost. They don't last long, they merely linger in the half-light and then disperse with the blink of an eye. But the spectre of playing, the ghost of doing the thing that I loved best, still looms large in my life.

The beginning of the 1976–77 season (the first time in over ten years when I wasn't getting ready to play) was a gruelling time for my family and me. I used the summer months as a shield to protect myself against the inevitable emptiness that was heading my way. Recuperation was slow, painfully slow, but the public gaze that had magnified my every groan in the first weeks after my operation lessened, and I was consigned to a welcome semi-obscurity. I knew that autumn, and missing out on the rush of rugby that came with it, would hurt – and it was a pain that stayed with me for many years. Standing on the rugby pitch, being with the boys, feeling the sinews stretch and strain, hearing the final whistle blow and trudging off, satisfied, full of achievement: how could I replicate those feelings? How could I fill the void?

The easiest option would be to watch, but I never enjoyed watching rugby; and being trapped up in the stand, removed from the action, only added to my torment. I did go and watch my fair share of matches, but I felt uncomfortable being so close, yet so far, from the game. I toyed with other sports, but my body let me down. Whilst recuperating I thought there might one day be another physical outlet to ease my sense of uselessness, but when I tried, my rather pathetic efforts only added to the frustration that I felt. I went down to a local golf club to play a round, but it was hopeless: I couldn't hit a golf ball cleanly because I had no sense of balance. I tried tennis and squash, but both balls moved too quickly and too erratically for my flailing, uncoordinated arm. And I saw little sense in playing sport if I could not win. I never played for fitness; I played for competition. I cannot stand pity, or the idea of someone giving me a chance by easing off, so I thought the best course of action would be to bury my sporting instincts completely.

I tried DIY – after all, there was always some task that needed doing around the house and I liked using my hands – but when I picked up a saw or a hammer those hands felt uncoordinated and unlike my own. The time it took to put up shelves or paint a wall, the false starts and clumsy errors, the dropped nails and bodged cuts removed any sense of achievement or satisfaction one normally felt for a job well done. A better man than I might have dedicated his free time to his young child, but I feared that I had little to teach him. I couldn't even beat Christopher at tiddlywinks and, when he got older, I was unable to offer practical, normal, parental help. All the little moments that we take for granted: teaching our children to ride a bike, to kick a ball in the back garden, to make model aeroplanes, or just to colour in pictures became so hard and complicated that I lost all heart in the attempt. When my daughter Laura was born on 25 September 1978, we were statistically an average family, albeit with Dad wobbling around and falling into ever-blacker moods.

Saturday afternoons became my purgatory: I initially spent them squirming at St Helens watching Swansea, or out in the country, walking . . . escaping. And there was one other place where I increasingly hid: the pub. I was often bitter and remote – not a nice man to be around. The initial relief I had felt about being alive in the middle of 1976 was soon replaced by annoyance and irritation that is best summed up in two small words with a huge and heavy implication: why me?

Within a year of my brain haemorrhage it became increasingly apparent where the limits of my physical recovery would end. I looked OK, tall and gangly as ever, though when my strength returned, the left-hand side of my body was considerably weaker. The biggest problem centred on my coordination: I didn't have any, well, not enough to play sport. The speed of thought and action, the instinct to react decisively to the ball suddenly appearing, the agility and spatial awareness that had been the foundation of my rugby . . . all that was gone. Suddenly, my whole world was filled with intense frustration, and being a private – indeed, a reserved – man I internalised much of what I felt.

What exactly were the physical effects of my brain bleed? Let me provide some examples. Imagine ordering two pints of beer from a bar and then walking ten yards to a table. I could pick up both glasses and turn and cross the floor and present one pint, held in my right hand, full to the brim. But the pint in my left hand would be half empty because of the constant 'wobble' I feel in that particular hand and the inability I have to keep anything stable. Another example would be the 'wall'. Imagine walking down a road and suddenly the way is blocked by a two-foot wall. If one is feeling particularly agile or sprightly, one could leap over it without breaking stride – or at least stop, hop up with one foot and push off from the top. I couldn't do that. I couldn't judge the size and distance of the wall and I couldn't instruct my left foot to act when I needed it to.

Another problem was negotiating steps; I found it tremendously difficult walking down stairs and took route one – straight on my backside – on more than one occasion. I have probably fallen over more since my brain haemorrhage than I ever did on the rugby field. These are not life-altering problems, admittedly; more a nuisance than a serious hindrance. I was lucky that I could function more or less normally – but as a 29-year-old man who had been the captain of his country, I felt like my life had been destroyed. In some ways, that challenged my ability to be a man.

Maybe it is a working-class thing. My father always worked in a hard, manual environment and therefore I may have equated manliness with physicality. I was brought up to believe that using one's brain was better than using one's brawn, but the man I respected more than any other, my father, used his muscle to provide for his family. Maybe that is how I wanted to define myself – through strength and physical effort. Working as a teacher or a sales representative, in the soft world of books and paper, had only increased my need to test my body. As a boy, I was always drawn to the idea of working with my hands, of learning a trade, but as is common with many first-born children, I was pushed more towards academia and a profession. My younger brother, Dyfrig, was never shoved at his exams like I was, and seemed to have enjoyed a very fulfilled life as an electrician. I never got any satisfaction from teaching, from sitting in a warm classroom talking to children. I had to test my manliness elsewhere and therefore embraced the physical challenge of rugby. When that challenge was taken away, I hoped I might find another arena to get rid of all that excess testosterone.

Given the choice, I would have retired from rugby in 1978 after leading the Lions to New Zealand and captaining Wales to (hopefully) the third of three consecutive Grand Slams. Given the choice, I would have gone out at the very top. Given the choice, I might have moved into coaching and used my experience to help a new generation of players. Given the choice, I might even have ventured into administration and tried to educate the archaic WRU into understanding the needs and expectations of the players. Given the choice, I might have made a difference to the game I loved. But I was never given the choice. *What ifs* and *maybes* are pointless, but I could not stop tormenting myself with what might have been.

My future active involvement in rugby was curtailed when I wrote my book *Number 8* in 1977. Once I signed the contract to deliver the manuscript I 'professionalised' myself and effectively cut myself off from the nitty-gritty of day-to-day rugby football. I have no regrets about writing that story: it was a thorough – though sanitised – version of my life, which managed to record the intricacies of my rugby experiences. But I wish I had waited a year or so, to see what other options in the game might have arisen. For me, coaching could never have entirely replaced playing, but I needed time to give myself a clearer perspective on what I should – or could – do. Instead, my publishers wanted to capitalise on my 'fame' and the deal was done. I didn't really write the book to tell my story, I did it to earn an extra few bob and support my family. I have leant heavily on the work I did then with David Parry-Jones for the preparation of this current book, and I can smile wryly at the way I viewed my future back then. In print, I was very positive and determined about my recovery, and it must have seemed as if I had shrugged off the hand that fate had dealt me with a philosophical air. But a miserable, bitter Mervyn would have been bad for sales, so I bit my literary tongue and played the battered – but unbroken – warrior.

By accepting the book deal in 1977 I also committed an act of ultimate betrayal to the amateur game – I made some money out of it. The WRU scaled great heights of paranoia in this particular area. It all seems so quaint now but back in the '60s, '70s and '80s there were spies everywhere waiting to report clandestine meetings in motorway service stations with league scouts from the evil north, or illicit boot deals being done with certain manufacturers. Whenever a player conducted an interview on TV, an official letter from the WRU would arrive within days 'reminding' him to contribute his fee to the Welsh Rugby Union Charitable Trust. Clive Rowlands tells the story of how he once accepted a set of golf clubs that must have been worth over £50 and, thus, 'professionalised' himself. No one cared more about the Welsh game than Clive, and he would have never done anything willingly to jeopardise his amateur status. There were scams and backhanders, sure – I remember some Welsh players being flown out to play incognito club matches in France, and they didn't do that because they fancied a game! None of us read the rules of amateurism, but we all knew the score: the WRU would watch us like hawks. Once I had agreed to write a book, I thought I might as well try to earn some more money from my 'fame'. I didn't particularly care what the WRU thought and I didn't believe that I owed rugby anything; actually, I thought the opposite was true. As far as the WRU was concerned, I was history and I got nothing from them except kind words and sympathy. My injury was not deemed a rugby injury, so I didn't receive any compensation or even a testimonial, but I did receive tremendous goodwill and help from many people outside the game, who went out of their way to look after me.

The trend today is for ex-players to seek work with the media when their careers end, and many do a good job bringing their recent expertise and their insight into the television studio. For most, it seems like a natural progression, but for me, it was an extremely uncomfortable experience. Despite the failure of my year-long dabble with punditry, I am still grateful to Onllwyn Brace and Dewi Griffiths at the BBC for pulling a few strings and getting me on board. And it was a pleasure, too, to work in the studio with my friend and former co-author, David Parry-Jones, and my former coach, Carwyn James. But the moment Carwyn started talking about 'static platforms', backed up by David asking me for my views, my moustache would bristle with confusion and I would struggle to make a semi-intelligent contribution. I was on TV because I was Mervyn Davies, ex-Wales captain, not because I had anything incisive to say.

Being with the media also changed the relationship I had with the players. Once I crossed the floor, I was no longer their mate or their ex-colleague . . . I was a bloke who was trying to file copy. I never had much time for interviews when I was a captain and would normally give my opinion under sufferance. In fact, I did view the media with some suspicion when I played and was painfully aware of those past hostilities when I joined the press corps. I never felt comfortable going back into the players' dressing-room after I retired, but I did, and by doing so I put myself in a place where I felt great angst.

I started writing for the *Daily Mirror* in 1978, intending to write about rugby the way I saw it, and there were times when my words came back to haunt me. I remember I once wrote a few negative comments about Clive Williams after he'd played for Wales and suggested that he wasn't, perhaps, Wales' best option at prop. Players have long memories and Clive certainly made his displeasure felt when he took umbrage at what I'd written and flattened me at a Swansea end-of-season dinner. I left early that evening feeling utterly humiliated but finally fully understanding a simple truth: when an ex-player writes for the press, he sacrifices his right to be seen as 'one of the boys'. Some players make the transition quite easily, while others find it more difficult: Barry John has never been afraid to be outspoken, whereas someone like Phil Bennett treads a more wary line and doesn't deliberately go out of his way to court controversy. Maybe that exemplifies the kind of characters that they are? There is a fine old yarn that Bobby Windsor spins about Barry and his outspoken opinions. Barry was lambasting Bobby for his lack of speed around the pitch in a particular match, a claim 'The Duke' memorably rejected with the terse response: 'He never saw me getting my fucking head kicked in two minutes earlier, did he?' But the worst experience I had 'on the other side' was probably the lowest moment of my entire convalescence period. It cost me a very dear friendship for a number of years, and, looking back now, I don't know why the hell I put myself in such a vulnerable position.

The highpoint of my career would have been to captain the British Lions in 1977, especially by taking them back to the place where I had experienced my greatest success: New Zealand. My ambition led upwards like a series of steps: first, play for Wales; next, play for the Lions; third, captain Wales; and then finally, accept the ultimate accolade and captain the British Isles. As Wales were about to claim the Grand Slam in 1976, John Dawes approached me a good year before the party was selected and asked me to be his man. I was reluctant at first, because I remembered all too well how tough it was touring in New Zealand. But when John said, 'You'd go as captain', I couldn't refuse. At that moment, Wales were untouchable in British rugby – streets ahead of Ireland, England and Scotland. It seemed fairly obvious that the main contingent of the touring party would come from Wales. And it did.

The man chosen to captain the British Lions in my place was the man who had succeeded me for Wales: Phil Bennett. Wales managed to win a Triple Crown that season but fell in Paris after failing to score a try for the first time in 18 internationals. Despite Wales having a mediocre season by their exacting standards, 16 Welshmen were named to tour. By all accounts, it wasn't an enjoyable experience and there were a number of factors that seemed to contribute to the sense of unrest. For a start, the weather was atrocious with both North and South islands battered incessantly by wind and rain. Believe me, there is no fun in training or playing when one does so in soaking-wet kit. And because so many of New Zealand's recreational activities take place outdoors, there was little that the squad could do by way of relaxation to help them get away from rugby. Second, the level of expectation thrust upon the Lions was huge. For years the British Lions had been an ambassadorial enterprise in rugby relations. No one expected them to win in New Zealand in 1971, but after that success – coupled with the exploits of 'the Invincibles' from 1974 – the expectation placed on them was immense. Third, there was a lack of real leadership. Phil has since gone on record and admitted that he struggled with the burden of captaincy:

> 'I should never have accepted the captaincy of the Lions tour in 1977. I have spent many a wistful hour thinking what may have been achieved had the leadership gone to someone far better equipped than I to deal with the all-engulfing pressures of a three-month rugby expedition.'
>
> Phil Bennett quoted in *The History of the British & Irish Lions*, by Clem Thomas and Greg Thomas

It takes a brave man to admit he was wrong, but Phil was also a victim of his own reputation. The All Blacks knew he was the creative catalyst of the team and they subjected him to some brutal off-the-ball treatment. When the New Zealand forward, Kevin Eveleigh, late tackled him in the Second Test, it caused a huge ruckus. Bennett was singled out and the effect of his roughhousing had a big psychological impact on him and therefore on the rest of the squad. Phil was a wonderful player, but his confidence was shot then. So, in many ways, was his performance and the Lions couldn't afford an under-par captain. What Phil and the team needed most were senior players to step forward, but few seemed willing to fill the breach.

Squad selection also created its own problems. In terms of experience (and ability) there was no Willie John McBride, Gerald Davies, J.P.R. Williams, Gareth Edwards, Fergus Slattery, Ian McLauchlan – and, dare I say, no Mervyn Davies. But my loss was something that the Lions had a full year to come to terms with: losing a man like Roger Uttley, who was earmarked to lead in the pack, damaged them more. A good squad also needs men who can raise the spirits with a song and a joke, and I have been informed that there were no 'characters' there with the wit of a Bob Hiller, John Spencer, Ali Biggar, John Pullin or Ray Hopkins. A number of factors therefore conspired against the Lions, but probably the greatest source of unrest was the poor relationship between the press and the Lions hierarchy of George Burrell and John Dawes. John was an experienced tourist and coach, and well aware of the pitfalls that can occur when spending three months away from home. Burrell didn't have that recent experience and many believed that he set the insular and somewhat touchy tone that dogged the tour. The relations between party and press worsened over the weeks, and it culminated in a very unpleasant incident right at the tour's end. Guess who got caught, unwittingly, in the middle?

I went to New Zealand at the back end of the tour at the invitation of former New Zealand player Andy Leslie. The purpose of my visit was to take part in a small lecture tour visiting rugby clubs – usually in smaller towns and villages – to talk about rugby life with the Lions. I never joined the official press party or stayed in the team hotels. In fact, I spent my evenings with local host families because I consciously wanted to see another side of this wonderful country and meet New Zealanders from all walks of life. I thought it would give me a buzz – talking about the game I loved and being so close to the action. But in reality, it made me as miserable as sin. I had never travelled on my own before, and I felt increasingly isolated and confused. I went to New Zealand to escape the frustration that had built to almost claustrophobic levels back home. I ran away; I fled to a place where I thought I belonged, but I didn't belong there any more because my day had gone. I was yesterday's man.

The culture of sports reporting had changed in the years since the last Lions tour, and the level of interest in the Lions story had increased, so the tour was front-page news back home. Whilst the squad was winning their games, everything was rosy. And, on the whole, the 1977 British Lions were a winning squad, enjoying success 21 times out of 25. Unfortunately, they lost the Test series three to one. The New Zealand press instigated a plan to unsettle the Lions and there were numerous lurid headlines, which proclaimed that the Lions were 'louts' and 'lousy lovers'. The British press picked up on the discontent, sensed a story and reported back home to the wives and families that the lads were up to no good. As we all know, bad news sells papers, but I never saw any evidence to back up the sensationalist claims. However, the damage was already done: a siege mentality within the squad had been created and many of the boys were furious and upset by the way they had been misrepresented. A few bad apples in the press pack soured the reputation – and professionalism – of the others, and by the time I arrived, I was perceived as Mervyn Davies, the pressman. I thought I was just Mervyn Davies, the mate.

It was the last night of the tour and I was invited to attend the official closing function by the New Zealand RFU. I only had minimal contact with the team up to that point because I didn't see what benefit my contact with the squad could have. But many of them were my mates and by the end of the tour I thought it wouldn't matter who I spoke to. I remember bumping into Derek Quinnell and Bill Beaumont, and Bill warning me that they – the players – weren't allowed to speak to me. These men were my friends and I couldn't understand what they were referring to, until they said that Burrell had decreed there would be no contact with the press. But, I insisted, I wasn't press.

What hurt me most was that it was left to John Dawes – my dear friend and mentor – to ask me to leave the function. I told John that I was the guest of the NZRFU and not there in any press capacity. A few choice words passed between us and I took my leave. Clem

Thomas – that great man of the press – was aghast at what he had heard: John had no right to ask me to leave and I was within my rights to stay. It didn't matter, the damage was done . . . the man I admired most in rugby had humiliated me. I was heartbroken when I left.

In his recent autobiography, Phil Bennett blamed the incident on me removing two crates of sponsors' beer from the players' room, but that is not how it happened. It was many years before John and I spoke again, and it was only when I was preparing this book that I talked to him about what happened between us that night.

The relationship between John and George had disintegrated, but being the good and loyal man that he is, John publicly stood by his manager. And he still does, in fact. George could be dogmatic, to say the least, and when he asked John to get rid of me, John did as his manager instructed. I was surprised that John didn't tell Burrell where to go, but on reflection I think the problem might have been deeper-seated than a disagreement over what capacity I was there in. I was John's first choice as captain, I was the man who had led his Wales team, and I was the bloke who had been his friend and his confidant since I first started playing. Just as he had endured his worst rugby experience – the only blip in an outstanding career – there I was, apparently with the press pack, the boys who had made the last few weeks miserable. The sense of betrayal felt by the Lions was compounded by the discovery that another of the journalists, whom they considered to be a 'good guy', had allegedly been writing critical stories under a pseudonym. When I turned up, it was the last straw. John carried out his duty to his manager, acting under orders, but I suspect he knew he had picked on a man who would never, ever betray him.

It is all water under the bridge now, and I must take the blame for any falling out between us because I should never have gone to New Zealand in 1977. What was I thinking of? Did I need to bask in a kind of reflected glory if the Lions won? Or inwardly gloat if they couldn't succeed without me? Physically – and mentally – I was still weak and unsure. I have made many mistakes in my life, but being in New Zealand then as a hanger-on, that was one of the worst.

Going to New Zealand, hanging around pubs, being sullen and

distant: those factors exemplified the Mervyn Davies' life story for a good few years post-1976. Replacing rugby was impossible and the quest for a similar buzz left me reeling. It cost me my dignity, my reputation and even my first marriage. There were stories circulating about me getting pissed in clubs and falling around on the street. Often, it was my clumsiness that caused me to fall, but there were plenty of times when I drank too much and sought solace in the bottom of a beer glass. But the comfort I needed wasn't to be found there; to get over the disappointment of losing rugby meant getting on with my life. It meant growing up.

XIII

Getting Back

Life is about living, not wallowing in self-pity. Life is about getting on with day-to-day business: being with people, sharing, thinking clearly, setting objectives and trying to be happy. Life is about what you do have, not what you don't. So I lost rugby . . . big deal: many people lose much more than that in their lives. I was physically impaired, but not incapacitated by my illness. Through the intervention of those present at Cardiff Arms Park that day and the skill and care of Mr Weekes and his team, I had escaped with my life. I didn't need other people to remind me of that fact, and I was convinced – despite many moments of anger and despair – that I would eventually work most of that pent-up frustration out of my system. Looking back, I think my pride was hurt as much as my psyche. Losing the joy of playing did hit me hard – as did losing the camaraderie in the game and the respect of others. But I had friends and family in my corner who tried to involve me in their lives, who tried to show me that Mervyn Davies the rugby player was only one tiny aspect of Mervyn Davies the man.

I did sink fairly low, but I do not want to give the impression that my life was one continuous downer during the years that followed my brain haemorrhage. The previous chapter detailed some of my distress, but there was a flip side. Going back to work helped me, and I returned to Blyths only six months after my illness struck. I mentioned in the previous chapter some of the people who went out of their way to offer support, and no one did more for me than Len and Norman Blyth. To ease my way back into my work schedule, they gave me a new sales patch away from the valleys, one based in and around Swansea, closer to home. It was a tremendous help that I didn't have to drive too far because my confidence behind the wheel wasn't great. And having an entirely new client base to focus on didn't allow me any time to brood during the working week. Being a man who loved a challenge – and competition – I would dearly like to report that I channelled all my energy into being Blyths' top sales representative, but I didn't. Away from the playing field, in business, I was an easy-going man, happy to build relationships with my customers; I saw them more as friends than as potential signatures on a sales order. Is it unusual for a man to be totally driven in one area of his life whilst a little more laid back in another? Perhaps if I had finished playing rugby at a time of my choosing and not been a victim of circumstance, then I might have channelled that competitive streak into another sphere. Len and Norman showed unwavering loyalty and kindly overlooked my average sales figures upon my return, although having a high-profile recovering invalid on their books didn't do them much harm and many new contacts probably invited me across their threshold out of a sense of curiosity.

There was, of course, for a long time afterwards, one topic of conversation that cropped up wherever I went: my health. 'How are you feeling, Merv?' became the constant soundtrack of my days and I'd say 'fine' and hope I wouldn't trip up in the street. It soon became obvious that the condition that afflicted me had blighted other people's lives too. 'Merv, I had one of them brain haemorrhage things. See?' and then they'd point to their heads as if willing me to see inside their skulls. It became a bit of a war story for me and fellow veterans wounded in the old cranial trench. It felt like there were bloody brain haemorrhages happening everywhere, but I had to better the competition by having lifesaving brain surgery. Beat that, then . . . and here's my scar to prove it! On the whole, people were kind and genuine – though sometimes endearingly insensitive – but it did help having a little bolthole like my local, The Cockett Inn, where I could seek refuge within its beery walls. And it was in the Cockett where I probably felt happiest at that time . . . it was a haven when I needed one most, a place where I was just 'Merv' and not the man who had played and lost his career. It was also a meeting point for a whole cross-section of Swansea society, from lunatics to lawyers, dockers to doctors – in its peculiar way, the Cockett was its own mini-universe.

I maintained my friendships from rugby, especially with the local Swansea boys like Neil Webb and Morry Evans. My visits to St Helens were OK, but I had to bite my tongue a bit when it came to Wales. When Wales won the Grand Slam in 1978 and the team was lauded as 'Phil Bennett's Grand Slam team', I harrumphed and pointed out that it was virtually identical to my bloody Grand Slam team. Luckily, landlord Len Smith and the boys at the Cockett punctured my posturing and spent a discourteous amount of time praising the replacement number 8, Derek Quinnell, as the key that turned a good Welsh team into a great one.

Fast-forward a decade or so and I reached the almost inevitable point when I got sucked back into rugby. What drove me back into my boots? Boredom, probably . . . plus a need to understand this new game that now called itself rugby union. The lineout had changed beyond all recognition and so had the laws around contact; I was itching to discover what effect this had on the forwards. I learnt that a good friend of mine (and fellow Penlan Old Boy) John Schroeffer, a leading coaching adviser with the WRU, was planning to run a coaching course at Swansea University. John is the type of coaching talent that a country like Wales needs. He was an excellent fly-half but desperately unlucky with injury. When he was forced into retirement at a young age, he didn't disappear into the realms of the bitter; he harnessed all his enthusiasm for playing and dived into coaching. His desire was quite infectious. I thought about signing up for a while, wavered, but then my curiosity got the better of me and I decided to get involved. Perhaps it was the nature of the course that appealed most: all us would-be coaches were expected to turn up in tracksuits and get stuck straight in. I remember the frisson of excitement that swept over me as I felt the ball in my hands again and breathed in the sweet smell of freshly mown grass.

Unfortunately, perhaps I was too eager – or too brittle – for my enthusiasm got the better of me and I broke my collarbone. But I had crossed a great divide, and I thought, 'Maybe, just maybe, I might give this coaching lark a go.'

My mind was made up when a fellow trainee coach from Hendy Rugby Club, who'd asked me if I fancied getting involved, contacted me. Hendy, just the wrong side of the Loughor for a Swansea man, is a great South Wales club, one of many that form the bedrock of our game, and the pedigree of players it has produced includes the late Terry Price, the exciting full-back who played union and league in the '60s. If I had stopped and thought about why Hendy wanted me, I might have said no. But I was flattered to be asked and I wanted to try to find that missing Saturday-afternoon buzz, so I agreed.

I can't say I was a natural coach, but I did spend four years in charge, four years in which Hendy enjoyed a fair share of success and of disappointment. My biggest issue was commitment: I expected 100 per cent from my players. Ironic, really, for I was never the most enthusiastic trainer as a player myself – but when someone didn't show up for training, I knew all the excuses in the book, so nothing washed with me.

Lower division teams like Hendy are normally made up from two distinct sorts of player: the older, experienced man dropping down a division to prolong his playing career and the younger, up-and-coming boy looking to move on. Hendy had a terrific reputation as a feeder club for Llanelli, so I thought my efforts might at least scupper the Scarlets' chances at uncovering new talent!

What did I learn about myself as a coach? Well, it is easier to play than to guide from the sidelines. A captain has to lead his team by example, he has to be the alpha male in terms of attitude and intent, but a coach can do precious little once the referee blows for kick-off. It was difficult to keep the playing staff happy: on one hand I wanted to promote youth and let all that raw enthusiasm shine through, but the need to win dictates the playing style – and to secure the win I had to turn to the older and more experienced players. It was these boys who were nigh on impossible to coach: they had enough rugby in their brains to play the game the way they wanted to. The little rebellions, the lack of real influence, left me feeling that the whole coaching experience was vaguely unsatisfying. The lack of commitment to the cause – and the difficulty in raising my best team week-in, week-out – persuaded me to walk away. Coaching might have been easier if I had belonged to a first-class team as an assistant rather than being the main man in charge, and I did speak to current Wales coach, Mike Ruddock (who was then the Swansea coach) about a more influential involvement with Swansea, but nothing really came of our conversations.

I believe that I left it too late to take up coaching. A coach needs to understand what it feels like to play the game: how much a tackle hurts, how small the spaces are, where the pressure points in the scrum materialise. Too many years away from rugby had dulled my rugby senses and I was a dinosaur, there because of an earlier reputation, talking about a game that was ten years out of date.

Coaching had confirmed my previous suspicions: it did not replace or come near to matching the enjoyment I took from playing. I entered into coaching on a personal search to see how different rugby was. And it was very different. When professionalism arrived in the mid-'90s, everything changed, and no one felt that change more than the smaller clubs. Suddenly, everyone wanted paying and the clubs started spending money that they just did not have. It all seemed rather distasteful – but, then again, am I speaking from jealousy? Do I wish I had been paid to play my rugby? Yes. Do I resent the modern-day player who is paid? No. Good luck, lads: fill your boots. At the highest level there are staggering amounts of money available, but one cannot condemn a player for recognising his value and reacting to market forces. One cannot compare the two eras: amateurism and professionalism are so fundamentally different that they should be viewed as two separate games. I believe a good player is a good player in any era, but the culture of rugby has been radically altered since my day. Men of my generation, the men who achieved incredible success in Welsh and British rugby, are sometimes criticised for not putting anything back into the game, but that is mainly down to the nature of amateurism. Most of us wrote books because we wanted to make money, and the ridiculous notion of being an outcast for 10 or 15 years because a player had tried to make the most of his 'fame' whilst he was still relevant, robbed Welsh rugby of a decade of shrewd guidance. By the time we were officially allowed back into the game, few of the younger players would have listened to us anyway. There is one school of thought that all we are good for is harking back to the '70s, which only highlights the trough the game went into in the '80s and '90s. I can genuinely sympathise with the crop of Wales internationals that had to play in our shadow, and I wouldn't have welcomed the sniping from a group of past players, but a few of us spoke out in desperation. Some are happy still to revel in their past exploits, but I honestly long for Wales to enter another Golden Age so they can put arthritic old duffers like me out to grass. At this rate, I'll be crabbing along on my zimmer-frame talking about John Taylor's conversion or Barry John's solitary tackle!

It must have been after the New Zealand tour of 1988 (which I'll discuss more in a later chapter) when this whole Golden Years industry sprang up. John Dawes once said to me that, 'The price of success is the fear of failure.' Now I don't know if that is a Dawes original – it sounds like it – but what is the price of failure? The search for success? Wales is a strange old place, quite backward-looking really, constantly willing to re-invent its perception of the past. Take my hometown, Swansea. Now its most famous son had a few choice words to say about the place, but get off the train today at Swansea station and a visitor would swear they are entering 'Dylan-land'. There is an insatiable need to hide in the past, to shift perspective on what was said and what was achieved, and to cherry-pick the good things. I'm doing it now, regurgitating long-forgotten tales 30 or more years old. But the 1988 tour to New Zealand (and losing 52–3 and 54–9 while there), coupled with a defeat to Romania six months later, was a real kick up the backside for Welsh rugby and the Welsh public. Nobody feared us anymore . . . we might still fight our corner on the European stage, and we went to the southern hemisphere as Triple Crown champions, but the All Blacks – the team Wales measured itself against beyond all others – had moved way, way ahead of us. In the midst of failure, the search for success began, and so the boys who had done it all a decade or so before suddenly found themselves with a willing audience. Just as the old

Arthurian legend tells of the King awaiting his country's call, so it was with us, but all we could do was remind people how good we used to be.

An industry grew up around the nostalgia of the success we had once achieved, and a few years later I climbed on the bandwagon and started giving the occasional after-dinner talk. It's a strange way to spend an evening, standing up at the head of a room and regaling a crowd full of (usually inebriated) rugby players with past experiences. But people seem genuinely interested in what I have to say, because that era shines in the annals of British rugby like no other. Even Scottish, Irish and English audiences are quick to praise the Wales team of the '70s for the way we attacked the game. I assume that we are part of 1970s culture: long-haired men in red, with big sideburns, cutting up the turf with glee. And the comment I most hear today whenever I attend a function is, 'What's happened to Wales?' There is a real desire for Wales to produce a consistently challenging twenty-first-century team. Those performances against England and New Zealand in the last World Cup created huge excitement across Britain. Wales is so embedded in rugby folklore, it is so synonymous with the sport, that people long for us to be up there with the best. But it's not just Gareth, Barry, Willie John or me who feed the need for old stories; the England boys who triumphed in Sydney in November 2003, they'll experience it too. Whatever happens, their exploits are trapped in time, and they are now marked down for evermore in the collective consciousness of the sporting public.

I don't quite know what type of speaker I am; I'm no joker, but I try to talk honestly about what it is like to play for the British Lions and for Wales. I try to capture the sights and sounds, the smell of fear on the pitch. Rugby is such a visceral experience, all about hard physical effort, about incredible emotional highs and draining, despairing lows. I try to tell them what it's like to glance up from a ruck and see Gordon Brown about to come crashing down on my exposed ribs. I talk about the good times, the laughter and the fun of being with the boys. It's an almost childlike happiness . . . and when I talk about the memories, they come to life again in front of my eyes. Riveting stuff, eh? Well, it depends on the age of the audience. The older members who saw me play, or know my story, listen with kind ears but the colts – the youngsters – well, I barely reach them! But that is what being young is all about: being cocksure and insolent and oblivious to the blabbering of an old-timer like me.

I don't spend much time driving around the country talking about my life; it's an occasional occurrence, but an enjoyable one. I still work; I'm still out on the road selling my wares. With some sadness I ended my association with Blyths in 1992, and I knew then that I would not find better bosses. For a short time I worked in finance, but for the last decade I have been self-employed – selling metal protection to industry. It's work I enjoy; I like being with my clients and I like the buzz of reaching my targets. Competition and camaraderie – some challenges are still there to be met.

My children have grown strong and healthy, and I am happily re-married. I lost my father a few years ago, but he played a good and full innings and all my memories of him remain fond. My mother still lives in the house where I grew up and she still sometimes treats me like a little boy. Often she complains that she cannot mow the lawn or finds it difficult bending down to pick up objects, and I have to remind her that I've been struggling with those simple tasks for the last 28 years!

All in all, my life is good. Old friends are close by and I am enjoying my time in the public eye again. There seems to be some big reunion every year or so, but they never get dull despite the same old tales being trundled out. The memories are always quick to return and the feelings of being blessed are strong. Now even the regrets seem dissipated and the 'what ifs' are now 'so whats'. If I could only carry a pint of beer in my left hand without spilling any, then I guess I could call myself contented.

XIV

Keeping the Past

In May 2002, the inaugural Welsh Rugby Hall of Fame dinner was held at the Marriott Hotel, Cardiff. I stood up that night on stage, after John Dawes had said grace, and made the official welcome speech to a room full of esteemed guests. For a moment I was almost tongue-tied, for stretched out before me, seated in and amongst many of Wales' leading businessmen and women, were some of the finest rugby players ever to have graced the game. And they all shared one common denominator: they were Welsh. Suddenly, it hit me: the sheer scale of what our small nation had achieved in rugby. We have treasure in our midst and we were drawn together that evening in celebration of eight decades of rugby excellence. We came to praise, we came to remember . . . we came to honour Welsh rugby's glittering heritage. The following players, chosen from their respective eras, were the first inductees:

> 1930s: Harry Bowcott and Vivian Jenkins
> 1940s: Jack Matthews
> 1950s: Bleddyn Williams
> 1960s: Clive Rowlands and Delme Thomas
> 1970s: Gareth Edwards
> 1980s: Ieuan Evans
> 1990s: Neil Jenkins

Wonderful players, each capturing the unique highs – and sometimes deep lows – of a particular decade. Each man stands out in the annals of the game. Harry and Viv were both London Welsh men and played in the first Wales team ever to win at Twickenham. Jack – the doctor who ran to my side all those years ago in Cardiff – played in the Victory Internationals after the war, just as my father had done. Bleddyn was one of eight brothers to play for Cardiff; he captained Wales five times and won each match. Clive . . . well, Clive covered just about every role a man could have in Welsh rugby: captain, coach, president. Delme – the only forward to be honoured that night, I should add – was a model of Scarlet steel and led his mighty Llanelli to a memorable win over the 1972 All Blacks. Gareth's many achievements are known and appreciated right across the rugby world. Ieuan was a beacon of try-scoring success in harsher times, and Neil – the great survivor of the modern era – was the first man to break the 1,000-point barrier in international rugby. Not bad for a small nation stuck out on the western limb of Europe. Not bad for a little land famed for sheep, song and rain. But looking around the room that evening and seeing who else was present, I realised that we could have inducted three, four, five or even six players of similar excellence from each decade alongside them. Such is the legacy of the rugby men that we produce.

The event was organised and staged by the Welsh Rugby Former International Players Association (in conjunction with our sponsor, Honda). I was speaking in my official capacity as chairman of the association, and it is a role that has given me immense pleasure over recent years. The Hall of Fame dinner was the first of many high-profile gatherings that we have subsequently organised, gatherings that included celebrations of the 1976 and 1978 Grand Slam winning sides, and the 1988 Triple Crown-winning team. We have inducted captains, number 8s and half-backs into the metaphorical Hall: each occasion recognises a unique aspect of Welsh rugby and we are effectively building a living museum that chronicles the importance of the union game to the people, and the heritage, of Wales. If we are going to wallow in the past – as we are often accused of doing – then let's do it properly; let's give rugby a platform, a museum to mark its dominant place within Welsh society.

Of course, this all sounds like a black-tie jolly for old friends, but there is far more substance to these events than just taking a stroll down memory lane. The Welsh Rugby Former International Players Association (WRFIPA) is the fundraising arm for the Welsh Rugby International Players Benevolent Association (WRIPBA). The key objective of our dinners (apart from a cracking night out) is usually an auction of rugby-related memorabilia – or sponsor prizes – so that we can raise money for ex-international players who have fallen on hard times. The WRIPBA is a registered charity with a remit to aid 'the relief of poverty and hardship of Welsh international rugby players and former players, or their families and dependants'. There are men in Wales who once represented their country and who are now suffering. The physical effects of rugby are usually long-term and painful, often felt in the back and the knees, or around the hip or in the hands. It has taken time, and a considerable amount of hard work, to establish ourselves as a viable working charity, but we are slowly raising our profile with ex-players and sponsors, with existing rugby institutions and with the public at large in Wales.

People involved in rugby tend to care. They care about their friends and their colleagues. Time often diminishes old rivalries, and words or punches that might have once been exchanged on the pitch can provide the basis for an unlikely friendship. There remains a tremendous sense of camaraderie and spirit amongst former players that endures across the years; we are part of an extended family that tries to keep its arms wide open. For years, the WRU has done exceptional work in the field of looking after those who have fallen – especially in cases where severe injuries occur – through the work of their own Charitable Trust. But the WRU Charitable Trust caters for all of Welsh rugby; we want to concentrate solely on former international players and we can only hope that we achieve half as much as they – and other charitable groups like the Wooden Spoon Society – have achieved.

The journey from idea to actuality is a long and often difficult one, and the people who helped shape the WRFIPA are a Llanelli-born businessman called Peter Thomas and two of my old international teammates, J.J. Williams and Allan Martin. Peter's involvement began when he did some fundraising work with a children's charity called SPARKS, which involved raising money from limited-edition prints signed by members of the 1974 Lions party and sold at auction. Through his involvement with leading business names and his relationship with ex-Lions players like the late Gordon Brown, Peter went on to meet and work with one of his Stradey heroes, J.J. They recognised that certain ex-players needed support and thought if they could establish a fundraising association that brought together high-profile ex-players, leading corporate figures and members of the public with a real interest in rugby nostalgia, then maybe they might find a way to help others. The real breakthrough came when Honda agreed to be a major sponsor: the WRFIPA already had strong rugby and corporate contacts but now it had the backing to match its purpose.

I came on board as chairman in 2001 because the Association sought an ex-player who had scaled the heights with Wales, had achieved much with the Lions and – let's be frank about this – had also experienced significant physical misfortune. In many ways I represented the hard fact that men who appear physically strong and fit sometimes break down. It took 25 years for it to work in my favour, but my brain haemorrhage could, at last, be put to good use!

However, there was another goal for WRFIPA to aim for: we wanted a room somewhere, dedicated to all those men who had once taken up the call and represented their country. England has one: it's called ERIC's (England Rugby International's Club) Room in Twickenham and it is only accessible to those players who have worn the red rose in an international match. For years, the powerbrokers of English rugby seemed light years ahead of their British counterparts in all manner of ways. The vision they had to fully realise rugby's growing commercial potential was evident in the way they transformed Twickenham from a windy, ugly old stadium into the heart and home of English rugby. When Cardiff trumped west London with its own splendid piece of modern sporting theatre – the Millennium Stadium – we knew the WRFIPA had found the perfect venue for our room. England had ERIC's, we wanted WREX (Welsh Rugby Ex-players). Getting it, however, was an entirely different matter.

The Millennium Stadium is, without question, the finest large-scale, all-purpose venue in the UK. It is a magnificent setting for sports events and music concerts, and really is the jewel in the capital's crown. I admit, like many of my countrymen, that when I first heard of the intention to build a state-of-the-art 75,000-seat stadium in the heart of Cardiff, I thought the ambition outstripped the reality. I thought that a project of such magnitude could never be finished in time for the 1999 Rugby World Cup and I feared its unfinished state would make Wales the laughing stock of the sporting world. But it was delivered on time and soon set the standard for sporting venues in the UK. It is difficult to remember the old stadium these days, and those who wailed about ripping up the past and stamping over our history when it was torn down now shed few tears for that lumbering old girl. Cardiff Arms Park – or the National Stadium to give it its official name – was a cold, unwelcoming place. What made it special was the rugby played on its green turf and the crowds singing in its stands or out on the open terrace. The Millennium Stadium is far, far superior. The immediacy of the place, the way the seats bank high but never away from the field, is its most striking aspect. And a roof . . . well there's a fine thing; imagine shutting the rain out on international day! As a spectator, one never feels that far from the action. All I can say is that I wish that I had played there. There is magic in the air in every game and I still believe that the Welsh rugby team has not yet learnt how to deal with playing well in such an awesome space. The Stadium is something that Cardiff should be rightly proud of, but, to this day, despite the rock concerts and the soccer internationals, despite Cup finals and play-off games, the Millennium Stadium is still not being used to its full – and quite fantastic – potential.

There is a fair amount of heated discussion in Wales about who should own and run the Millennium Stadium. The WRU guard it jealously but the cost of building and running it is having a draining – some say disastrous – effect. Many believe that the WRU would be better off selling the Stadium, taking the money to tackle its substantial debts, and concentrating purely on running rugby. There are consortiums circling who want to realise the venue's full potential but other influential groups believe it would be dangerous to pass what was envisaged primarily as a rugby venue onto non-rugby people. It does fill me with sadness to see such a great space being underused. The Millennium Stadium should be at the very heart of Cardiff life. There should be shops and restaurants, bars and boutiques, cafés and crèches open all along its concourse. Both locals and visitors ought to be encouraged to come in and share the experience. It should be the new home of Welsh rugby – and not just present-day Welsh rugby, but also Welsh rugby of the past. Newlands in Cape Town houses an excellent rugby museum that contextualises the importance of rugby union in South Africa's sporting past. Welsh rugby needs this kind of home too . . . we need a museum where the story of Welsh rugby and all its glorious ups and downs can be presented for posterity's sake. We have the perfect venue. We have the perfect story. We need to bring them together.

But as well as a museum, we at the WRFIPA felt that we needed a dedicated space where former Welsh internationals could gather, meet and reminisce. No city embraces international day quite like Cardiff. The crowds gather early in the mornings and stay late into the night and because the Stadium is slap bang in the heart of the capital, there is no need for that horrid canter from the pubs and restaurants before kick-off like there is at Twickenham, Murrayfield or Lansdowne Road. The pubs and bars in Cardiff absorb thousands upon thousands of people, stoking them up from opening time and coughing them out some 30 minutes before the match starts. When I was playing for Wales in Cardiff, the short walk from the Angel Hotel was an exhilarating (but rather intimidating) affair and we players seldom reached our destination without being pawed and pulled about by well-intentioned – though also well-oiled – fans. If you played international rugby for Wales, then there is a strong likelihood that someone will remember your face and that means that international day can still be a daunting experience. What a lot of ex-players want to be able to do is go up to the game with their wife or their girlfriend, their son or daughter, their friend or colleague and enjoy the day without being victim of a furious bout of backslapping (or in J.J.'s case, abuse from disgruntled Pontypridd fans!). If I sound overly sensitive, then forgive me; nothing pleases me more than chatting about rugby, but being in a public bar, warily surveying the swarming crowds, fighting the constant intrusion and trying to have a conversation with my wife or my mate, is not the best way to spend an international day.

After an endless round of lobbying, pleading, backtracking, false dawns and fevered discussion, the WRU finally allowed WRFIPA access to a room within the bowels of the Stadium. We were granted a lease to use a space that was, and in all likelihood would still be, standing empty. But we could only have the room provided that we sponsored, decorated, furnished, ran and controlled it all ourselves. To set it up we needed backing, and here another ex-Wales and ex-Llanelli man – Phil May – came into his own by helping us secure the support of Diageo, a leading international premium drinks business. Diageo own well-known brands including Guinness, Smirnoff and Johnnie Walker, and their backing has helped propel the WRFIPA forward.

WREX is a marvellous place to be on international day. The walls are filled with photos of Welsh teams throughout the ages. There is a Hall of Fame board marking out certain individuals' exceptional achievements and there are areas that commemorate the Grand Slam and Triple Crown-winning sides. The bar (of course!) and kitchen help to give WREX its appeal, but without the men who gather there it would be just another room, sunk in the depths of the Stadium. What brings us together is our shared experience, and it does not matter how many caps a player won in his international career: if he crossed the touchline and took the field in a capped match, then providing he has his invite, he, and a guest, can use WREX to relax, unwind or just catch up with old friends. It can be a place of great laughter, too: I remember on one occasion a group of lads, Allan Martin amongst them, all lined up at the bar wearing their Barbarian ties, waiting to taunt Clive and Norman Gale – two men who never joined that exclusive club. What WRFIPA does is put a badge on our achievements. Nothing matches the honour for playing for one's country, and an hour or two spent in WREX, catching up and sharing a drink, reminds us all just how special – and fortunate – we once were.

There are still obstacles that we must overcome. It is important that if the WRFIPA is to be seen as an inclusive body, open to all who played for Wales, so we must break down the barriers between then and now. It is an organisation created to cater for all players from all eras. The fact that J.J. and I play a key role does not make it a '70s Old Boys club: Cliff Morgan, our president, is an outstanding figure from the '50s. But we must get the younger players involved – the boys who played in the '80s and '90s, retired players from the current generation. Only when we've achieved that will we show that the heritage of Welsh rugby is all-encompassing and not restricted to one or two eras. I don't know if this will happen but I am encouraged when I see the involvement of a man like former national captain, Paul Thorburn, and I only hope that other high-profile ex-players will join in and share the good work. All I can do is commend what the WRFIPA has given me in terms of personal enjoyment and satisfaction: it feels as if the players are finally taking control of their own experiences. We are working together to build a citadel of achievement, a place where all our collected memories can live on.

Hopefully we'll also make life a little easier for the men who wrecked their knees, or stuffed up their shoulders playing for their country. And we'll ease the burdens on their families too. We too easily forget the toll international duty takes on the waiting wives and children – the Saturday afternoons on the sidelines and watching Dad go through his painful recovery on the days that follow matchday. Playing international rugby affects many people – not just the man who actually took part. We hope we can help where help is needed. Not every player who played for Wales enjoyed the breaks – or opportunities – that came to some after their playing days were over, just because they were famous. Most played their matches, saw out their career with their clubs and then carried on working. Not all got involved with the media or were offered positions because of who they were. Is it right that some men should suffer now because they gave so much of their physical self to a sport 10, 20, 30-plus years ago? Is it right that players who gave so much pleasure – and pain – to a watching nation now languish in uncertainty? And rugby men are proud men, reluctant to ask for support . . . but if they must seek help, then surely it is better that they seek it from their own kind?

Returning to that night in May 2002, the memories now feel more poignant because Viv Jenkins, full-back, Lion, sportswriter, left us in 2004 at the magnificent age of 92. In a sad, yet strangely fitting way, that night can now never be repeated: the team we selected for our first Hall of Fame dinner has broken up. But the memories linger and the photographs are proof that great men from eight different decades once shared the spotlight together. That is why the WRFIPA matters. We are intent on being the keepers of the past, so we can use the memories of better times to help the same men who once made them. That is what Peter, J.J., Allan, I and countless others are working so willingly towards.

XV

Pub Talk

Who are the greatest players to have played rugby? Well, there's a provocative question; hence the name of this particular chapter – Pub Talk. Let's take some time out for a spot of punditry, let's pull up a metaphorical stool, sit around and pit one player's merits and attributes against another's. This is my book, therefore my rules apply and my criterion for selection is simple: I must have played with, against, or witnessed my chosen 30 in action. What I'll do before I begin the selection process, however, is create a level playing field for these superstars to operate on. So we will take a giant leap of imagination and believe that all the players coming into this imaginary game are 'professionals' and have benefited from the modern training methods and indulgences that swathe the twenty-first-century rugby player. Call me old-fashioned (please), but I still believe a good player back in my day would make a good player today. I might fiddle around with traditional positions such as tight-head and loose-head prop, right and left wing, and the back row, but these are the men I would pay good money to go and see. Let the debate begin: two teams comprising the best of Britain and Ireland against a World XV. I'll start on home soil.

Full-Back
Scotland have produced two great full-backs in the last 30 years in Andy Irvine and Gavin Hastings. Andy was a supreme footballer, a

191

wonderful strike runner and possessed an astute kicking game. Gavin wasn't quite as exciting roaring up from the back, but he was solid, dependable and ever accurate with his boot. What really made both men shine in their respective eras was their ability to captain a side from a notoriously difficult position. Hastings' record for his country and the British Isles speaks volumes for the respect he got from his teammates. Few men are chosen to lead the Lions, those who are must earn the honour. Tom Kiernan, a massive figure in Irish rugby, also led the Lions from full-back and was very much an established star when I first arrived on the international scene. Other short-listed candidates for the number 15 jersey include Jason Robinson and Gareth Thomas, but they are not specialist full-backs; they represent the modern-day utility back who can play anywhere across the back three. Good players all, but none can claim the full-back berth in my home XV. That choice for me is easy, arguably the easiest decision (along with scrum-half) that I have to make. I choose **J.P.R. Williams**.

Throughout the course of this book, I have written about the success I enjoyed with London Welsh, Wales and the British Lions . . . and much of that success was built on the rock that stood behind me in each one of those three teams. I doubt there has ever been a more influential full-back in international rugby than J.P.R.; certainly not in British rugby. Perhaps he was fortunate to hit the game at a time when the laws governing kicking changed, transforming full-back play from a defensive, covering role into a more attacking one. Good job for us, and a good job for J.P.R. too – his kicking was never the strongest feature of his game. It didn't have to be; his running and his bravery (going forward and in the tackle), and his sheer bloody-minded determination to win, set him head and shoulders above all other British full-backs.

Wings

Gerald Davies flies in on one wing. I have gone on record as saying he is the finest player that I ever played alongside, and I have not seen a better British wing three-quarter. He epitomised the flair and derring-do of Welsh – and British – rugby in the halcyon days of the 1970s. His side step, his swerve and his ability to ghost tight to the sideline were touched with genius. He was never the biggest player on the park but his agility and rugby brain more than made up for his lack of bulk. Wing play nowadays is more about size and strength, and that is why men like Ben Cohen do so well. And I agree that there is something beneficial about having a strapping lad, built like a number 8, out wide. But in my team I want wingers who can soar into space on jet-engine heels. J.J. Williams comes tantalisingly close to inclusion, especially when I recall the way he played for the Lions in 1974, as does John Bevan from an earlier Lions tour. In many ways, John was the forerunner of the big aggressive winger, and he made a terrific impact when he first burst onto the scene. Another Welsh winger who is a little lost in time is Maurice Richards, a clinical finisher who enjoyed many a fine day in the red shirt.

From the other home nations I might muse over the Irish boy, Simon Geoghegan, but his meteoric ability too often seemed checked by unfortunate injury. Jason Robinson gets close for his speed off the mark and dazzling footwork. However, the final wing position is a tough choice between two old adversaries, Ieuan Evans and Rory Underwood, and a much admired former teammate David Duckham.

Ieuan's career is remarkable in the modern game and I feel he would have been a staple in the Grand Slam winning teams of the 1970s if he had been born a generation earlier. What I liked about his play was his uncanny ability to know exactly where the try-line was. He scored a record number of tries for his country during a period that saw both success and strife. He featured in three Lions' tours ('89, '93 and '97) winning two ('89 and '97) and returned from horrendous injury on more than one occasion. He captained Wales impressively from a difficult field position and deservedly became a much-loved figure in the game. But he just misses out on my team . . . and Ieuan, I swear, your omission has nothing to do with you being a Scarlet.

Rory Underwood played for an England side that was often criticised for having no sense of adventure. His try-scoring feats counter that particular criticism. Again, here was another winger who instinctively knew where the try-line was and the sight of Rory taking off on an arcing run, skinning his opponent on the outside, was perfect proof of what a great winger with guts and balance can bring to any side. Welshmen like to point to his lapse in February 1993 when he lost out in a one-on-one race with Ieuan. But two years later Rory returned to the scene of his famous blunder and produced a virtuoso performance, scoring two tries and helping England to a comfortable win. Rory gets close – probably closer than Ieuan – but he doesn't get in.

Whenever I played with or against him, I found **David Duckham** to be a splendid player. He had all the attributes a first-class winger needs to succeed at the highest level: strength of character, clarity of thought, speed of foot . . . in many ways, he was one of a kind. He and Gerald would book-end my back line nicely, just as they did in New Zealand in 1971.

Centres

As a playing partnership, the fulcrum in defence and attack, my centres have to complement each other. My inside-centre requires excellent hands, good marshalling skills and an ability to think about the shape and the structure of the match as it unfolds around him. The outside-centre should have a spark of creativity, a quick turn of speed and a killer eye for a gap. Looking down at the pantheon of greats who have occupied the centre-pairings in British and Irish rugby over the last three or four decades, I could happily nominate two from Jerry Guscott, John Dawes, Allan Bateman, Keith Jarrett, Ray Gravell, Steve Fenwick, Ian McGeechan, Jim Renwick, Scott Gibbs and Will Carling.

Carling and Gibbs go for the inside-centre spot just as they did in New Zealand in 1993 when the bullocking Welshman shocked the armchair pundits and usurped the English captain in the Test side. I am close to reversing that decision for my team because I think that Carling suffers the same fate as John Dawes in terms of how his playing ability is assessed. He was, primarily, England captain and was brought in to the national set-up to do a tough job at a tender age. He grew into the role and improved massively as a player, and he remains, like Dawes, one of the most underrated British backs to have graced the sport. But he just misses out.

My two centres are two Irishmen: **Brian O'Driscoll** and **Mike Gibson**. I like O'Driscoll: I like his drive, his attitude, his wonderful ability to be brave and take the game to the opposition. He is a superb player and carries the hopes of Irish (and perhaps Lions) rugby with him. There are no better shoulders for his nation's weight to rest on.

Mike Gibson is rightly regarded as an all-time great. He was a fantastic footballer who possessed nothing less than magic in his game. He could run, he could kick, he could think and he could act decisively. What a wonderful addition Mike Gibson would have been to the Wales back line of my day . . . something we saw a tantalising glimpse of in New Zealand in 1971, when he slotted in so smoothly with Edwards, John, Dawes, Davies, Bevan and Williams. Gibson's longevity also deserves praise – five Lions tours is an impressive feat – and his dedication to his rugby paid dividends: he has been afforded the twin accolades of 'rugby legend' and, arguably, Ireland's greatest player.

There is a very powerful case to select a Carling–Guscott axis in the centre but for me Driscoll and Gibson shade it – just. There can be no sleep for my starting pair, however, with the other two breathing down their necks from the bench.

Outside-Half

This remains the greatest source of debate in the Welsh game; who is the best outside-half of them all? Well, there are the usual suspects lined up – all with impressive playing CVs – Cliff Morgan, David Watkins, Barry John, Phil Bennett, Jonathan Davies. It is difficult to split that lot but the Welsh don't have dibs on the number-one number 10. That is why I shall risk exile and look outside Wales for my key playmaker. And I don't have to look very far. He is English, he is young, he is magnificent and he has the world at his feet. His name is: **Jonny Wilkinson**.

There is something very special about the way that young man plays rugby. Even if we ignore his outstanding kicking game, we are still left with a player who can run, who can pass, tackle and make the correct decision 99 times out of 100. His inclusion – and blossoming – in the England XV affords his coach the luxury of picking a dynamic, interchangeable back three. Wilkinson's player selection – in terms of who he brings in off his shoulder – is supreme; he reads the game better than any other outside-half I can name. His aura, too, forces the opposition to check their play and that slight hesitation in defence usually creates gaps for other Englishmen to exploit. My one bone of contention with young Jonny is his tackling: ease off, son. You are going to rewrite all the record books in rugby so let your back row and centres put in those crunching hits. I have criticised certain fly-halves in the past for not tackling their weight but a Jonny Wilkinson tackle is unlike any other fly-half tackle: it is an explosion of energy. When he is fit, he is the most focused – and important – player in the British game. The appeal he holds for youngsters cannot be underestimated. I hope the world of rugby enjoys the unfolding tale of Jonny Wilkinson for many years to come. It promises to be quite some ride.

Scrum-Half

One man takes the number 9 shirt and he is, of course: **Gareth Edwards**.

Terry Holmes possessed a rumbustious physical game, Robert Jones was a master technician, Rob Howley bullet-fast, and Gary Armstrong a real battler . . . but Gareth had all their qualities and more. His legend looms large over the Welsh game and he has produced three or four of the sweetest moments ever witnessed on the field. Ironically, the closest competitor to Gareth in the Mervyn Davies Home XV is the man who spent much of his playing career in his stocky little shadow: Ray Hopkins. Sorry, Chico . . . yet again, Gareth gets the nod.

Props

I'll skirt around who should play tight and who should play loose and base my selection on the two men who best exemplify the dark art of propping. It is, arguably, the most radically altered position in the union game. Props are now expected to rampage through the loose, have soft hands and an eye for a gap. Modern-day exponents like Phil Vickery and Tom Smith are good examples of the way the role has been redefined, and Wales has a good stock of young, mobile props. But I still believe a prop's first priority should be his traditional front-row duties. It is all well and good popping up on the wing in support of the backs but it is a prop's effectiveness in the scrum and in the tight play that influences my choices. My list includes a cauldron's worth of cast-iron Celts: Sandy Carmichael, Ray McLoughlin, Ian McLauchlan, Syd Millar and Graham Price. But in the front row, the two men supplying the grunt in my Home XV are two proud Englishmen: **Fran Cotton** and **Jason Leonard**.

With a sheepish glance to my old mate Graham Price by way of an apology, Fran is the finest prop I ever played with. He might not have been the best scrum technician and he certainly wasn't fast in the loose, but he was durable, determined and destructive. His weight, and his jutting jaw, epitomised his strength, and he needed every ounce of it to survive – and ultimately conquer – the most sapping position of all. Off the pitch, Fran was – and remains – excellent company. He is an articulate, thoughtful man whose intelligence extends far beyond what happens in and around rugby. By all accounts, he was a hugely impressive manager of the Lions in 1997 and a worthy heir to Doug Smith and Alun Thomas, who paved the way for good tour management all those years before.

Jason Leonard is the arch survivor of the modern game, a man who began his career as a good-time amateur and finished it as the consummate professional. He could play tight or loose, and few deserved to get his hands on the Webb Ellis trophy as much as the affable Harlequins veteran. To play international rugby over 100 times – and to do it in the front row – demonstrates huge ability and heart. I also like the stories of Jason seeking out his opposite number for a beer and a chat after each match. He does feel like a throwback to our more sociable times, but he remains a survivor, which illustrates the true pro that he is. Cotton and Leonard together: two of England's canniest front-row practitioners . . . pushing in unison.

Hooker

My hooker must be a firebrand, an aggressive bundle of non-stop action with a fair bit of the verbals thrown in for good measure. Bobby Windsor was the best hooker I played with, although John Pullin and Jeff Young also had admirable qualities. One player I do like, a very underrated player in my opinion, is Jonathan Humphreys. Like Ieuan Evans, he captained Wales through stormy times, but he always led his country with genuine pride and passion. His Indian Summer at Bath made very interesting viewing and I feel Jonathan has a long and successful coaching career ahead of him, should he decide to take that route. But Jonathan just misses out on this occasion – as do Bobby, John and Jeff. My hooker, my choice to stand tall between Cotton and Leonard, is: **Keith Wood**.

What I most admired about Keith Wood was his relentless pursuit of the cause. He overcame injury, loss of form and club disappointments to give his all for his country and his teammates when it was required. He reached his zenith with the winning Lions in 1997 when, as the talismanic figure in the scrum and in the loose, he became the pulsing heart of the whole squad. Few players epitomise drive and desire like the charismatic Irishman and he would be a worthy addition to any team from any era.

Locks

Into the boiler room and the candidates loom as large in my reckoning as they did on the field: Willie John McBride, Brian Price, Delme Thomas, Bill Beaumont, Geoff Wheel, Allan Martin, Robert Norster. All big men, all big match players, but they are left in the shadows of two of the best rugby men ever produced by these isles: **Martin Johnson** and **Gordon Brown**.

As well as being the undisputed ace player in my pack, Martin Johnson is also my captain. He is the consummate rugby animal and is a player after my own heart. There is little Martin Johnson would ask others to do without being prepared to do it first himself. As a lock, he is ruthlessly efficient, deploying his phenomenal strength to batter and subdue opponents. Once he was a furious young man whose temper could be a liability to those around him, but he learnt to channel that aggression, to harness its primal force and put it to the collective good. As a leader he stands without parallel, skippering the Lions, England and Leicester to the highest honours in the game. Martin Johnson would be the first name on my British XV team sheet because he sets the physical and psychological standards that other players have to strive to reach.

Gordon Brown, baby-faced and strong-boned is a much-missed friend. As a lineout forward he was big, athletic, strong and utterly fearless, as he needed to be to conquer Colin Meads. The second row is such an important part of the team, and I believe my two choices – Johnson and Brown – would have the sound and the fury, the balls and the brains, the guts and the gumption to sweep all other contenders aside.

Flankers

I played with some of the best back-row forwards of them all. John Taylor and Dai Morris were certainly two of Wales' finest flankers – they had to be to keep Tony Gray out of the national team – and they made my life in the red shirt a lot easier. Tony Neary was another talented wing-forward and desperately unlucky not to play in the Lions Test side of 1974, although another member of that squad, Roger Uttley, performed splendidly and contributed significantly to the best pack I ever played in. Modern-day contenders include Richard Hill – England's biggest unsung hero – and Neil Back, a man whose ability overcame the problem of his size. And Simon Easterby is developing nicely for Ireland, as is the rest of the Irish pack. But my two flankers of choice are: **Lawrence Dallaglio** and **Fergus Slattery**.

I like Dallaglio because he is bullish, arrogant and full of unwavering self-belief. He always stands tall on the field and seems to view each match, each confrontation, as a test of his manhood. The jury might be out on his captaincy – Johnson's void remains a huge one to fill – and I am inclined to think that Dallaglio operates better without the burden of leadership – but his ambition for Wasps, England and the Lions pours from him like sweat and there was no way he could ever turn down the invitation to lead his country when it came. He has played the majority of his rugby at number 8, but he is versatile enough to pack down on the blindside (as he has done when required throughout his career). The choice between Dallaglio and Hill is exceptionally tight, but Lawrence's prominence as a ball carrier and his dynamism around the field swings selection in his favour.

On the other flank, I have to go for Fergus Slattery ahead of John

Taylor. In game after game, Fergus was primed and launched like an exocet missile from the back of the scrum, and there have been few players who possessed his fury and competitive spirit. I discovered on two tours that Fergus had to be the best at everything he attempted: from singing on the tour bus to scything down opposing outside-halves. I much preferred playing with him than against him – joining his charge rather than stopping it – and would pick him willingly in any selection I had to make.

Number 8

Who should wear my old shirt? Do I go for one of the men who came before me, like the late, great Alun Pask? Should I look at the two men who gave me the biggest run-around of my career: Andy Ripley and Ken Goodall? Would I be best served selecting from the era of the English juggernaut and pick the truculent Dean Richards? Or should I opt for the boy who happens to be my godson – Scott Quinnell?

I'll cut the choice down to two: Ken and Scott. As I stated earlier, Goodall set the standard of what great international number 8 play was about and he would have gone to New Zealand ahead of me in 1971. It was my good fortune that he went north, leaving the way clear for me. If one had to compare our games then I would say that Ken was a better ball user and I the better ball winner. But I watched him play and I learnt from him, and I still regard him as one of the finest northern hemisphere number 8s.

Scott Quinnell burst onto the international scene in 1994 when he scored a stunning solo try against France. It was a forward's try, second only to the one I saw Ian Kirkpatrick score in the Second Test at Lancaster Park in 1971. Scott's try had the hair standing up on the back of my neck and, by God, I wish I had had a charge like that when I played. Throughout his international career, Scott seemed to be the only Welsh forward who was willing – and able – to make hard yardage with the ball in his hands. Going to Wigan and league was a sensible move and it helped him get fit, which benefited Wales – and Graham Henry – on his eventual return. Without allowing any bias to interfere, and admitting that I am a little envious of the attributes he has as a number 8 forward, I select **Scott Quinnell** to be the rudder of my pack.

Here it is, then – the Mervyn Davies British and Irish XV.

15. J.P.R. Williams (Wales)
14. Gerald Davies (Wales)
13. Mike Gibson (Ireland)
12. Brian O'Driscoll (Ireland)
11. David Duckham (England)
10. Jonny Wilkinson (England)
9. Gareth Edwards (Wales)
1. Fran Cotton (England)
2. Keith Wood (Ireland)
3. Jason Leonard (England)
4. Martin Johnson (England) captain
5. Gordon Brown (Scotland)
6. Lawrence Dallaglio (England)
7. Fergus Slattery (Ireland)
8. Scott Quinnell (Wales)

Six Englishmen, four Welshmen, four Irishmen and a Scot . . . and each one a Lion. It is a mix of the old and the recent, and therefore my coach must span both eras, which is why I pick **Ian McGeechan**. Why choose Geech ahead of coaching luminaries like Carwyn James, John Dawes and Clive Woodward? Well, Geech has a wonderful perception of how the game is played and his man-management skills are exceptionally astute. He was also clever enough to move with the times and, being a players' coach, he never allowed himself to get bogged down in set patterns and plays. His tenure in charge of Scotland wasn't easy; the raw materials he had to work with often failed him. But his guidance of the Lions in 1989, 1993 and 1997 proved his coaching credentials. Lions tours are never easy to run; grown men can pout and sulk like children, but McGeechan's success ratio is two out of three and it signifies the way his players respond to his call. I'd take that track record for the man I'd entrust my boys to.

And what of the opposition? Let's see what I can conjure up!

Full-Back

Just as J.P.R. stands like a colossus over British full-backs, one man has the same stature as full-back in my World XV: **Serge Blanco**. Pierre Villepreux, André Joubert and Christian Cullen all had wonderful playing qualities but none could match Blanco as an out-and-out entertainer. As a player, I always enjoyed playing against the French because I never knew what they were capable of: they could either play like heroes or flounder like a bunch of dopes. Blanco's unpredictability was beguiling. On his day, he was one of the brightest talents on the world stage. His audacity and his sense of adventure were the key to his success, and when the mood was with him, he was a joy to behold.

Wings

My wingers pick themselves and I defy anyone to select better: **David Campese** and **Jonah Lomu**. Campo had much of the Barry John about him: a marvellous, unpredictable talent that had crowds clinging to their seats in anticipation. In some ways, he was the first – and arguably still the best – of the southern hemisphere showmen . . . hitch-kicking and dummying his way to rugby superstardom. His mischievous spirit is still prevalent, especially when it comes to Pommie-bashing, but it's all good fun and part of the add-ons that now market the global game.

If Campo was a superstar, how do we assess Jonah Lomu? For a start, he sometimes carried New Zealand in the mid- to late-'90s and made them appear a better side than they actually were. His monstrous presence terrified opponents and his destruction of England in the 1995 World Cup finals filled nine-tenths of the rugby world with utter joy. Credit must be given to the individual – or individuals – who saw this giant thundering around in the back row and decided to re-assign him to the wing. In doing so, they changed the course of rugby history and unleashed the most potently destructive force who ever set foot on a field.

Jonah's quest now does not centre upon rugby but on a personal battle for health and fitness. His kidney problems are well documented and as one ex-player who saw illness blight his career to another, I hope Jonah finds good health and peace of mind. But whereas I might be regretfully remembered as the man who crumpled to the earth, Jonah Lomu will forever be known as the 'freak' that trampled over half of Will Carling's England one scintillating day in South Africa.

Centres

An easy choice . . . two men who would form a dream centre-partnership: **Phillipe Sella** and **Tim Horan**. Sella was tall and rangy with a penetrating burst of speed, a big crunching tackle and an almost indestructible essence that put him in the French side on over 100 occasions. Inside him would be Tim Horan, the thinking-man's rugby player. He helped to guide the Aussies to glory in the Millennium Stadium eight years after first tasting the ultimate rugby success, and there are not many players who can point to two World Cup-winner's medals on their CV. He won 80 caps for his country and was absolutely vital in the establishment of Australia as the leading southern hemisphere nation of recent times.

Outside-Half

So far, so easy . . . two Australians, two Frenchmen and a New Zealander all selected from the mid-1980s to the late '90s: a decade when the southern hemisphere seized the initiative from the north. But choosing my outside-half becomes a little more complicated. Two wonderful place kickers come into contention: New Zealander Grant Fox and Diego Dominguez – the little Argentinean who helped take Italy into the Six Nations. Two Australians with two vastly different playing styles – Mark Ella and Stephen Larkham – also enter my reckoning. Ella was another naturally gifted performer who deserved greater success than he enjoyed. Larkham isn't everybody's cup of tea as a fly-half, but the man is a proven match-winner. When I think about France and contenders from the boys in blue, I automatically think of Thomas Castaignede and the day he obliterated Wales at Wembley. I remember that match and still shudder . . . it was the only time I ever walked out on my nation in disgust as that little magician made monkeys of the Welsh boys.

However, my outside-half is another champion antipodean:

Michael Lynagh. Not a darter or a dasher but a man who never hurried, was never rushed and always appeared to be calmness personified. Lynagh and Horan were the precision part of the smooth-running Australian machine and their work together is an example to all young players of how an inside-centre and his stand-off should dove-tail. He wasn't a bad goal kicker, either!

Scrum-Half

Joost van der Westhuizen played some Herculean matches for South Africa in the mid-1990s and was one of the tournament stars when the hosts memorably won the World Cup. Fabien Galthie improved with age and wore the mantle of French captain well; he was part of the new, focused France that appears to be far more consistent and professional, harnessing their natural flair and aggressive forward power towards a more clear and measured purpose. His '70s predecessor, little Jacques Fouroux, also made a huge impression on French – and Five Nations – rugby. Nick Farr-Jones of Australia and David Kirk of New Zealand led their nations with aplomb. But the man I select is a man I had my fair share of battles with: **Sid Going** of New Zealand.

Difficult man, Sid: tough to play against, tougher to know. He caused us a fair few problems in 1971, so much so that Carwyn had to re-think our game plan to contain him. Derek Quinnell did a mighty job on Going to quell his blindside breaks but choosing one player to effectively man-mark an opponent shows what kind of threat that man posed. Going played like an extra back-row forward and craved the physical stuff more than any scrum-half I have seen. I have plenty of respect for Sid Going, and, much as Gareth did for Wales, he cast a giant shadow over New Zealand scrum-half play.

Props

I could cheat in my World XV front row and include Graham Price because he was born in Alexandria and I feel bad for leaving him out of my British and Ireland XV – but I won't. I don't have much detailed knowledge of the props I played against and will therefore rely on the words of men who reported back from the front line;

based on those reports, I select **Ken Gray** of New Zealand and **Hannes Marais** of South Africa.

One cannot overstate just how dominant the All Blacks pack of 1971 was. It was built on supreme scrummaging power, ruthless rucking, immense mauling and ram-raiding lineout peels. Gray was one big granite block in a solid granite wall and part of the most powerful group of forwards I ever competed against. Marais is in for different reasons. When the Lions went to South Africa in 1974, the Springboks believed themselves to be all-powerful up front . . . but they weren't. In their captain, however, there remained a spectre of what had gone before. He was drafted in on past reputation to face the Lions in that Test series and was one of the few South Africans to hold his place in all four encounters. Off the pitch too, he appeared to be a nice chap . . . perhaps too nice, in those difficult circumstances.

Hooker

One man stands out in my opinion as the best hooker to have played the game, and he is **Sean Fitzpatrick**. The most glowing compliment I can pay him is that he would have held his own, and thrived in, the New Zealand pack of 1971. His New Zealand team were the form team of the 1995 World Cup and losing the final to a Joel Stransky drop goal in extra time must have been absolutely galling. But Fitzpatrick responded with typical resolve and took his side back there to clean-sweep the world champions three nil. What a hooker, what a captain . . . in my opinion his leadership abilities are second only to those of Meads.

Locks

I have Johnson and Brown in the second row for the British and Ireland XV, so I need two men who would happily want to meet that particular confrontation head on. Strangely, there are two men who stand out and, in certain ways, mirror the British pairing in style, attitude and reputation. In my World XV I have another two shoe-ins at lock: **Colin Meads** and **John Eales**.

What a pairing: icons both for their respective nations. One was hard and ruthless and the other a genuine rugby athlete. Both were natural leaders and both inspired respect from their teammates by just getting on with their jobs. My captain will come from this pairing: let's keep it nice and symmetrical, and put the leadership with the locks in both teams. John Eales – like his great rival Martin Johnson – lifted the World Cup, but my World XV leader is the Pine Tree – Colin Meads.

Flankers

The choices thus far have been fairly clear-cut, but now it gets tough. There are fleet-footed New Zealanders like Josh Kronfeld and Michael Jones in contention, there are Australians like George Smith and David Wilson, there's South African Francois Pienaar and excellent French fliers like Serge Betsen and Laurent Cabannes. But in choosing my two World XV flankers, I'll go for two old foes I bashed it out with and select **Jean-Pierre Rives** on the openside, and **Ian Kirkpatrick** at blind. Both men have the speed, stamina and strength to wreak havoc in opposition lines and would undoubtedly be a major factor in the success of this team. Rugby cannot be played without the ball and that is why Rives and Kirkpatrick excelled . . . they nearly always emerged with the ball.

Number 8

The position that is closest to my heart is the one that caused me most deliberation. Certain players lobby hard for inclusion: Willie Ofahengaue, Pat Lam, Dauga and Spanghero of France and even the young Imanol Harinordoquy – who probably excites me more than any other number 8 in the current game. Then there is Zinzan Brooke, who did things that no other number 8 ever did. He wasn't what one would quite expect from a traditional New Zealand forward, being a superb entertainer and beautiful ball player. But my choice of number 8, nudging Brooke out, is the best number 8 I have ever seen: another New Zealander by the name of **Wayne Shelford**.

I would have loved to have gone toe-to-toe with 'Buck' Shelford. When he led the All Blacks on the UK tour in 1989 – a tour in which they won every game – he dished out a magnificent example of battleground leadership. Ferocious, unflinching – scary, even . . .

I look at my World XV pack and see a New Zealand spine of Fitzpatrick, Meads and Shelford, and I shudder at the mayhem those men could create.

The Mervyn Davies World XV
15. Serge Blanco (France)
14. David Campese (Australia)
13. Phillipe Sella (France)
12. Tim Horan (Australia)
11. Jonah Lomu (New Zealand)
10. Michael Lynagh (Australia)
 9. Sid Going (New Zealand)
 1. Ken Gray (New Zealand)
 2. Sean Fitzpatrick (New Zealand)
 3. Hannes Marais (South Africa)
 4. Colin Meads (New Zealand) captain
 5. John Eales (Australia)
 6. Jean-Pierre Rives (France)
 7. Ian Kirkpatrick (New Zealand)
 8. Wayne Shelford (New Zealand)

Seven All Blacks, four Australians, three Frenchmen and a solitary South African. And as coach I'd choose **Bernard Laporte** – the current French coach – a man who seems to specialise in smoothing down rough edges and bringing together difficult personalities. Any coach who can curb the natural indiscipline of a French side is worth acknowledgement, and I can't help but feel that Laporte is laying the foundations for a new dynasty of French dominance.

They are my teams . . . and while I am sure that there is some computer software available somewhere that could assimilate all my players' individual stats and run a like-for-like game, I prefer to let my imagination play out the action. I view the forward battle as seismic – especially the confrontation between locks. And as was so often the case in my own career, I think the World XV forwards might just shade it . . . Fitzpatrick, Eales, Meads, Kirkpatrick, Rives and Shelford at their peak would be damn hard to contain. And I also give my World XV ascendancy in one other area: out wide. I can't quite imagine Gerald bringing down a rampaging Jonah Lomu. But then again, I am sure J.P.R. would have concocted some fiendish plan to stop him.

In a match between the two teams that I have chosen, the World XV might nick it by a point, unless Jonny Wilkinson gets the ball in the opposite half with the seconds running out. He's done it once . . . and I dare say he'll do it again.

XVI

Once We Were Kings

Welsh rugby . . . now there is as much sport to be derived from analysing the pitfalls and pratfalls that surround Welsh rugby as there is from the game itself. Pity the poor fan in Wales, for we have been on the receiving end of much turmoil in the last two decades. We have seen professionalism, we've seen the temporary exile of our biggest clubs, we've witnessed player power, Grannygate, new stadiums, spiralling debt, flashy kits, rock music, rock-bottom performances, big-name sponsors, absent sponsors, sugar daddies, new leagues, old scores, the arrival of regions, the disbanding of a region, coaches coming and coaches going, ludicrous salaries, threatened receivership, bonus points, fitness advisers, pod systems, players going north . . . and then coming back again, World Cups, whitewashes, task forces, EGMs, AGMs, bleep tests, bankruptcy, backbiting, bitching and farce. One can call Welsh rugby many things but never, ever call it boring. Both on the field and off we have been routed, ridiculed and even redeemed for a short time. But through it all, with a handful of notable exceptions, the lacklustre performances of the national team has seen Wales fall, unceremoniously, from the top table of the world game. I can't put my finger on exactly what went wrong – brighter men than me have tried – but I have a few hunches.

The single worst moment that I can recall, the match that sums up the despair that too regularly consumes the national game in Wales, didn't take place in Cardiff but at Wembley Stadium – the home of English football. I shall never forget the abject misery I felt on that day in April 1998, when France walloped us 51–0. It was the only time that I ever walked out on a Wales team and despite the pain of the occasion, I still, to this day, feel a sense of shame that I fled. I wasn't the only escapee; there was a seething, sorrowful exodus walking down Wembley way that afternoon and I wonder how many of us seriously considered walking away for good? But us Welsh are a breed of masochistic dreamers when it comes to our rugby: we expect pain but we hope for pleasure. Yet that particular Sunday felt very, very bad. By the way, what possessed the administrators to schedule international matches on a Sunday? Do they have any consideration for the fans? Sunday fixtures have bitten hard into the spirit of the Six Nations. Gone are the balanced trips: arrival on Thursday, departure on Sunday with a match perfectly poised on Saturday. I felt even more dejected trudging out of Wembley knowing I had to go to work the next morning.

It wasn't just the manner of the defeat against France, because Wales had become well practised to the undignified thrashing. What I resented most, what angered me was the lack of pride being shown in the red shirt. Wales gave in. A group of well-paid professional players, handsomely rewarded to play a sport that better players than them previously did for the honour, just gave in. Defeat was (grudgingly) acceptable but surrender was not. Admittedly, Thomas Castaignede had a dream day at outside-half for the French and ran the show with style and verve, but I would have thought any Welsh team – any rugby team for that matter – worth its salt would have found a way to either work him out or to stop him completely. But we didn't . . . we never touched him; we seemed to be absolutely devoid of either instinct or ideas. Being in Wembley felt alien, too: it was a difficult place to get to and totally lacked the international day atmosphere one could expect to enjoy in Cardiff. I'd never been there before and thought I would buy into the novelty of seeing my country play beneath the famous Wembley towers. But within 20 minutes of kick-off I was asking myself why the hell I had bothered. Why was I there? Why was Wales there? We were there because the

WRU in all its wisdom decided to invest all its money, all its hopes, dreams and its reputation in a brand-new stadium. The men who controlled the national game made a decision to invest in bricks and mortar, in pomp and stature, at the expense of people and players. Congratulations, we have the greatest stadium in the world but we have no team to grace it. I feared then what I fear now: the decision to divert money from the grass roots of the game will haunt us for decades to come. As I made my way back to the train station that afternoon, a taxi driver took note of my accent and burst out laughing. This is what we had become: a Welsh team being humiliated 'at home' in England. I doubt my taxi driver was the only one who thought the country that was once at the vanguard of European rugby was now little more than a laughing stock.

But let's rewind a little: when the injured captain, J.P.R. Williams, left Cardiff Arms Park on 17 March 1979 with a gash in his calf, he left with his country well on the way to winning a fourth consecutive Triple Crown. Wales would beat England with considerable ease by 27 points to 3. It was a fitting end to a decade that saw Wales achieve terrific, almost unparalleled, success. And throughout, J.P.R. had been ever present. He had seen it all and outlasted every single one of us. With the flags flying and the ground a sell-out, everything seemed rosy in Welsh rugby and it was widely felt that the coming decade could match, perhaps even exceed, the '70s. Welsh rugby believed it had a God-given right to succeed. As we collectively sang 'Cwm Rhondda', we took off our laurels, laid them out before us and sat our fat backsides down right on top of them. Never had such a rugby nation been heading for such a great fall.

When time and space and history finally place Welsh rugby of the 1970s in context, I believe that the players from that era will be regarded more as the exception rather than the rule. We managed to produce a once-in-a-generation collection of internationals, unique in British rugby. Not that the boys who came after us weren't up to it . . . far from it. Terry Holmes was an exceptional scrum-half; very different from Gareth but a hard, physically imposing player who always impressed me with his play. His successor Robert Jones was the scrum-half's scrum-half . . . a true master-craftsman. His half-back partner Jonathan Davies ranks up there with the best to play in that most debated of positions. Robert Norster was a supreme lineout forward and Richie Collins was another back-row player who honed his ball-handling skills on the basketball court. We still had the heroes in place who could inspire the youngsters but soon, when the darker recesses of '80s economics hit Wales hard, those youngsters who would have to go on and take the game forward, were not so easily found.

Losing the heavy industry, the mines and the steelworks, the factories and the docks certainly damaged the tough working-class identity that had, for so long, defined the Welsh. Admittedly, there weren't that many international players coming from a heavy-industry background but it still provided a hard base upon which rugby was built. Tough men played a tough game. The schools provided another kind of base, a base where skill and flair and thought prevailed. Losing the school influence meant losing the future of our game. Welsh rugby depended on the eyes and awareness of schoolmasters and games teachers, men who were in prime position to spot the good and mould the mediocre. For years, those same teachers had given their time willingly to their young sides and it reached a point where they felt they were being taken for granted. In the 1980s, giving anything away for free became an anachronism. Life got harder in the '80s, money for most got tighter and teachers (understandably) wanted paying for their time. They wanted a little more remuneration for the lunchtime training sessions, the after-school coaching and the Saturday morning matches. When the money didn't come, neither did the rugby. Suddenly there was a generation of younger players who weren't being exposed to rugby in a way that their forebears had. Wales was starting to lag behind.

The great coaches of Welsh rugby had been schoolteachers: Clive Rowlands, Carwyn James, John Dawes and Tony Gray all knew how to motivate, educate and inspire children. And sometimes, rugby players are little more than children, eager to impress and show off, willing to prove their worth to their coach. But all these fine coaches, and other exponents of the rugby art dotted throughout Wales, had a gift; they knew how to pass on ideas, they knew how to help, they knew how to fire the imagination of those who were willing to listen and learn. Once we lost the teachers we lost the means to access and involve the young. Rugby growth became centred solely around the clubs and what they could do for local boys on a Saturday or Sunday. Funding was never very good and soon the bandwagon that had carried Wales along a golden road for so many years finally slowed and stopped.

The great watershed moment in Welsh rugby, the time that initially gave us a reasonable perspective of where we actually stood on the world stage, occurred between 1987 and 1988. In 1987, Wales disastrously lost to France, Scotland and Ireland in the Five Nations but then went to the inaugural World Cup, won five out of six matches and finished third behind New Zealand and France respectively. The first World Cup, hosted in Australia and New Zealand, was seen as a novelty item and was miles away from the stunningly successful – and very slick – commercial enterprise that millions around the globe enjoy today. Curio or not, Wales went there to win and group-stage victories over Ireland, Tonga and Canada – played out at breakfast time for the munching masses back home – served the national mood well. In fact, the feel-good factor continued and for proof, most Welsh people pointed gleefully to a defeat of England in the quarter-finals and the third-place play-off win against Australia. Adrian Hadley's try and Paul Thorburn's injury time conversion ranked Wales up there with the best in the world. Not everyone was convinced; my attention was drawn more to the 49–6 drubbing from New Zealand in the semi-final. A divide had formed and never had those dark clouds looked blacker. David Kirk's All Blacks went on to win the World Cup, but Wales returned as heroes. The nation was once more buoyed by success and the children had new heroes to emulate in the parks: men like Jonathan Davies, Robert Jones, Mark Ring, Ieuan Evans and Paul Thorburn.

A Triple Crown followed in 1988 and suddenly the game looked good. Wales had a team comprised of useful forwards and skilful backs, marshalled by an excellent coaching team of Tony Gray and Derek Quinnell. All that was needed was to go and show the world champions that the previous semi-final defeat was a mere glitch. The boys flew out confident and serious; they travelled with intent and revenge on their minds. There are echoes of 1969 in what happened next: a winning Wales team going to New Zealand full of hope. But as it was in 1969, the tour was a disaster and the Triple Crown boys were once more sent packing. We used the 1969 tour as the springboard into our Golden Era, and we used the excellence of the All Blacks as our rugby benchmark: they led, we followed and we aimed to surpass. Regrettably, history did not repeat itself – the 1988 squad imploded. The defeat against Romania – a defeat that must rank with those against Western Samoa in 1991 or Italy in 2003 as one of Wales' worst – was the final straw for some. Jonathan Davies, the great hope of Welsh rugby who received more criticism than most for the Romanian debacle, cashed his chips in and went north to Widnes. Wales had not only lost one of her genuinely world-class performers, but she had lost a role model. Other players from that (and a slightly later era) went north too: Dai Young, Adrian Hadley, John Devereux, Mark Jones, Jonathan Griffiths, Allan Bateman, Paul Moriarty, Scott Gibbs and Scott Quinnell. A team cannot consistently challenge without its best players . . . and in the late '80s and early '90s, Wales kept losing hers.

Wales could not afford to lose players of that calibre, players who could have shaped and supported the national team through the lean years of the '90s. As a small nation, we will always suffer because of our relatively small player base. England and France dominate us in terms of population and therefore should dominate us in the number of players actively playing rugby. The pyramid gets stronger: bigger base, better competition, and higher summit. The reality of the situation is clear: France and England can compete six, seven, eight or more deep in every position. Clive Woodward can pick a challenging squad for any tournament or tour. OK, his 'lesser' teams might not always win, but at least they compete and his players show a genuine hunger for improvement. Wales struggle to find 20 players who can be honestly regarded as hardened internationals. If that sounds harsh, ask yourself this question: how many Welsh players from the recent Six Nations would genuinely challenge for a place in Clive Woodward's England team? How many are good enough to supplant a World Cup winner?

Forces did conspire against Wales in the '80s and '90s (retirement, stringent rules of amateurism, loss of industry, school disputes, rugby league, declining player base), that much is true, but we did go through that time with our heads rammed right in the sand. Tony Gray was replaced as coach by John Ryan, who in turn was replaced by Ron Waldron, who saw his side concede over 60 points to Australia. The 1991 World Cup arrived and Wales quickly departed, humiliated at the Arms Park by Western Samoa, who taught us a lesson in physical rugby. To try to pull us onto an even keel, the WRU looked outside of Wales and selected an Anglicised Welshman, Alan Davies, as coach. For a while, the ship settled and Wales turned into a conservative – but effective – unit that knew, and worked within, its limitations. They squeezed past England in Cardiff in 1993 (which made everything rosy once again) and then went on to win the Five Nations Championship the following year. Not a Grand Slam or a Triple Crown – England put paid to those twin ambitions – but something for the public to celebrate, something very welcome in a barren time. But no sooner had Alan Davies looked to be slowly achieving something tangible with the national side than his Wales team were whitewashed in the next Five Nations, and the WRU made the first of its big southern hemisphere errors and chose Australian Alex Evans to lead a battered and confused Wales to South Africa for the 1995 World Cup.

We will draw a veil over that particular campaign, but the fallout from South Africa had, in my opinion, one totally catastrophic effect on the Welsh game: professionalism. Wales lurched from one crisis to another, reacting sloppily to change, panicking. But when the game went 'open', it all hit the fan. To be blunt, we never had a hope of coping.

If Welsh rugby is a business, then it lacked business acumen. When the International Rugby Board proclaimed professionalism had arrived, the first reaction in Wales was to throw money right, left and centre at everything. The players had a field day; clubs panicked and paid way over the odds to build up their squads. And it wasn't just in the higher echelons of the game either: clubs in lower divisions were paying silly sums of money per week to secure the services of certain players. I was never against the notion of a player being paid for his time and efforts, but the pay on offer in the first throes of professionalism was too much, too soon. Division One clubs could not afford rising wage bills based on gate receipts from crowds of 3,000 or 4,000. Not every club possessed a rich benefactor like Peter Thomas of Cardiff, and when clubs started wobbling they had to rely increasingly on the WRU. By then however, the WRU was committed to building the Millennium Stadium. Where else would the money come from? Sponsors? Yes . . . although the national league went without a sponsor once Heineken switched its patronage to the European Cup. Imagine the Premiership in soccer without a sponsor. It is unthinkable, but the showpiece domestic league in Wales could not muster the interest of a commercial backer. One can only suppose the price was far too high for the potential return.

What about television money? Great, yes please, but television money comes at a cost. Suddenly the key clashes were played out on a Friday or Saturday evening, and the traditional 2.30 or 3 p.m. kick-off on a Saturday afternoon was gone. Fixture times would change at the drop of a hat to satisfy television requirements, and it became an ongoing source of frustration for the ordinary fan that there was no consistency about when their team would play. The big televised games between Cardiff and Newport or Llanelli and Swansea would often have a detrimental effect on the gate. If it was wet or cold, many potential attendees would prefer to watch from the comfort of their own home or from down the pub. I do sound like a 'pipe-and-slippers moaner' about the random scheduling of games, but I find it intrusive, unnecessary and infuriating. Just as international matches should be played on a Saturday afternoon, give the derbies back to the fans at a time that suits them.

Panic spending gripped rugby like wildfire, and the appointment of Mr Henry is the prime example of waste. The influence of Graham Henry and Steve Hansen upon Welsh rugby will divide fans for years to come. Was it a bold step on behalf of a forward-thinking Union, going outside Wales in search of success? Or was it an expensive folly borne of desperation that came with price tag of something like £250,000 a year?

I do not believe that Graham Henry did Wales any great favours during his tenure. Kevin Bowring went after the 51–0 France defeat and by the time South Africa had beaten Wales 96–13, we would have followed anyone in the hope of buying some kind of success. There have been those in the last year who have criticised the way that Gareth Jenkins was treated when applying for the national coaching role post-Hansen. I share their misgivings. Gareth is an honourable man and deserved due consideration when the WRU surprised everyone and selected Mike Ruddock seemingly from nowhere. It is interesting to note that if anyone could understand the frustration that Gareth felt, then it is Mike Ruddock because the WRU did exactly the same thing to him in 1998. Mike is a very good coach and I firmly believe that he is the right man for the Wales job. His record with Swansea and the Newport-Gwent Dragons is good and the time he spent in Ireland with Leinster certainly broadened his horizons. But in 1998, just as he was about to take charge of Wales, the job was given to Graham Henry from the Auckland Blues.

The Great Redeemer arrived in Wales and captivated the Welsh public. For a year (from his debut in charge against South Africa at Wembley to the start of the World Cup in Cardiff) the Welsh finally found reason to believe in rugby again. We beat France in Paris for the first time since 1975 and then again in the Millennium Stadium. We beat Argentina in a Test series in Argentina and memorably took the South Africans (something I never did with Wales) again in Cardiff. But what really cemented Henry's place in the public's hearts was the win over England at Wembley in 1999. That victory was money in the bank for the Henry dream – he could do anything on the back of that success. But what had he done that was really different from previous coaches? He brought in Shane Howarth and Brett Sinkinson (New Zealanders both, who mistakenly believed they were Welsh, qualified) and Peter Rogers at prop, but the other players he selected had largely been the same players who had been at the disposal of Alan Davies and Kevin Bowring. What Henry actually did was make his players believe in themselves and in him. He was a schoolmaster by calling and used his persuasive skills to tell them they could match anyone. It worked for a while – and his methods would only ever have a short shelf-life – but when he stopped persuading them, he lost them. By the time of his departure however, he had greatly improved his bank balance and managed to bag the Lions coaching job to Australia – a tour which, I believe, revealed his deficiencies as a coach. When he left, he left a team that was easily beaten. At time of writing he is currently head coach of New Zealand: the Wales job proved a useful stepping-stone on his career path. So who got the most from the Graham Henry years? Wales, very much back to chaos and defeat, or Graham Henry – a coach winging his way back to New Zealand with a unique insight into northern hemisphere rugby? With international rugby now centred around winning World Cups, there was no way that New Zealand would let Henry's insider knowledge slip away.

And what of the Great Redeemer's great replacement, Steve Hansen? Well he lacked his predecessor's charm but at least he had the honesty to tell the nation that Wales were not very good! His record certainly backs up his claim and one must respect his candour. Hansen appeared to be more of a players' man and certainly (with the exception of a few high-profile dropouts) seemed to earn their loyalty. One must praise him for backing youth, for concentrating on fitness and conditioning, and trying to confront the drinking culture that afflicted the Welsh game. I suppose he should also be praised for not quitting when he had ample opportunity to do so. His time in charge will largely be remembered for two defeats in the 2003 World Cup against New Zealand and England. Wales played quite brilliant rugby during those two matches and frightened the life out of the two tournament favourites, but I cannot buy that their sudden transformation into a dazzling attacking side was part of Hansen's World Cup game plan. Does a team really have the balls to play with such abandon in the two most crucial matches of the tournament? Or was it a case of the players dictating the style out of desperation? Whatever the reason, Wales suddenly reverted to a more traditional Welsh game, where forwards tried to avoid contact and fast three-quarters spread the ball wide. We are not southern hemisphere (nor English) juggernauts and we cannot play the crash-bang-wallop game straight up the middle. Wales need to move the ball quickly and decisively, just as we had always done. Maybe we are starting to realise that there might be something useful to learn from the past?

Hansen and Henry are gone. Intriguingly, they now coach together for New Zealand; they've got the jobs that they always wanted. The Lions tour in 2005 will make fascinating viewing. I am glad that they have gone because I believe a Welshman should coach Wales. It requires a Welshman to understand Welsh rugby and the Welsh psyche. I can't quite put my finger on what it is a Welshman brings to the post, but I trust and hope that Welshmen will now take control of the national team's destiny. I also hope the parochialism and age-old club loyalties that have dogged previous Welsh coaches are a thing of the past.

As for the domestic game in 2004, well, it's a bit of a mess. Regionalism came in a bizarre hotchpotch of ill-conceived partnerships that catered to certain clubs' (and their owners') egos and therefore shattered the whole balance of the enterprise. I am sad for Pontypridd and Bridgend that they have lost their Warriors, but we should never have entertained the idea of five regional sides. We cannot afford to run them. I would have split Wales from north to south in three, and gone with East, Mid and West regions . . . three strong teams built to feed the national squad. I fear the traditional first-division club sides (Swansea, Neath, Ebbw Vale, etc.) might wane beneath the existing regional set-up because it resembles a closed shop. Where are the talented youngsters going to play when so many regional contracts are taken up with southern hemisphere players looking for a pension pay-out? Shut the door on them; invest in youth; build for the future. At present, the Celtic League is a bit of a farce. We are happy to measure ourselves against mediocre Scottish sides and Irish teams who keep their better players for the European competitions. But it is not just at the higher levels of the game where disharmony rules; grass roots rugby is on its knees and still the WRU is involved in publicity stunts. The great Iestyn Harris fiasco should shame all involved; imagine wasting all that money on one player – another pretend saviour – on a man who never really delivered. I can think of far better ways to spend £800,000.

And across the border, despite recent results, our English neighbours are basking in the success of total club and country domination. The World Cup victory has had a tremendous trickledown effect on the English game (just look at what London Wasps achieved in 2003–04) and the youngsters appear to be buying into rugby in swathes. I wish it were the same in Wales. It saddens me to see the playing fields around Llandaff, Cardiff, or Ashley Road, Swansea, quite empty on a weekend. Two decades ago, teams would queue up on the touchlines to get a game. Will we see those days again? I fear not.

Two decades of decline has done much damage to the game I love. I do not know where to begin in terms of fixing it. I'd like the WRU to sell the Millennium Stadium – it is a millstone around the Union's neck – and start clearing the debt. I'd like them to pour more money into the grass roots of the game. Let the people with the commercial nous run the facility and let the rugby men run the game. I'd also like to do something about professionalism. In my day, rugby players gave all they had to their rugby but they also had an occupation, a trade, a calling to concentrate on. To make a choice between one's rugby and one's career is difficult. How many talented young rugby men do we lose to this dilemma?

The best rugby I saw in Wales in the last ten years was when Swansea and Cardiff crossed the border for a season and chose exile in England. Playing the big English clubs like Bath, Leicester and Gloucester every week lifted the standard of both Welsh teams and certainly swelled the crowds. When I was playing for London Welsh, the matches we played against the leading English clubs enhanced our playing skills and the teams we played in Wales gave us fierce and intense competition. Where is the real competition now? Where are those skills to be truly tested? In Europe? In England? The only real hope I have for Welsh rugby is if we start competing vigorously on those levels.

I do not think we will win another Grand Slam . . . I hope and pray that we do but I just cannot see it. I think we will always be a team who can upset the odds occasionally, and pull off a surprise defeat against a bigger – and better – nation. If the pride comes back, the instinct, the adventure, the common sense, then maybe, just maybe, the shocks will come more frequently. But right here, right now . . . I view Welsh rugby with a sense of fear and dread.

XVII

A Lucky Man

When I look back on my life, I have to concede that I have been a lucky man. I grew tall and strong and bloody-minded, and managed to use what natural sporting talents I had to propel myself onwards. I never went into rugby with any ambition to make it to the pinnacle of the game; I merely played to test myself. It just so happened that each test took me to a higher level. It is a long way from the gangly youth who couldn't get into the Swansea Schools XV to the man who captained his country. If someone had asked me back then in the early '60s, as I trudged my way homewards to Trewyddfa Road, whether I could follow my father and wear the red jersey of Wales, I would have scoffed 'no'. It was merely the desire to play that motivated me. Initially, I only ever thought about Saturday, about leaving the field as a winner. But when I settled in at London Welsh – and a few weeks later with Wales – I started to yearn for the ultimate rugby goal: the British Lions.

Luck played its part too, and I hold my hand up and acknowledge good fortune. I was lucky that London Welsh needed a tall man in the lineout to feed their fizzing backs. I was lucky John Jeffery wobbled against the All Blacks. I was lucky Dennis Hughes was too injured to trial. I was lucky to pack down between Dai Morris and John Taylor. I was lucky that I took a good beating at the hands of New Zealand at an age when I was young enough to learn the valuable lessons that can be obtained from defeat. I was lucky to play with a Wales team that set the standards for British rugby in the '70s. I was lucky that I played with – and against – the very best of men all over the world.

To some, I will always be the man who nearly died on the rugby pitch. To others, I'll be 'Merv the Swerve' – number 8, tackler, jumper. But I don't feel like either of those men. So much of my life seems based around events that happened 30 years ago. It is preposterous really; only my rugby stopped, whereas my life went on. For a good while I could not make much sense of what happened to me after my brain haemorrhage but somehow, I moved on and found a place where I could enjoy my life. I missed my rugby, I missed the physical release of playing and competing, but one cannot wallow too long in what was. I hope the journey we've just taken down memory lane hasn't felt too much like a wallow. And I hope, too, that the memories and the stories are clear and correct. Some bits remain scrambled but my intentions are honourable and this story is written in good faith.

As I approach my 60th year I do so as a man with few regrets. I have made my share of mistakes, but there isn't much that causes me sleepless nights. The only real regrets that I have from rugby are quite small, piffling almost, when I put them in context with my playing achievements. First, I wish I could have had a say in my retirement. If I had been granted that decision then I might have plotted my immediate future in a slightly different way and channelled my energies into coaching or administration at a time when my playing experience would have been useful and relevant. My other regret is the Lions: I cannot imagine a greater honour in rugby than to be a captain of the British Lions. Yet these things were not to be; fate – or a small vessel in the centre of my brain – determined another path. And again, I must thank good fortune that I fell from Cardiff Arms Park straight into the arms of the best medical care available. Typical Merv, always in the right place at the right time – even when flirting with death.

We spend so much of our time in Wales staring into the past. I sometimes long to escape what was and welcome what is. But I cannot; I am locked in a time when rugby was fast, romantic and delicious, when it was the people's game, when it pulled us through the depths of winter and into eternal spring. I hope that my fellow countrymen, the young boys who now shoulder what once went before, experience what I did. There is no feeling quite like it. There is no joy like winning for Wales. There is no moment to match that final whistle when your body feels like disintegrating but your heart and spirit soars up to the heavens.

So here I am: Mervyn Davies, captain of Wales; British Lion; father; husband; friend; chairman of the Welsh Rugby Former International Players Association; businessman. A man who had the strength to compete with the best in the world. A man who flirted in the shadows. Part of me hates being the centre of attention but another part feels proud of what my achievements have given to my family and my friends. The day I received my OBE from the Queen is a case in point. I felt privileged to be at Buckingham Palace but also acutely embarrassed that the man who was part of a team should be singled out for such an individual honour. But that day wasn't for me; it was for my family and it made the time spent in the spotlight worthwhile. And when I was featured on *This Is Your Life*, I sailed through the whole experience bemused by the good words and goodwill coming from others. I couldn't grasp that it was me who was the subject of such attention. And when Colin Meads – the greatest of the great – emerged from back stage after flying all the way from New Zealand, a small voice in the back of my head convinced me that I wasn't that bad a player after all. But both those events were a long time ago. The goodwill, however, still remains and the people I meet on my travels are warm and kind in their welcome.

Of all the memories that sometimes steal into my thoughts, there is one that will remain with me. Strangely, it is of the last moment from my last international game. I still hear that whistle now and sense the utter exhaustion of winning a Grand Slam for Wales. Being lifted high and carried from the field of play through a joyous, approving crowd is a great way to finish a playing career. It's not a bad way to finish a book, either.

XVIII

Afterwards

When my autobiography came out in the autumn of 2004, I was a little nervous about the type of reception it would receive. I wanted people to enjoy my story but, more than anything else, I wanted them to appreciate that it was an honest tale told from the heart. I hoped that I hadn't done any of my ex-playing colleagues any disservice; I just wanted to tell it as it was from my perspective. One area that didn't concern me was my assessment of Welsh rugby; I wanted to stir up a hornet's nest. I wanted to express the frustration I – and my fellow Wales fans – felt at the demise of the game in our country. And when I wrote the words: 'I do not think we will win another Grand Slam . . . I hope and pray that we do but I just cannot see it . . .' I did so with utter conviction. Well, maybe. There was a slight, nagging hope that Wales might just do it in a few years' time. Thank heavens I got it wrong.

The moment Martyn Williams kicked the ball up into the stand of the Millennium Stadium on that beautiful spring day in March 2005, a nation celebrated. Of all nine Welsh Grand Slams since 1883 this was, perhaps, the sweetest. What made it so good were the bad times that preceded it. What made it so breathtaking was the way Wales took hold of the ball and sidestepped the defence-driven drudgery that international rugby had become. Suddenly, we had forwards who could run into space and off-load in the tackle, and we had backs who were implored to play on their instincts. Us dinosaurs from the 1970s watched on and smiled. For years we had droned on about how the game should be played. We wholeheartedly believed that rugby worked better when guile and cunning were allied to adventure and intent. And when Wales finally cut the shackles, it was plain to see: running rugby works.

When I handed my manuscript in to my publisher in mid-2004, I anticipated, 12 months on, that I would be contemplating a revision for the eventual paperback release. What I never anticipated was the complete change in fortunes for Welsh rugby. In recent months, I asked myself: should I trawl back through my book, tempering my criticisms and drafting on references to what had just passed? Or should I leave my words in a kind of metaphorical time capsule, frozen before the events of 2005? After much soul searching, I settled for the latter approach. I still stand by what I wrote. This chapter therefore, written in the summer of 2005, is a chance to reflect on the last 12 roller-coaster months.

When I voiced my doubts that Wales could ever win another Grand Slam, I added a caveat which read: 'If the pride comes back, the instinct, the adventure, the common sense, then maybe, just maybe, the shocks will come more frequently.' So maybe, just maybe, Merv's crystal ball worked. Pride, instinct and adventure: the class of 2005 had that in abundance. I have been highly critical of the WRU and the Henry/Hansen influence on Welsh rugby but I must concede now that these two New Zealand interlopers set the renaissance in motion. It was the work being done behind the scenes, the conditioning and fitness training, the development of a professional attitude, the hiring of men like Scott Johnson and Andrew Hore that proved so crucial to this brave new Wales. What gelled it all together was the appointment of a Welshman to the helm. Mike Ruddock was undoubtedly the right man at the right time. He told his boys to back their talent, to give it a lash, to enjoy it. And believe me, the only way to truly enjoy your rugby is to win.

The Welsh public had a taster of what was to come when Wales lost 26–25 to New Zealand in that coruscating game in the autumn of 2004. So this is how it was going to be under Ruddock: quick taps, running from deep, athletic forwards and spirited backs playing high-risk rugby at break-neck speed. But still it ended in defeat. We pushed South Africa to within two points but we still lost. Wales's reputation as a genuine rugby force was growing but so was our inability to finish matches off. We could challenge but not finish. Everything changed on 5 February.

Reading on from my reflections 12 months ago, I come to another part of the world game that I got wrong: the apparent decline of England. In the last Six Nations campaign, they were quite obviously a team in transition. No team, no matter how good, could readily cope with losing the juggernaut forces of Johnson, Dallaglio, Hill, Leonard, Back and Wilkinson. If coach Andy Robinson had said that his team was in transition, then the pressure would have been off him and some of the younger players he selected. He didn't: they were world champions and therefore fair game. The Wales–England clash under the Millennium Stadium roof was a lovely night for the Welsh fans and a highly significant event for both sets of players. The fans got the gloating rights and the Wales players shook that monkey off their backs by finally nailing one of the big teams in world rugby. The English fans saw the chariot stall and the English players had to ask themselves who is worthy and able to fill the shirts of World Cup-winning giants?

Grand Slams come down to moments: J.P.R. tackling Gourdon in '76, John Taylor's conversion at Murrayfield in '71 . . . moments, that's all. In 2005, for John, see Gavin Henson and his booming penalty. Great kick, epic moment, but I don't think many people (even Silverboots himself) that night thought 'Grand Slam'. Amidst the wild celebrations, my thoughts were grounded in dour realism: if England had had a Johnson, a Dallaglio, a Hill, Leonard or Wilkinson on the field, they would have won. Despite Welsh bravery, defiance and unquenchable willingness to run, the overriding feeling was that England lacked leadership. They lost. We won. We were in the ascendancy.

Grand Slams come down to moments and as much as Henson's kick may well be the defining image and poster shot of the 2005 Grand Slam, it was the second-half display in Paris that made winning a Grand Slam possible. Two Frances turned up that day: in the first half, they were rampant, and in the second, outclassed.

Wales showed a resilience I thought I would not witness again in my national team. I was immensely proud of the young men carrying the fight to the French, riding the passion of the fans, refusing to bend. By the time we came back from Scotland with another stirring win for the inevitable decider against pre-tournament favourites Ireland, I knew the Grand Slam would be ours for the first time since 1978. Irresistible forces were at play, Cardiff was crackling, nothing could stop the inevitable . . . On Saturday, 19 March – match day – I wrote an article for *The Independent* that stated:

> As a team we were very much of the people, for the people and this Welsh team has definitely connected with the fans. That is their biggest achievement under Mike Ruddock. The innate Welshness of the side has come to the fore. Whatever the outcome today, they have achieved what many thought impossible – to restore pride and credibility to national sport.

When Wales win, the nation rejoices and few Welshmen felt happier than the stumbling ex-number 8 who had been proven so comprehensively wrong. I celebrated that night with a few beers and a late supper out. The mood of the city was electric and I received my fair share of joshing about the damning words that I had written in my book. The curry was excellent but humble pie tasted better.

The next test for Wales is to move on and consolidate the good work they have done. Winning breeds confidence and confidence makes good players great. And what is so pleasing about the current Wales set-up is the number of very good young players who have a genuine shot at greatness. What helps them immeasurably is the professional attitude they have towards their sport. They train hard, play hard and look after themselves off the pitch. Regional rugby appears to be working (sorry again there, Mr Moffett), certainly in the case of the Neath-Swansea Ospreys it is. What the domestic game in Wales needs now is success in the European competitions. It's been too long coming.

But the most heartening aspect of the Grand Slam win is the effect success is having on Welsh kids. They don't want to be Ryan Giggs;

they want to be Shane Williams, Gavin Henson or Dwayne Peel. The game is hitting the headlines for all the right reasons and long may it continue.

It's been a strange year all round, though. I didn't foresee Wales doing what they did and I certainly didn't think Clive Woodward would have struggled with the British and Irish Lions. Just as the exploits of Wales have gladdened my heart, the plight of the Lions has saddened it. Who would have believed that the very existence of the greatest of rugby institutions is now being questioned? And who would have believed that a World Cup-winning coach, a man whose rugby thinking and beliefs elevated him to the status of knight of the realm, would be taking all of the flak?

I experienced real rugby highs and lows in New Zealand. Winning in '71 was made all the sweeter by defeat in '69. But away from the pitch it was the experience of being there, of rubbing shoulders with the fans and the players, getting out into the community and enjoying the country itself that was truly enriching. What the Lions of 2005 saw was what all players across the ages have seen: the New Zealand psyche is defined by the aura of the All Black jersey. I thought the Lions had a real shot at winning the series but it soon became apparent this was not to be. I think Woodward got his selections wrong, very wrong in some cases. I thought he took too many players and advisers and played far too few games. But above all else, he got the tone wrong. He failed to grasp that a touring side runs like a finely balanced machine. The players need more than rugby to make them succeed but rugby is why they are there. I am writing this before the inevitable fall-out and I don't want to add to Sir Clive's woes, because he is an honourable and decent man. He should have coached the Lions in 2001 instead of Graham Henry. The Henry tour failed because a New Zealand coach failed to manage a squad of strong personalities. Ironically, Clive's tour failed because the personalities were not allowed to shine through. They were a tired touring team against a rampant All Blacks side and there was always going to be one winner once the real business got under way. The aftermath of Lions tours should be about players not coaches and spin doctors.

For the Welsh players who went (and, yes, there should have been more), I feel it will be a valuable learning experience. They returned with reputations intact, if not fulfilled. It was encouraging to see Ryan Jones establish himself on the world stage and I hope he continues to be a leading light. But I'm not going to venture too far into the soothsaying game any more . . . I'll just sit back and see what unfolds.

Rugby is a wonderful way to bring people together. Rugby lovers are tribal and ferociously loyal to their team, their interests. With the rise in rugby websites and fan forums, opinions and arguments fly through the ether with alacrity. We all have opinions now and a stage on which to present them. But the 2005 Lions appeared to fracture further the sometimes uneasy relationship between Scottish, Welsh, Irish and English fans. As usual, everyone gangs up on the English but, my Welsh friends, no one gloats more than a happy Welshman. No one feels they have a more God-given right to claim the spoils of rugby like the Welsh. Celtic and English fans alike may have blamed over-inflated reputations or poor selections for the New Zealand debacle but I guarantee the players on tour would have relished the adventure. Friendships would have been formed, rivalries instigated, frustration felt, but Lions were born.

When all is said and done, rugby is just a game. It is sport. But it remains a marvellous obsession and an intoxicating release from real life. Events of the last year have drawn me back into the fold. It's a place where I want to be. Rugby has defined my life yet the last time I played was over half a lifetime ago. I can live with that. I'm still happy with my lot. I can talk about the game and analyse what I see. I can criticise and champion but when I see what I have seen in the spring of 2005, days when Wales played with a wonderful chaos, I feel pride and envy. I see it in the faces of a triumphant squad, bonded together, setting off a great journey, buoyed by the hopes and dreams of their people. Once a game is played it is consigned to memory. But the games to come, they must provide the spur; they are what matter now. Next time Wales take the field, I will feel the way I did during the Grand Slam season: how I wish it were me, not Michael Owen, picking up the ball from the base of the scrum and powering into a solid wall of defenders. I know what he knows: there will be men on each shoulder, men to rely on. In my mind's eye, that's where I am . . . brothers by my side. Waiting for the ball.

Bibliography

Bennett, Phil and Thomas, Graham, *Phil Bennett: the Autobiography* (CollinsWillow, 2003)

Billot, John, *History of Welsh International Rugby* (Roman Way Books, 1999)

Curtis, Tony (ed.), *Wales: the Imagined Nation* (Poetry Wales Press, 1986)

Davies, Mervyn with Parry-Jones, David, *Number 8* (Pelham Books, 1977)

Edwards, Gareth, *Gareth Edwards: the Autobiography* (Hodder Headline Audiobooks, 1999)

Edwards, Gareth with Bills, Peter, *Tackling Rugby* (Headline, 2002)

Jackson, Peter, *Lions of Wales* (Mainstream, 1998)

John, Barry, *The Barry John Story* (Collins, 1974)

John, Barry (ed.), *Rugby '76* (Christopher Davies Publishers, 1970)

Richards, Huw, Stead, Peter and Williams, Gareth (eds), *Heart and Soul* (University of Wales Press, 1998)

Thomas, Clem and Thomas, Greg, *The History of the British & Irish Lions* (Mainstream, 1998)

Thomas, J.B.G., *The Roaring Lions* (Pelham Books, 1972)

Visit: www.wrfipa.co.uk
www.red10creative.co.uk